Praise for Deborah Threadgill Egerton, Ph.D. and

KNOW
JUSTICE
KNOW
PEACE

Deborah lays out the background and possibilities in the healing of "othering" while also providing an excellent introduction to the Enneagram. Doing this all in one book is no small feat! More importantly, she lays out how the methods of inner work are crucial for doing social justice work and racial healing, and how our awakening demands our participation in the healing of the world.

— **Russ Hudson**, co-author of *The Wisdom of the Enneagram*

Know Justice Know Peace is a brilliant new field guide, based on an ancient spiritual blueprint, that will inspire a new generation of activists to work with love—that is, the greatest force in the universe and heartbeat of the moral cosmos—to bring about social justice, end racism, and create a better world for us all.

— **Robert and Hollie Holden**, creators of Everyday Miracles

Dr. Egerton's revolutionary book illuminates the Enneagram in a way that has never been done before. A must-read for all who want to encourage real justice and peace within themselves and the world.

— **Catherine R. Bell, MBA,** founder of The Awakened Company, and best-selling and award-winning author

In working with Dr. Egerton over the past couple of decades, I have been awe-struck by her understanding of the most complex and challenging organizational issues, her sensitivity, and her incredible common sense in solving problems. She gets to the heart of people's motivations, and her input has enabled me to set the direction for my agency and for myself.

— **Gwen Wright**, director of the Montgomery County Planning Department of the Maryland-National Capital Park and Planning Commission

Dr. E is diligent, nuanced, and brave in the way she does Enneagram and anti-racism work. The work she does comes from a deep spiritual and loving place within her. I've learned so much from her around healing my own heart that I now have the capacity to really be effective in the DEI work that I do.

— **MILTON C. STEWART, MBA,** founder of Kaizen Careers, Coaching and Consulting, and host of *Do It for the Gram: An Enneagram Podcast*

While many have cautioned Dr. Deborah Egerton not to highlight the issues of IDEA with the Enneagram, she's elected to bravely expose all the reasons why it has to happen now. The exploratory dimensions of Enneagram combined with viewing the constructs of race and "other"-isms lead us to unimaginable levels of healing. Her book serves as a light to guide us through the journey using these two lenses. Dr. Egerton serves as the Enneagram harbinger for our times; for this, we are grateful.

— **ERLINA EDWARDS,** board president of The Narrative Enneagram

Dr. Deborah Egerton brings to her work with the Enneagram powerful and persuasive insight into how best to infuse workplace culture with compassion and innovation. Her unique talent and wisdom help establish greater communication among teams, resulting in better diversity and inclusion outcomes for all. Working with her inspires confidence in her teachings as she approaches her informed lectures with warmth, intelligence, and, above all, kindness. Deborah's brilliant, funny, and highly effective manner is simply the best.

— **CHARLES JOHNSON,** executive producer at CBS Television Studios

KNOW
JUSTICE
KNOW
PEACE

KNOW JUSTICE KNOW PEACE

A Transformative Journey of Social Justice,
Anti-Racism, and Healing through
the Power of the Enneagram

DEBORAH THREADGILL EGERTON, Ph.D.

WITH **LISI MOHANDESSI**

HAY HOUSE, INC.
Carlsbad, California • New York City
London • Sydney • New Delhi

Project editor: Melody Guy
Cover design: Lisi Mohandessi
Interior design: Claudine Mansour Design
Interior photos/illustrations: Lisi Mohandessi

Names and identifying details of certain individuals have been changed to protect their privacy.

The author of this book does not dispense medical advice or prescribe the use of any technique as a form of treatment for physical, emotional, or medical problems without the advice of a physician, either directly or indirectly. The intent of the author is only to offer information of a general nature to help you in your quest for emotional, physical, and spiritual well-being. In the event you use any of the information in this book for yourself, the author and the publisher assume no responsibility for your actions.

The Library of Congress has cataloged the earlier edition as follows:

Names: Egerton, Deborah Threadgill, author. | Mohandessi, Lisi, author.
Title: Know justice, know peace: a transformative journey of social
  justice, anti-racism, and healing through the power of the enneagram /
  Deborah Threadgill Egerton, Ph.D. with Lisi Mohandessi.
Description: 1st edition. | Carlsbad, California: Hay House, Inc., 2022. |
Identifiers: LCCN 2022018026 | ISBN 9781401967161 (hardback) | ISBN
  9781401967178 (ebook)
Subjects: LCSH: Enneagram. | Social justice--Psychological aspects. |
  Anti-racism--Psychological aspects.
Classification: LCC BF698.35.E54 E34 2022 | DDC 155.2/6--dc23/eng/20220509
LC record available at https://lccn.loc.gov/2022018026

Tradepaper ISBN: 978-1-4019-7418-3
E-book ISBN: 978-1-4019-6717-8
Audiobook ISBN: 978-1-4019-6718-5

10 9 8 7 6 5 4 3 2 1

1st edition, September 2022
2nd edition, September 2023

Printed in the United States of America

This product uses paper and materials from responsibly sourced forests. For more information, please go to: bookchainproject.com/home.

For all the lives lost while humanity watched with eyes that would not see. We honor you and continue the work so that humanity can know justice and know peace.

TABLE OF CONTENTS

An individual has not started living until he can rise above
the narrow confines of his individualistic concerns
to the broader concerns of all humanity.

— **MARTIN LUTHER KING, JR.**

I've learned that people will forget what you said,
people will forget what you did,
but people will never forget how you made them feel.

— **MAYA ANGELOU**

If you want a love message to be heard, it has got to be sent out.
To keep a lamp burning, we have to keep putting oil in it.

— **MOTHER TERESA**

God created us for love, for union, for forgiveness and compassion
and, yet, that has not been our storyline. That has not been our history.

— **FR. RICHARD ROHR**

FOREWORD

In my many decades on this planet, I have had the opportunity to travel widely and interact with people from diverse cultures and backgrounds. And while that diversity makes for so much of what is beautiful and delightful about humanity, there are also some striking truths that I find pretty much everywhere I go. Deep down, everyone wants to love and be loved. Everyone wants to contribute something worthwhile to this world. Everyone wants to know that their life matters.

Yet, despite the universality of this shared knowledge that we are here primarily to love and help each other, it is tragically rare for human beings to consistently live according to these values. We can all agree about the importance of kindness, compassion, wisdom, love, and generosity, but for some mysterious reasons, these qualities elude us with regularity. Even people who have been on genuine spiritual paths or who share such truths professionally would, in a moment of honesty, have to admit that they fall short more often than they would prefer.

As a young man, I became fascinated by this strange paradox—that we all knew much deeper truths about human nature than we were able to live. This led me into an interest in science and our great spiritual traditions. Some social scientists argued that aggression and competition were built into our instinctual nature just as much as were care and affiliation. The great religious traditions accounted for the problem with the idea of humanity's fall from grace or with the idea of karma. Classical psychology spoke of conditioning and how we were largely programmed by previous experiences that tended to overwhelm the possibility of free choice. I explored theories from various scientific, philosophical, and sociological perspectives as well as immersed myself in studies of the mystical traditions of the world. All these ideas were interesting, and each accounted for different elements of the issue, but what was often lacking was a method for transforming this tendency. Seeing our inability to live our real values, what are we to do?

As I continued to expose myself to different takes on the problem, I became aware of the concept of inner work. My own introduction to this was through the writings and teachings of the Greek-Armenian spiritual teacher Georges I. Gurdjieff. Gurdjieff arrived in Russia just before the First World War and began teaching a profound system of transformation that he had acquired through many years of studying in monasteries across Africa and Asia. Gurdjieff, who was raised Greek Orthodox and identified as Christian, shared that the inner work was given so that we might be able to live the commandments of Christ—to love God above all things and to love one's neighbor as oneself. He seemed to be addressing very directly the question that had so captivated my attention. Gurdjieff passed away in 1949, before I was born, but after some patient inquiry and searching, I located teachers who had worked directly with Gurdjieff and were able to pass on some of his methods and teachings. I felt quite fortunate to have had the opportunity to study with some of his direct students. What emerged from this long apprenticeship brought together much of what I had come to understand from psychology with what I had learned from spiritual tradition.

Gurdjieff agreed with the modern psychological notion that we human beings are programmed, much more than most of us realize. We are programmed, for better or worse, by our culture and its assumptions, by our family and its dynamics and issues, by our school experiences, by what works and doesn't work in our relationships, and of course by our traumas and difficulties. Literally, no one escapes this process. Our personalities and our sense of identity are shaped by so many factors, most of which are beyond our control. Very few of them are chosen. And much of this programming is exactly what prevents us from living from the deeper truths that in our better moments we know are there.

The good news, from Gurdjieff's perspective, and from the perspective of inner work, is that we are more than our programming. There really is a profound beauty, dignity, and wisdom in every human being, waiting for the conditions in which these gifts can flower and be fully expressed. For this to happen, the tradition of inner work suggests three necessary ingredients.

1. Being willing to see ourselves as we actually are—not as we wish to be or as we fear to be. We have to see what we are really up to, and this is more difficult than it might sound. It is difficult in that there aren't many places where we can acquire the necessary knowledge to see more deeply into ourselves, and also in that our personality has more defenses against seeing certain aspects of our character.

2. Developing the capacity to truly show up in our lives. In spiritual traditions we speak of this as the capacity to become more present: to be more awake in the moment. It is here and now, in this living moment, that we have the possibility of encountering the true gifts of our soul and the action of grace upon our lives.

3. When the first two come together, we need to develop the ability to see our programmed reactivity; to relax and breathe when we notice it; and, from the more grounded and spacious perspective that this moment of recollection can bring, to respond freshly to what is happening rather than react from our programming.

By engaging in this inner work, and with the help of our allies, teachers, and friends, we can free ourselves from some of the damaging programming of our past and our culture and learn to show up in our lives in new and creative ways.

The other great gift that I received from Gurdjieff was the Enneagram. As you will learn in this book, the Enneagram grew out of the contemplative traditions of Western spirituality, and different threads of it can be found in the mystical teachings of Judaism, Christianity, and Islam. The aspect of it that has currently captured public attention is more of a modern development, but one that in its original intent, was part of the tradition of inner work. The Enneagram offers us a profoundly accurate and insightful map into the inner lives of human beings and, when combined with the practice of inner work, can lead to powerful change and transformation. It helps us see the aspects of our personality that need our love and attention as well as areas we need to be careful around.

You may ask, "What does this have to do with social justice and with healing racial divides in our world?" As you will see, quite a bit!

Working with the Enneagram for many years, I came to see that human beings do have the ability to bring awareness to their issues and to the underlying emotions that create them. The Enneagram work brings much specific knowledge to our search, and helps us see what exactly we want to be aware of for our growth and development. We learn to bring honesty, humility, kindness, and courage to an ongoing exploration of our inner life, and in the process, we learn to release a lot of the old programming that has dominated our lives and sometimes held us back from being our best selves. It would be lovely if this were a one-shot deal, and after one beautiful experience we were no longer plagued by our old reactions. But that only happens in the movies. In real life, we will have many opportunities to "catch ourselves in the act" and to choose a response rather than a reaction.

Generally speaking, people don't want to be racist or to turn human beings into "others" in the various ways we do. While many of us set out with the best of intentions, we still have programming in our personality and therefore we get triggered. We see someone who does not look like our own peer group, and a flood of associations and assumptions appear. In some cases, these reactions will be negative—based in fear, suspicion, and past conditioning. We do not choose this—it just happens. And with the many centuries of "othering" that have occurred in pretty much every part of the world, we should not be surprised that we have such reactions. While we certainly do need to see our wish to make a better, more harmonious world, we need to realize that being able to truly "walk our talk," to truly live the values of love and compassion, we need to meet these unhealed parts of ourselves. We need to bring presence and awareness to the parts of us that are still lost in these deeply rooted reactions. While our good intentions are a good start, it is through the powerful combination of self-knowledge and presence that we are able to embody the principles we want to bring forth in our world.

As we learn more about our true qualities and capacities and see our limitations with more kindness and patience, a real spirituality starts to grow in us. As it does, we realize that true self-knowledge and the discipline of inner work brings about feelings of inner peace and courage we could not have imagined. We find in our own hearts many of the spiritual truths we had learned about since our childhoods—but now they are our direct experiences. It doesn't mean that our problems are over, but it does mean that we have a positivity and an equilibrium for dealing with those problems—and for truly taking in the good moments—that change our life in amazing ways.

And, if any of this is real, we want this for everyone else. It no longer feels okay if I am doing well but my brothers and sisters are still in terrible suffering. We learn too that while we cannot fix every problem we encounter, we can be a force for integrity, kindness, and healing that this world sorely needs. And we find a new family of friends across the globe who have similarly been touched by the flowering of their true heart. Knowing this, living this, changes everything.

———

I am very happy and delighted to call Dr. Deborah Egerton a dear friend and to introduce her to you. We have had the opportunity to work together on a number of occasions but also to share our wonder and joy for this life. If you have taken the time to read this foreword, I can also tell you that Dr. Egerton is a human being who has truly walked this journey. She has been on the front lines of racial healing and social justice work for many years, and she has a masterful understanding of the Enneagram and how it can be applied to help people truly meet each other. She understands deeply and intuitively how the principles of inner work can help us make the necessary crossings in our wish to know each other. She knows how this method of self-understanding can guide us through some of the difficult conversations that necessarily come up on the road to healing. Her skill and wisdom are rare and precious treasures.

Yet I suspect most of the people who have had the good fortune to get to know Dr. Egerton would agree that her main transmission, her great gift, is her capacity to love. She helps us see that, as scripture says, "with love, all things are possible." Her kindness and capacity to understand the pain that can drive us to do things we may later regret—her absolutely genuine human warmth—offer a context and container in which we can feel what we need to feel, receive each other's pain, and dare to open to a new level of heart. I have seen this over and over again. She knows how to transmute her own difficult feelings into the fuel for this work and for the benefit of others.

This remarkable book, Know Justice Know Peace, is the result of a lifetime of dedicated work, and carries all the qualities of compassion and wisdom I was just describing. Deborah lays out the background and possibilities in the healing of "othering" while also providing an excellent introduction to the Enneagram. Doing this all in one book is no small feat! More importantly, she lays out how the methods of inner work are crucial for doing social justice work and racial healing, and how our awakening demands our participation in the healing of the world. She provides moving stories of transformation—some fascinating and some heartbreaking—and keeps the theoretical frameworks employed here connected with real people and real life situations. It is a very down-to-earth book. But just as importantly, the book is full of practices and suggestions that will help you begin the process of bringing inner work into your own life.

We are in a pivotal time, not just in our country, but perhaps for the entire human race. More than ever before, we are within reach of having a society that truly reflects the deepest and most beautiful human motivations and values. Yet we also know that we are in a time where a great deal could be lost—and quickly. Clearly, many structures in our societies need to change, and are changing. Yet in this era of change, we want to see that the transformations that do occur reflect the best in us. For me, this book is arriving at a time when it is really needed. It is bringing self-knowledge and awareness to the activist communities and activism and involvement to the spiritual communities, and with enough specificity and power to go beyond platitudes and manifestos to offer something that can actually make a difference. I hope you will be as moved and inspired as I have been reading this book, and I wish you every blessing on your journey with the Enneagram and with the work that lies before us.

—**RUSS HUDSON,** co-founder of The Enneagram Institute
New York City
April 2022

PREFACE

In July of 2016 I planned to attend the Annual International Enneagram Association Conference in the Minneapolis-St. Paul metropolitan area. The conference was a yearly pilgrimage where those of us who study, teach, and practice the Enneagram assemble and connect. As I packed for my journey, that year was unlike any other. I was anxious, conflicted, and reluctant to attend an event that I had always looked forward to, knowing that I would take a deeper dive into the ever-evolving depths of the Enneagram. I tossed and turned that night. I arrived at the airport with plenty of time to check in and grab a coffee at the airport lounge. I noticed a tremor as I raised the cup to my lips. *What is wrong with me?* I was familiar with the symptoms of anxiety. I had experienced them before, but this was different. I could not identify anything that was going on in my life that would account for this discomfort. It was unsettling and confounding to say the least.

The flight was uneventful. We landed on time in Minneapolis, and my luggage was already making its way around the conveyor belt by the time I reached the baggage claim area. Now I simply had to grab a taxi and make my way to the hotel. The taxis were lined up right outside the door where I exited the baggage area. The driver got out to help me with my bags. There it was again. A little tremor. I slid into the back seat and said a little prayer that my taxi driver wasn't the chatty type. He was. "Where are you flying in from?"

"Baltimore," I answered, hoping that my one-word response would indicate that I did not want to talk.

"Guess I need to ask where you're going first," he chuckled. I gave him the name of my hotel and settled back in the seat. "Baltimore? You live there?"

"No. It's the closest airport."

"Well, then, where do you live?" It was clear that this was not going to be a quiet, peaceful ride. "I guess if you live anywhere near Baltimore, you are used to these shootings. It's a damn shame. That Castillo boy didn't deserve to die like that."

I looked down at my hands and realized I had a death grip on my cell phone. "Excuse me, what did you say?"

"That Castillo boy, Philando Castillo. I may not be saying his name right, but I'm pretty sure you heard about it all the way in Baltimore. You folks get a lot of shootings up there too, don't you? I'll drive you by where they shot him."

I didn't speak another word until we got to the hotel. I paid the driver, thanked him, and offered a meek explanation for my behavior. "I'm sorry. Yes, I'm aware of the recent shooting. His name. . ." My voice was barely a whisper now. I began again, but my voice was still betraying me. "His name was Philando Castile."

"I'm sorry, ma'am. Did you know him?"

"No, I didn't," I replied, "but I know his name." I checked into the hotel and made my way through the crowded lobby as quickly as possible. It all made sense to me now. The tremor, the uneasy feeling, the exact same feeling that I had when I watched the video footage of the police murdering Philando Castile while he was sitting in the car with his girlfriend and four-year-old daughter. Another Black body gone. Taken too soon by the violence inflicted by inadequately trained law enforcement humans. All spiritual beings in human form who were dominated by fear, colliding at a time and place where a life or lives would be taken.

I pushed my way into the elevator, went up to my room, and wept.

This was the beginning of a painful transition in my relationship with the Enneagram community. While my love for the Enneagram remained intact and continued to grow, I was becoming increasingly aware of my Blackness in a sea of White bodies. I went to sessions at the conference looking for familiar faces as usual, but familiar was not what I really wanted or needed. I was longing for someone, anyone, to give voice to the confluence of feelings that were welling up inside me. I have gotten used to being the only Black person in rooms full of White people for most of my life due to the nature of my work, so this feeling was not unusual. What was different at this particular moment in time was my acute awareness of my sense of loneliness, isolation, and pain. I was grieving, and there was no safe space, no container, no community holding me. I felt as if I had wandered into the wrong place, a place where my ethnicity, ancestry, and pain did not belong. I was grieving alone.

No one mentioned Philando Castile. I kept thinking that someone would express the desire to walk to the place where his life was taken from him. If not that, perhaps a moment of silence? Every day during the conference, I watched and waited for something that did not come. I was attending a panel discussion on the last day and the moderator opened the session up for audience participation. I do not recall actually getting up and walking to the microphone. I do recall clutching the mic and speaking these words: "Look around you. Where are the Black people in the Enneagram community, and what are we going to do about the obvious lack of diversity here?" I waited for a response. When someone finally attempted to give an answer, it felt inadequate. Too little, too late. I was back from my out-of-body experience by then with full recognition that no one had an answer for this unanticipated grenade. I had pulled the pin and walked away fully aware that people in that community might not ever look at me the same way again. That was not my concern. A White woman came up behind me and chastised the community for not responding to my question. She was outraged, but I was free. It was long past time to follow my own path. In 2016, accepting that truth set me free. The Enneagram was central to all my diversity, equity, and inclusion work, and now it was time to raise the bar. It was no longer enough to be an Enneagram practitioner. It was time for me to become an Enneagram activist.

Part I

THE
AWAKENING

Chapter 1

BENDING THE MORAL ARC TOWARD JUSTICE

If you are reading this book, know that right now is the moment for human-kind to come together to bend the moral arc of the universe toward justice. We need to cultivate new skills if we are going to put our world on a better course for present and future generations, and the Enneagram is well positioned to help us transform our way of being with each other in the world.

There are those who believe the Enneagram is a spiritual tool steeped in ancient wisdom from various sources, some who would categorize it as a psychological personality assessment tool, and others who see its utility as a personal, business, leadership, or team development tool.

And then there's me. While I believe that all the above are true, it also happens to be the most useful and most underrated diversity tool on the planet. I've been doing IDEA (inclusion, diversity, equity, and anti-racism) work for more than three decades. When I first started incorporating the Enneagram into this work, there wasn't much conversation about its capacity for healing the disconnects that separate us. I would present these ideas at International Enneagram Association conferences and a few brave souls would gather with me. I would guide them into this strange new world as they tried to understand the intersectionality of the Enneagram and social justice. Initially, it wasn't an easy sell. The intersection of the Enneagram with social justice was not necessarily on people's radars. However, we've learned that as we evolve as a global community of Enneagram practitioners, consultants, and curious enthusiasts, the utility of how our own inner work breaks down the walls that divide and separate us becomes obvious.

The concepts of bias, bigotry, and racism are unimaginable to me. Why would otherwise seemingly reasonable individuals continue to subject certain groups of people to the indignity of malice and disdain? I chose those words intentionally. Malice is the desire to cause pain, injury, or distress. Disdain is a feeling of contempt for someone or something regarded as unworthy or inferior. Both definitions are aligned with the actions that fuel racism, marginalization, and *othering*. Racism is a power dynamic that perpetuates the attitudes and behaviors aligned with the belief that one group of people is to be treated with respect and deference based on the color of their skin. This group holds this conscious or unconscious belief and has power over what they consider a lesser-than, thus subservient, race of people. Marginalization is the act of being treated as insignificant or peripheral. Othering, a process we explore in depth later, is the process by which we treat and view people as intrinsically inferior, different from, and alien to oneself.

If your choice is to move away from programmed bias and bigotry, then the inner work aligned with exploration of the Enneagram can be a transformative and healing experience. It takes time to explore which of these archetypal personality structures resonates with the way you show up in the world. By discovering where you fit in the landscape of these personality archetypes you can strengthen your resolve to become radically active within the human mosaic. The understanding of humanity as a mosaic is a stark contrast to the long-held view of humanity as a melting pot. I like to consider the Enneagram archetypes as the setting for the beautiful gems that we are when we come together as a complete yet ever-evolving depiction of our collective mosaic. When combined with IDEA work, the

Enneagram brilliantly illuminates our soul connections, and justice and peace can prevail.

The Enneagram invites you to explore your own way of being and opens the door to understanding many of the personal mechanisms behind the way you function, such as *why* you do the things you do. Understanding your own basic motivation, values, fears, and the strengths you have to offer are gifts that keep on giving. At the same time, there are things that are intrinsic to our egoic structures that trip you up, preventing you from being a person who can operate from a place of wellness and love. This book is specifically designed to help you focus on finding *your place* as humanity moves toward activation as connected Allies and Advocates. It will be our evolution from apathy to engagement on the path to reconnecting our global society that will ultimately heal humanity.

In life we all occupy different perches of a societal hierarchy of "power, position, and privilege." Some of us can walk through life unencumbered by the limitations associated with certain dimensions of our diversity, while some of us constantly struggle to overcome or endure daily indignities based on how our bodies show up in this world. When we acknowledge these barriers and obstacles that divide us, we gain understanding as to how they contribute to the marginalization or advancement of our global society. For the purpose of our exploration, we will examine three distinct "categories" of how our society has historically separated people within the social hierarchy: people with automatic advantage, people who develop positional power, and people pushed to the margins of society based on some dimension of their diversity—this is the group we have respectfully deemed the *Love Warriors.*

Automatic advantage is a term we will use throughout this book to cover the concepts of privilege, position, and power. Many people think the term *privilege* indicates entitlement and guilt. Privilege is an advantage, a special right, or immunity granted or available only to a particular person or group. While the term may elicit a negative response from some, the reality of having privilege should be an irrefutable fact. Acknowledging or admitting your privilege does not imply guilt, nor does it automatically lead to condemnation. The realization that many people live with automatic advantage and exist with inherent rights, opportunities, and possibilities that "others" do not seems to be a concept that creates conflict and pushback from the very beginning. So, let's take the stigma out of the word *privilege* and call it what it is: an *automatic advantage*. An automatic advantage may be any factor of a person's diversity they are born into that places them at a higher or more advantageous perch within the social and cultural hierarchy. This includes but is not limited to: being born into a body that is White, heterosexual, cisgender male, nondisabled, socioeconomically influential, physically and mentally nondisabled, or anything deemed "culturally dominant." This is not to say anyone who does not occupy these specific dimensions of diversity cannot or will not have automatic advantage. The concept of automatic advantage is relative and fluid. However, in our society the term historically refers to the value placed on the aforementioned dimensions of diversity.

If you do not experience observable marginalization in your everyday life and have some sort of automatic advantage, you may be reading this book in search of a way to become a better Ally to stand on the side of truth, justice, and advocacy, or to help you better understand how you have been complacent in your position within the human mosaic. Your automatic advantage, in whatever form it may take, has placed you higher on the social or cultural hierarchy. The automatic advantage you carry may open certain doors, grant you immunity from certain inequities, and absolve you from the daily indignities that flourish within our society. It is important to note that to not acknowledge your position, power, and automatic advantage is tantamount to using your position, power, and automatic advantage to perpetuate the systems put in place to oppress, marginalize, and discriminate.

In order to step into Allyship and authentic Advocacy, it is vital to acknowledge and manage your automatic advantage to create equity for those pushed to the margins in any system or situation. Using your automatic advantage to balance the scales, so to speak, is a fundamental step in bridging the divides many of us are currently facing. When we use our automatic advantage to either maintain our complacency or to fulfill self-seeking motives, we are essentially perpetuating the systemic inequities and reinforcing the social hierarchies of perceived race, gender roles, socioeconomic status, and other forms of value placed on dimensions of our diversity. Having automatic advantage is not a signifier of a biased or prejudiced person, but it does hold a degree of accountability to acknowledge the reality that the automatic advantage you possess affects those around you, even at an unconscious level. If you are reading this book and you have an automatic advantage, first understand that you are not to blame for the privilege, position, or power you were born into. You are, however, responsible as a human being to explore your automatic advantage and the effect it has on how you navigate through life. Fr. Richard Rohr teaches us, "The journey to happiness involves finding the courage to go down into ourselves and take responsibility for what's there: all of it."

As a person with automatic advantage, this book will help you explore:

- your self-identification as a human across a multidimensional diversity spectrum

- what it looks like to transform into an Ally and Advocate

- how you can begin to acknowledge aspects of your own unhealed trauma

- how you view, or are blind to, the various dimensions of diversity

- how the lens through which you view "others" may have been formed and affected

- the implicit biases you may be holding on to and how they can be uncovered, addressed, and overcome

- how your automatic advantage can be used to heal the divides we face as a global community.

The next "category" we explore consists of the people who have been historically, systematically, and perpetually pushed to the margins of society by systemic disparities, including discriminatory laws and practices, the prevailing acceptance of social "norms," the passing down of biased messages on value and power, and the perpetuity of stereotypes. This space is occupied by the *Love Warriors*, a term we have intentionally adapted in place of socially constructed labels such as "marginalized," "disenfranchised," "oppressed," and "minority." A Love Warrior is someone who faces discrimination, prejudice, and/or inequity as a hierarchical penalization for some dimension of their diversity. Much of the marginalization and discrimination that takes place in the world is directly connected to our physical form, the body that we inhabit from birth. You did not choose your physical body, and yet you are judged, labeled, elevated, or demeaned by how your body shows up in this world. For example, if you have been subjected to racism, homophobia, xenophobia, sexism, ageism, ableism, or any form of othering and "ism" based on how people perceive and label the way your body shows up, you are or have been marginalized by definition. While most people have experienced some form of discrimination in their life, Love Warriors are a distinctly defined group of individuals who experience daily indignities that fundamentally affect how they move through the world. These are people who face obstacles in situations where there is a conscious or unconscious inquiry into their value and position.

If you reside on the periphery of society based on some dimension of your diversity and find yourself explicitly restrained to your position despite your efforts, you may be considered a Love Warrior. Words have power, and I choose them intentionally with the awareness of the energy they carry. Do not think of yourself as a minority or a marginalized person. You are a warrior. Love is your arsenal. This book will serve as an introductory guide along your path toward healing and recovering hope in the humanity of people.

As a Love Warrior you will have opportunities throughout this book to begin your exploration into:

- your internal trauma and the wounds inflicted by systemic oppression and inequity
- the biases you may be holding on to as a result of your experience of being pushed to the margins of society

- shifting into a position of power through compassionate self-reflection and intentional activation

- occupying a space of hope, connection, and healing.

The final category we explore spans a diverse spectrum of people who reside in the middle ground between those at the highest level of the social hierarchy and those who have been forced to the lowest levels. If you have been born into this middle ground, you may have developed "positional power." This middle ground is difficult to occupy and can affect where a person resides within the social hierarchy. The situation or circumstance determines their placement. Even in considering this as a category, the people who reside in this space are in fact being marginalized. This is unfortunately an unavoidable concept as we make progress toward dismantling the systemic inequities that fabricate this middle ground.

As a person who may have positional power, this book will serve as an introductory guide in your exploration of:

- your self-identification as a human through a multidimensional diversity spectrum

- uncovering aspects of your own unhealed trauma

- how you view, or are blind to, the various dimensions of diversity

- how you navigate your intersectionality and the value you place on certain aspects of your own identity

- how the lens through which you view "others" may have been formed

- the implicit biases you may be holding on to

- how you can use your positional power to bridge the divides we face as a connected global community.

Regardless of how your body shows up in this world, this book is intended to:

- help you begin to explore what you may need to heal,

- help you begin your evolution as individual Allies and Advocates for Love Warriors, and

- advocate for collective unification and movement toward eliminating racism, gender and sexual diversity discrimination, classism, and all forms of othering.

I am extending an invitation to you, the reader, to explore your personality archetype and to activate as Allies, Advocates, Love Warriors, and compassionate humans within a beloved community—a community that acknowledges that, while we were created in many diverse forms of body, color, ethnicity, gender and sexual diversity, manners of worship, abilities, and more, we are all part of one race: that race is called human. Together we are, as intended, a complete collective creation of the Divine.

As we work together to strengthen our ability to show up as strong Advocates for racial and social justice, we can begin to envision a future where, together as Allies, we become the change in the world that eradicates the "isms" that threaten the cooperative and collective connections of our species.

To manifest this miraculous feat, we must acknowledge the current state of *what is*. In the words of Fr. Richard Rohr, "transformation is often more about unlearning than learning."

Chapter 2

THE INFLECTION
POINT

EARLY MESSAGES AND MESSENGERS

We can witness the genesis of distinct patterns when people are asked to recall their very first memory of experiencing a feeling of being diminished. If we consider the racialized side of discrimination, some have a vague recollection of an event occurring around elementary-school age; some people of color have very vivid and early memories of personal racial trauma, and some people may share a collective racial trauma with their families or communities. There is a similar dynamic that exists for individuals who carry the pain of being Love Warriors based on who they choose to love, how they choose to worship, how their bodies show up in the world, and what ethnic/cultural group they claim as part of their identity. Regardless of a person's background, nearly everyone harbors a memory occurring early in their childhood of marginalization seeping into their lives through learned societal behavior, family experiences and messages, or even through unconscious patterns of processed data.

To illustrate this, I'd like to share a story from my childhood.

Our flight landed in Birmingham en route to Mobile and then finally to Fort Deposit, Alabama, to visit my grandmother. The thud and the screech and the smoke indicated it was not a normal landing. I heard people speculating around me. Perhaps the plane had blown a tire or lost a propeller or the landing gear had malfunctioned. I was a five-year-old girl taking my first flight, so this was a new experience for me. My head hit the seat in front of me, my rear end hit the floor, and I found myself peering up from under the seat. I still have the vivid memory of thinking, I'm in trouble now.

"What the hell are you doing down there! Get up! Next time I take you on a trip, you are going to be old enough to take care of yourself!" Momma snapped. I watched as she adjusted her hat, smoothed her dress, and put on her trademark movie-star sunglasses. As I quickly scrambled back up into my seat, I realized that the seatbelt that I had not fastened must have been pretty important. My mother looked visibly distressed, and I just assumed that it was the unnerving landing. She loved to travel, but this was her maiden voyage in the air. I had no way of knowing what was coming next.

We deplaned in Birmingham for the connecting flight to Mobile, and we waited inside the terminal. I don't remember much about the physical structure of the building, but I clearly remember what happened next. Momma looked me over and smoothed my rather unruly hair to the best of her ability—hairstyling was never her strong suit. My hair was ungraciously tamed, and my unfashionably ugly hat was pulled down tightly over my coppery coils. Momma looked at me sternly and said, "Go into the bathroom and be quick. I'll wait for you right here." I knew not to question my mother. Momma was a force to be reckoned with.

"Momma, aren't you going to go?" I asked.

"No, I'm not. I just want to get the hell out of here."

Something was happening, but at the time I didn't understand it. When I came out of the bathroom, my mother was not there. When I looked for her across the hallway, my eyes brought her into focus. She was there, exactly where I left her, and yet I barely recognized her. My mother was a strong, proud, flamboyant woman. A woman whose strength no one dared to question. Momma's sunglasses were in her hand, and she had removed her hat. She had her head down, and everything about her looked and felt uncomfortable and unfamiliar to me. I had always seen my mother as fierce and unshakable, but somehow, in this moment, she seemed diminished. She appeared to be smaller, sad, and subdued. I had no idea what was happening. I was frightened by her sudden transformation.

It took me well into my adulthood to understand what had happened that day. How could I ever have understood how she felt? She had just successfully made me into a passable little White girl so that I would not have to go into the "colored" bathroom. She had made herself small so that she could sell the lie, positioning herself in a humble and nonthreatening posture. My mother was browner than I was, so the strategy was to appear as my nanny. Even though I couldn't explain what was happening, I experienced an inner knowing at the tender age of five years old that something had subdued this force of nature that was my mother, and whatever it was, it felt deeply wrong. I wanted it gone.

I looked at my mother, and when I spoke, my words came out in a whisper. "Momma, are you okay?"

She came back from the other world that she had been transported to in her mind. Momma looked at me with tears in her eyes, and her voice trembled, "Yes, Debby, I'm okay. Did you wash your hands? Was there anyone else in there?"

I started to speak, but when I noticed she wasn't really listening to me, I asked again. "Momma, are you okay?"

The tears gathering in her eyes were beginning to spill across her beautiful high cheekbones. Until this very moment, I had never seen my mother cry. She put on her sunglasses, a signature move that I would learn to recognize as her way of disguising *her tears. She began to speak, a quiet tremble in her voice. "I just want to get the hell out of here."*

I took her hand in mine and replied, "Let's go, Momma," and led my mother out of the airport terminal.

The sun was blistering hot on our faces and the air was inescapable and uncomfortably heavy like a tortuous metaphor of what we had just experienced. I have come to recognize the smothering air of oppression. It was unfamiliar to me that day, but since then I have experienced places where that air became familiar.

As we ventured outside, Momma put on her wide-brimmed hat and pulled herself back up to her full height. She looked at me and managed a weary but reassuring smile. I have replayed that moment over in my mind countless times. I knew that I must have done something right by taking the lead and getting her out of that building. She had followed me and gone along with the temporary reversal of roles. I had been the protective mother, and she was pleased with me. I watched her strength return, and I felt relieved and safe once again. My mother was back. We smiled at each other. I asked, "Can I take my hat off?"

Her face tightened once again as she looked around us, and she touched the top of my head. "Not just yet, but soon, baby. Soon."

From that day forward I continued to have an acute awareness of marginalization and othering. I have spent most of my life being a part of projects, programs, and organizations with a focus on helping Love Warriors. I have always worked to engage people in challenging marginalization and othering, even in my adolescence. When I was 10 years old, I started a neighborhood charm school for the other children in my area. It seemed like the right thing to do. I had been given an opportunity to have experiences that were not accessible to little girls like me, and I knew I had to appreciate and cultivate that opportunity. My life took many twists and turns from there. I married a West Point graduate, became an army wife, and gave birth to our first child while my husband was in Vietnam. When he returned from the war, he decided to go to medical school. I worked, took care of our baby, and went to school at night so that I could complete my undergrad degree and he could go to medical school.

When the marriage failed after a decade, a new and unforeseen chapter of service began for me. Now single and with two small children to raise and a full-time job, I went back to school. I took on an additional part-time job as a special events coordinator at a department store in El Paso, Texas. This gave me purview over Joske's Teen Board, a group of beautiful, talented high school girls, most of whom were Latina. Once again, I was involved in a way where I could have an impact on young Love Warriors. My teen board girls watched me fall in love again, begin a new life, and marry the love of my life (40 years together and still smiling). My next assignment was working with at-risk youth in El Paso, culminating in my appointment as consultant to the city manager. My work in the social services arena led to my discovery that El Paso had difficulty maintaining a runaway shelter. I was able to cut through the red tape and logistics challenges, identify a venue, train the staff, and get the doors open. I went on to become director of the runaway and emergency shelters for the city, another opportunity to get involved in bringing people back in from the margins.

My heart was deeply affected by the painful conditions of runaways and abused children, my mind was deeply immersed in my graduate school studies, and my body was reeling from the task of adjusting to my new marriage and raising two children with another on the way. From El Paso, the next stop was Augsburg, Germany. My new husband was an army doctor, and I was on the road as an army wife once again. In Germany, I taught psychology and was the counselor for the cooperative work experience program at the Augsburg American High School. I loved the students and managed to find creative ways to keep them educated, employed, and engaged as young people in a foreign land. When we returned to the U.S., my husband was assigned to the United States Military Academy (USMA) at West Point as the brigade surgeon for the corps of cadets. Talk about coming full circle! I was hired to work with the research project that was a joint venture between the USMA and the Albert Einstein College of Medicine to study the effects of stress on the student population. I learned so much about how stress affects the body. Little did I know how significant that information would be as my career path continued to unfold.

It was with great reluctance that I gave up that position; I was painfully aware of the limited number of women and students of color who were enrolled at the USMA. This was also before the Clinton administration enacted the "Don't Ask, Don't Tell" military policy for anyone who identified as other than heterosexual. My husband and I were grateful for the time that we spent there, as we knew that we could provide a safe space for those who needed support. These students were "others," and they carried the stress of that status right along with the rigorous demands and discipline of the environment. I'll admit that it did keep me up at night.

I would approach every new space that I entered like a soldier commanding my own army. My husband had his orders, and I had mine. The problem was that I was beginning to feel like that old military slogan. I was an army of one, and it was wearing me down. I left West Point after accepting a psychotherapist position at the State University of New York at New Paltz. Once again, I carved out my niche and found myself with students who were struggling to balance college life and the underlying burden of being "other." My position came along with the additional responsibility of being co-coordinator of the Mentorship Scholars Program (MSP). The MSP was designed to provide psychological, academic, and social support for economically disadvantaged students of color. I carried a caseload of students who needed therapy, taught classes in the Black Studies department, and was the lynchpin for the MSP. I took on the responsibility of being the advisor to the president of the university for multicultural affairs. This swan song "assignment," as I have called many of the jobs that I held over the years, was the pinnacle of my career as an employee. I experienced that something was happening with our young people, which gave rise to a feeling of sadness that was inexplicable for me. I listened to the students and did my level best to support them when they were in crisis—marginalization and othering emerged as common themes for their suffering. I had an awakening that opened an awareness in the core of my being that there was something missing from the therapeutic process. I connected with the students by creating a safe space for them to be authentic and vulnerable on their journey to heal the broken parts of their hearts and souls. It was much like the experience of reaching my hand out to help my mother when the pain of her past experiences came flooding back to her in front of me in that airport in Alabama. I knew once again that I was being called to continue my journey. My husband received orders to command the health facilities at Aberdeen Proving Grounds in Maryland, and I had a decision to make: find another job or create an opportunity. Out of the stillness the answer came. I was to start my own business and name it "Trinity." I didn't receive much more direction than that . . . so that is exactly what I did. Trinity Transition Consultants was born and there was no looking back.

Shortly after my business was established, I received a phone call from Army Family Services. "Hello, uh, Dr. Egerton. This is AFS calling, and we were told that Colonel Egerton's wife is a psychologist. We have a team of contractors on site here at Aberdeen Proving Grounds that wants someone to help them with team building. Do you do that?"

"Yes, I do," I responded. From there it became much clearer as to what I was getting myself into with this new career venture. I accepted the consulting position to work with those contractors. There were nine of them. After working with them for a few months, I felt that they were ready to take the next steps on their own. In my final session with them, I explained how I could see them continuing their work of being a high-performing team, bringing forth their best talents to support one another. This is what I shared with them: (The names are changed to respect their privacy.)

"Joe, you are the moral compass of this team. You will point out the things that challenge the integrity of the team. Martin, you have a heart for the people. The project does not define the way you treat one another, and you will always bring the team back together with kindness. Charles, you are the go-getter, a can-do kind of guy. You are resourceful and will find ways to make sure that the best outcome is achieved. James, you are unique in the way that you view the tasks that lay in front of you. You add depth and creativity to the team's mission. Bernard, you are the team's researcher. You will always make sure that all the information is brought to the table so that credible decisions can be made. John, your capacity to see what may be needed at any point in time is uncanny. Your backup plans have backup plans. You are a walking safety net. Len, thank you for all the ways that you have managed to keep it light even at times when this felt like a heavy lift. Continue to keep your team positive. Rafael, your gift is your fearlessness and relentless capacity to keep it real. You so often say what others are thinking but would not give voice to, even when no one really wants to own it. And finally, Jerry, you are the team peacekeeper. You don't always seem like you are paying attention, but when you speak up you bring the team to consensus. Speak more and don't hide in the shadows. This team needs your peacemaking ability. And with that, gentlemen, carry on with what you have begun here, and take good care of one another. That is every bit as important as the work that you came here to do."

When I did the team-building work with this group, I did not yet know the Enneagram. I went home that evening and began searching online for more information about team-building tools and personality assessment, which brought me to the Enneagram Institute.

Fast forward many years, and I continue to design ways to engage people that provide the possibility for positive outcomes. My training as a psychotherapist and my work as an executive coach and organizational development consultant allows me to hold on to my heaven-sent belief that we really can uncover the best in ourselves and others. I believed it as a child, and I hold fast to that belief today. I love my work because it affords me the opportunity to make a difference in the lives of the people that I encounter. It's the age-old concept of leaving a place a little better than you found it. That "place" for me is in the people that I meet, work with, and encounter, even if it's only in passing. And still I felt that I needed something more. Something that would make the work more sustainable. In working with one of my long-term clients, the director of the organization made a comment that sent me straight back to stillness. She said, "You know Dr. E, it's amazing how much better we all behave when you come around. It's like you have become our spiritual mother." I wanted to be flattered, but I understood exactly what that meant. They were not doing their own work, and I needed something that would help people continue to "do the work" after I had left the building. The Enneagram was the answer, but I did not expect the Enneagram journey to lead me down a path into the heart of humanity.

Ultimately my work evolved, and I transitioned to more executive coaching and less psychotherapy. My company became more actively focused on consulting and coaching in the IDEA space. I believed that this was the place where I could help to create a safe space for individuals to speak their truth and be who they were created to be. My experience as an Enneagram practitioner helps individuals find the blueprint as to why they do what they do, which often includes looking at the depth of their hatred and fears. Hatred and fear—these two gangsters walk hand in hand.

I am still on the journey, as that is how life is meant to be: a continuous exploration and endless unfolding of the evolution and intersection of our human and spiritual nature. We will not evolve without the exploration of why we react, respond, and behave as we do. Evolution is a necessity for the survival of the human species. We must evolve beyond racism and othering for our very survival. Every nation has its historical and institutional demons to wrestle. Much has been written about human beings' inhumanity toward fellow humans and the need to dominate to feel better about oneself. I don't want to regurgitate what is already out there. I do want to illuminate the path of peace and reconciliation and help all humans wake up and rebuild the bridges that bias, bigotry, and hatred broke.

In the safe space that is created when I work with people one-on-one, the unfolding of the divine order begins to show itself. We were not intended to harm or hate one another. How did I know this as a child? How do I know it now? Because it is true. We hear this message frequently from parents, teachers, and spiritual leaders such as pastors and preachers, reverends and priests, rabbis, monks. Many of us are taught to love one another, and yet we proceed to leave that message behind and move forward like zombies who've forgotten everything good that we have been taught. Compassion and empathy are essential human qualities, and somehow, we teach ourselves to switch them off. Many have defined 21st-century existence through a lens of fear, apathy, and separation. We have hardened our minds and our hearts to create the imperfect armor against harmful attitudes and actions. In the United States, the climate of racial injustice is riddled with conflicting narratives that have divided families, destroyed friendships, and alienated entire communities. Perhaps we are just trying to protect ourselves against real and perceived threats.

So once again, we leave behind the messages we received of love and compassion and ignore the light that resides within us. In spite of our efforts to rationalize why "I am right, and you are wrong," we cannot justify the end result: chaos, confusion, loss of trust, and division. We can know justice and know peace when we go deeper into understanding how to do the inner work and how each of us can contribute to eradicating racism, gender and sexual discrimination, classism, and all forms of marginalization. By utilizing our gifts as Allies who stand with BIPOC (Black, Indigenous, people of color) and all the targets of marginalization and discrimination in communities, we can activate as Advocates for inclusion, diversity, equity, and anti-racism.

Perhaps it is time to humble ourselves and really do the work so that there is something left for future generations. We have to take a leap of faith to fight for and heal humanity, and begin to build the bridges to reconnect to one another. With my faith as my strength and the Enneagram as my road map, I have been able to continue working on those bridges to reconnect humankind. The negative behaviors and beliefs that continue to be perpetuated and go unchallenged ultimately create a strong desire to retreat and withdraw. This is the opposite of what is needed to breathe life back into our global society. If we are going to eradicate all forms of othering now and in the future, it will take more than a village. It will require a global army of Love Warriors, Allies, and Advocates taking a stand to stop the hatred and division born of bias and bigotry.

COMMUNITY OR CHAOS

The Enneagram, when studied and implemented correctly, teaches us how to be together in community through connection and interrelatedness. Our ability to relate to one another is dependent on how we invest our time and efforts into understanding the connections. When asked, "How can I improve my relationships?" my answer is, "The more you know about yourself, the better the quality of your relationships." As individuals, we have a natural tendency to look toward the external to correct things that are not working well for our individual way of being. If I were to ask you, "Whose attitudes, behaviors, and beliefs can you control?," your response is likely to be, "Only my own." While we know the correct answer to this question, we do not live our lives in a way that is aligned with that response. We may know that this is true; however, our tendency is to expect other people to change their behavior to fit our personal wants and needs. Let it suffice to say that there are few among us who cannot come up with a list of ways that we would like for the people around us to change their behaviors. Especially if those behaviors affect you personally.

The Enneagram can help us to peel back the layers of our individual internal programming to do the work of releasing what no longer serves us for our individual growth and the greater good. Inner work involves waking up and becoming present to how you show up in the world. When you begin to pay attention to how your attitudes, behaviors, and beliefs have you trapped in a fortress of judgmental binary thinking, you are beginning to do inner work. Inquiry without judgment and expansion of your heart space is the resulting awareness from this work. Learning about and understanding yourself in terms of what drives and motivates you is essential. Becoming more open and accepting that we do not all have the same way of moving through the world and understanding how you relate with others based on what drives and motivates them is all part of doing your inner work. It is how we are able to move beyond dehumanizing people by no longer seeing them as objects or pawns in the game of life and move toward honoring the humanity of every individual, thus regaining our own humanity. We can allow ourselves to experience the world around us in a new way. A kinder, more compassionate, and more loving community must emerge. This can only happen if we do our individual work and come together as a community that treats no one as less than but rather seeks to elevate each individual to reach their highest and best. This is how we come to know peace.

The Enneagram can help us to become fully present as we grow and learn how to be connected to one another across differences. Remember: *presence is not a privilege; it is a necessity.*

THE ROAD MAP

An army needs a map and a strategic plan for how to approach and defeat the real or perceived enemy. And make no mistake, we are an army of Love Warriors, Allies, and Advocates. In this book, we explore how the Enneagram can serve as a map to guide us through the understanding and appreciation of the similarities and differences across all of humanity. The capacity to give and receive love is a precious gift. It is this gift that allows you to thrive and function in community and to love others as you learn to love yourself. The wisdom encapsulated in the Enneagram becomes a powerful framework for creating authentic Allies, Advocates, and Love Warriors who lead with love and compassion. The exploration of the nine different Points on the map allows us to fully engage our inner work to strengthen our capacity for seeing people for who they are as human beings and not as objects. In other words, the Enneagram allows us to see and understand human beings based on how their core motivations and basic fears express themselves in the world, rather than viewing them as detached entities with preconceived motives and habitual behaviors. There is so much more to a person than we give them credit for. I am reminded of a billboard that I would drive past frequently on the highway that read, "If you knew my story you wouldn't hate me." The Enneagram opens you up in a way that allows you to see how you truly show up in the world. This can be very different from the way that people experience your behaviors. Unfortunately, we also have created a value system that focuses the gaze to the external, and the resulting outcome is destroying our humanity.

Racism is the original sin among the many ways that we have been taught to demean, dismiss, and disrespect "others." The social construct of race continues to be a destructive force that has poisoned the minds and hearts of our collective humanity. There is no way to soften or reinterpret this reality. We have all been duped; the truth about the human struggle to survive and thrive and at what cost is quite a bit different from what we were taught in our history books. Systemic racism has left a legacy of death and destruction within our collective cultures. Sexism, homophobia, xenophobia, and dogmatic religious discord have villainized, demonized, and destroyed lives and communities around the world. We can choose any dimension of human diversity and culture and explore the ways that a dominant culture has impeded progress and ultimately subjected "others" to inhumane treatment in order to force them to occupy a lower place in the hierarchical structures of society.

We, as a communal species, are at a pivotal point in our human evolution; we are faced with the need for a critical course correction. Our reality is changing, power dynamics are shifting, and marginalized communities are redefining their place in this world. This metamorphosis, like all aspects of change, naturally creates fear and conflict as the current dominant culture clings to and fights for the familiar comforts of *the way things were.* Inherent in the definition of the word *culture* is *the way that people do things.* Culture defines what is acceptable and what is not. We explore culture through the lens of White bodies and bodies of color and how we have been taught to categorize certain aspects of these bodies, to lay the foundation for how we have treated and viewed one another.

A fundamental flaw in our foundation is the failure to pick up the mirror and do the work of coming to fully understand ourselves as individuals who ultimately become part of a collective community in a societal structure. The foundational aspect of evolution is the survival of the fittest through natural selection, but the broader view of this concept is that *communities rather than individuals are more likely to survive.* Communities rely on cooperation and mutually beneficial practices; generosity, compassion, contribution, and support are key elements in determining a community's survival. The social construct of race and the ensuing process of classifying humans—we use the term *othering*—are designed to divide our communities into dichotomous hierarchical systems that directly oppose successful human evolution. If we choose *not* to come together as a species to address these threats to our existence, the outcome will result in a rapid descent into complete chaos, which only reinforces the divides. The healing process for humanity begins with doing our own inner work as individuals and identifying and uprooting the origins of our divisions; divisions held at an individual level and sustained at a collective level. We must find a way to address where these divisions dwell within us and how they have affected the way in which we navigate our world.

WAKE UP

Many have embarked on the Enneagram journey in search of the secrets to maintaining healthy relationships. The first step is the recognition that change only happens when you are willing to let the work begin with you. Much like the message in Michael Jackson's song "Man in the Mirror," when you truly look at yourself, you unlock the capacity for significant transformation that extends to everyone around you. The people closest to you will know that something has changed. Your family, friends, co-workers, partners, and acquaintances will experience the change that comes from taking off your metaphorical mask and opening your heart. The work of the Enneagram opens you up from the inside out. The authentic desires and experiences of your heart will begin to reveal themselves in the outside world. Your *authentic self*, as opposed to your idea of the best version of yourself, will begin to emerge. Give it a chance. Once you begin to truly know yourself, you can find empathy, compassion, and love everywhere. It is indeed possible to open your heart to all of humanity.

The inner work that you engage with the Enneagram has universal application. I have brought the Enneagram to neighborhoods, schools, communities, and organizations that are looking for ways to align their diversity and social justice strategies with their achievable goals in a way that honors the dignity and respect for every unique individual. My work has earned me the affectionate moniker the "Enneagram JEDI" (Justice, Equity, Diversity, Inclusion). I love my work and I believe that there are more positive people around the world than any one person has the capacity to identify. I will admit to being on a mission to find all of them. The challenge is that "good people" who are passive and inactive are unknowing contributors to the societal scourge of othering, racism, bias, and bigotry. When it comes to racism and othering, *there is no middle ground.* Being oblivious or indifferent to it qualifies as being complicit and aligned with guilt by passive association.

Perhaps you are experiencing a persistent call to wake up or maybe just a flicker of light in the darkness of our current cultural climate. If you are experiencing an awakening in the stark reality of the disruptive forces of othering, bias, bigotry, and racism: don't go back to sleep! Stay awake and occupy the space that is designed for you to show up at this critical moment in time.

So let's begin. Every journey begins with a first step. If this is your first step, please take my hand. As I said to my mother: let's go . . .

FINDING THE PATH

Whether you are new to the Enneagram or you have studied it for many years, you might ask yourself: *To what end is this exploration? What is the purpose of this deep dive?* Your answer may be that you are trying to intentionally engage on the journey to find that place where you can embrace your authentic self. You may be in search of a way to heal your own trauma, unearthing and acknowledging the wounds inflicted by racism and othering as you have been pushed to the margins of society. Perhaps you are feeling the need to wake up and challenge your inherent attitudes, behaviors, and beliefs. Maybe you have come to the realization that it is not enough to say things like "I don't have a biased bone in my body; I embrace everyone." First of all, statements like that are problematic primarily because they are not true. We all have biases. I have never heard of anyone who identifies themselves as unabashedly biased; however, their actions demonstrate quite clearly that they are racist, homophobic, xenophobic, and sexist, among other things.

Only your authentic self has the grace to accept this conviction and make an intentional shift away from those biases. Actions will always speak louder than words, and silence and no action are perceived as an affirmation of the status quo. All bias comes with a cost. The acceptance of the biases formed in the margins creates additional wounding on the journey toward healing. Everyone has wounds to heal.

When viewed through the lens of the Enneagram, race as a social construct, the effects of systemic discrimination based on all dimensions of diversity, and subsequently how we have all been gaslighted into accepting this as our reality becomes painfully clear. The established perspective of "race" as it pertains to our society in the United States of America begins with the documented enslavement and subsequent destruction of multiple civilizations and continues throughout our complex and tumultuous history. Since the beginning, we have all lived in a biased society that thrives on the othering of its people. Some people who argue that racism (or sexism, homophobia, etc.) isn't a big deal fail to recognize that the engineered reality we live in is based on the foundation of systemic oppression. If you doubt that we are still experiencing the effects of slavery, religious persecution, medical experimentation on bodies of color, the oppression of the gender and sexual diversity community, or the inequities in the justice system, I invite you to take a moment and look around you.

Many people exist in the margins of our society, forced to the periphery by systemic inequities that affect how and where they live and work, who they love, how they worship, their ability to improve their situation, and even the extent to which they are able to function within society. If you resonate with this concept, you may fall into a category people refer to as minorities, marginalized, disenfranchised, disadvantaged, or oppressed. As stated earlier, I refer to the people who reside in these categories as *Love Warriors*. I have intentionally adopted this terminology to move away from labels that are intrinsically dismissive and demeaning. *Minority* implies that a group of people are inferior by the very nature of the word. People who are forced to exist in a world that constantly pushes against their survival and well-being have earned the right to be identified respectfully. To show up and face daily indignities and continue to persevere takes the strength of a warrior. The strongest warriors of all understand the reality that love is the most powerful armor and shield to protect you from real or perceived adversaries. It is also a sword to wield that will render every adversary defenseless. It takes time, faith, strength, and a resilient spirit to win this battle. Many people who occupy this space do not choose love as their weapon or protection. They assume the posture of warrior but reject the concept of love as a mechanism of engaging in this ongoing battle.

There are many who have come before us that have left their legacy and lessons to guide us on this journey. This path is long and treacherous without the motivation and protection that is available through a spirit of love. We have a thorny and tangled history to uproot. For this journey toward uprooting systemic treachery, we begin by expanding on the social construct of race. In many ways this illustrates how we as a society have adapted the components of categorization to fabricate the hierarchical system that forces people to the margins. This practice, developed over generations and reinforced by a series of grievous events and policies, has enabled our collective demise as a society. We will continue to use the word *othering* as an umbrella term to define this process of assigning meaning and perceived value to a group of people based on some dimension of their diversity—assumed race and ethnicity, gender and sexual diversity, socioeconomic status, religion, age, geographical location, physical and mental ability, skin tone, culture—compounded with the stereotypes, biases, and unconscious patterns ingrained into the societal perception of the value assigned to each category of "other."

The process of othering was constructed to elevate one's own value by devaluing *dissimilar* people; the process is systematized by nature and hierarchical by design. The addition of intersectionality facilitates and emboldens the growth of othering on the foundation of a myriad of dimensions of our diversity.

As we continue to unlearn and reeducate ourselves, it is important to differentiate between having an automatic advantage and gaining positional power: both concepts are rooted in a biased system, but positional power denotes that a superior way of being exists and one should strive to assimilate to gain access to this level of socially constructed value. This is obviously a toxic and detrimental praxis to address and dismantle. We have witnessed positional power as the "offer" available to people pushed to the margins, as automatic advantage is guarded by those who already have power, position, and automatic advantage. The intention here is to shine a light on these unfair and biased practices and create a shift into a more equitable way of navigating through the world—to move away from the divergence of power, position, and automatic advantage and into a fair and equal existence for all humans.

Intersectionality is the key factor that contributes to the complicated and fluid identity of this particular group of positional power. *Intersectionality* can be defined as the "oppression and discrimination resulting from the overlap of an individual's various social identities." The intersectionality of a person's identity designates their unique place within the social construct of the value hierarchy—the more complex the identity, the more complicated the placement.

Let's consider a few hypothetical identities to illustrate this complex group dynamic. Pay attention to each dimension of diversity and consider how that may place the person higher or lower within the social hierarchy of value. Reflect on how positional power and intersectionality can manifest.

Let's look at a Black, cisgendered, heterosexual, light-skinned, upper middle class male with an advanced degree in the United States of America.

Black/African American	Marginalized norm
Cisgendered male as identified at birth	Dominant norm
Heterosexual	Dominant norm
Skin color lighter vs darker	Tolerable norm
Upper class/middle class	Advantage norm
Advanced degree: M.D., J.D., Ph.D.	Advantage norm
Professional career status	Advantage norm

While all of the factors listed above may give this Black man a level of positional power that may allow him to have a voice or measure of societal influence in a life or death situation, in the face of active othering, it will be the marginalized norm that determines his fate.

Continue this exercise by considering these identities:

- A multiracial woman who identifies as a member of the gender and sexual diversity community may have access and opportunity to readily advance her socioeconomic status. She may also use her voice and have a measure of societal influence. In a situation of active othering, her gender and sexual diversity and multiracial genetic background can limit the extent of her influence.

- A White male, living with a nonvisible disability, whose partner identifies as Latino, and who is a parent to multiracial children, may enjoy a high level of unencumbered access as he navigates the world as a solo entity. When he discloses his sexual diversity status and appears with his multiracial family, his value in the societal hierarchy is affected.

- An Asian nonbinary humxn resides in the upper class of society and holds a doctorate. They use their advanced knowledge and mental abilities to create opportunities for advancing their career and gaining a higher social standing. When this humxn speaks at a conference, their knowledge and expertise may increase their social value, but their gender and sexual diversity affects their position as they reside outside of the social dominant norm.

These people would, by definition, have positional power over groups of people who do not share similar dimensions of diversity, while also still having a specific dimension of diversity that places them lower on the social hierarchy of position and power. As you can see, this "category" is deeply complex and contains a multitude of juxtaposing elements that affect a person's identity. When people in positions of power are recognized by the dominant culture, the marginalized norm has a tendency to affect their level of positional power. Certain aspects of a person's identity could place them in different positions of power while offsetting other dimensions of their identity. The underlying concept that certain dimensions of diversity can "outrank," "redeem," or "make up for" other dimensions is a destructive paradox we must decipher and address while on the path toward equity. People with positional power, while occupying a paradoxical space, can play an essential role in rebuilding the bridges that our differences broke. The unique perspective of occupying a fluid position allows this group to connect polarities and create the space for dialogue, healing, and reconnection.

A common theme among people who reside in this space is the struggle for "acceptance" by their own community. The very nature of the complex identity of their existence threatens the collective identity and homogeneity of already marginalized communities. They may have the experience of "not being Black enough to be Black," or not being accepted based on their fluency in the native tongue of their community, or having a diverse/blended/"nontraditional" family which complicates their identity when out in public. One of the most common occurrences people in varying levels of positional power face is the experience of being "too much of one thing" to fit into a particular group; as in being "too mixed," too light, too dark, too much of one culture, too outside of the norm of their marginalized community, and so on. This experience of being too much or too little of one or more dimensions of diversity to be accepted into whatever group they reside within puts these individuals on their own margin within a margin. Their position in the group can be called into question and called out. It is a gray area that has compounded polarities. If you reside within this gray area, it is important to first find your identity and analyze the complexity behind the paradigm of positional power.

PROGRAMMING

We have been programmed to categorize people as "other," like computers programmed with an external code. Othering serves as the mechanism by which we dehumanize people and begin to view them as objects—as in "you are not like me and therefore you are not connected to me." This programming is immediate and seems to manifest shortly after we enter this world; later in life the programming mutates into an amalgam of toxicity and dehumanization. Let's start at the beginning of this process. There has been quite a bit written about the outdated practice of slapping babies upon their arrival to elicit the startled cry—what a way to enter the world! I am mindful of the fear that little ones experience when someone rushes the process of taking them away from Mom or Dad in an attempt to hold these little bundles of pure love. It usually produces two different experiences: a well-intentioned interaction for the adult and a traumatizing encounter for the infant. Having bonded with the familiar sense of their close family members, any other well-intentioned humans entering too close into a little one's space can be frightening and unwelcome. And so the bonding and othering begins; the reassuring embrace from Mom or Dad feels very different from the clinical slap on the butt or the fear instilled by an unfamiliar face or experience. Some othering is instinctive or learned, as with a baby going through the phase of parent attachment. Consequently, some of these behaviors are learned-instinctive responses. They are taught to us at the beginning of our development as little humans. We learn who to trust, who to be fearful of, and who we are to avoid at all costs. Most people can recall a moment in time where there was an instinctive fear-based response to a stranger. Often these fear-based responses come from things we have taken in as micromessages about whole groups of people. Left unexamined, this disconnect becomes our "normal." Left unexplored it will be our undoing. It will take the return to our innocence, to remembering the heart of the child you embodied before you were taught to disconnect from "others." It will be our intentional return to that state of consciousness that restores our world. Our connection is always there; however, we will not experience it until we look deep within to see with a new perspective. When we are able to see past labels, descriptors, and judgments, what appears is a message of "you are me, I am you, we are one."

Take a moment to pause and consider your self-identification as a human. This reflection will take considerable time. Do not rush through the identification of facets of your intersectionality and of those around you.

A UNIVERSAL CALL

The lockdown that accompanied the COVID-19 pandemic presented all of us with a huge opportunity to experience a collective awakening. Waking up is coming out of a state of nonawareness. You can't force it to come; however, you can be open to its unexpected arrival. It is having the experience of sight, smell, sound, taste, touch, and all accompanying sensations in an entirely different way. It is letting those sensations inform your being. Fear cannot thrive where there is an abundance of love, hope, and understanding. I am full of hope today. I am aware of my inner knowing that something powerful and meaningful has shifted. My studies and experiences with teaching the Enneagram have granted me the honor of witnessing transformational results and moments of awakening that still leave me awe-struck and inspired by those who have chosen to take this path.

You may feel a strong call to this path that comes from a source that you cannot identify or describe. It may be the collective spiritual energy of your ancestry. If you later choose to venture outside of the designated dogma, denomination, or spiritual heritage of your culture, this powerful call continues, as the call is universal. Every individual has access by the very nature of the call—which is to wake up. If we choose to acknowledge the call, we advance a little further along the path. There is a basic need for something to light the fire inside, and once it ignites, it burns and becomes something that you cannot ignore. It is not easily explained as it is a personal experience for each individual. It is the moment where you pause and acknowledge that something bigger than your own personal empathy, curiosity, and will has led you to a space where you will be guided to do your own work. If you are open to accepting the invitation, the grace to access the wisdom, courage, and preciousness of being brought into your own inner sanctum allows you to begin the work.

I remember vividly one of the stops along the way of my personal journey where I had encountered Russ Hudson, my first Enneagram teacher and lifelong friend. I have never forgotten the words that he spoke to me early on the journey. This was long before I knew we would continue down this road together. Russ said, "Deborah, if you would just stop competing with God, things might go a little easier." At that moment I knew why the words "be still and know that I am God" always stopped me in my tracks. This was my call to enter into a space of learning and an experience of true humility. The awakening to having an experience rather than a cognitive awareness is often overlooked as a necessary step toward activation and healing.

To follow the path means a surrendering of sorts that comes from the recognition that you don't have all the answers. It is in the silence of that surrender where you discover you have access to a greater source of wisdom, a compassionate entity that loves you more than you could ever imagine. This source has many names and forms, and for me, it is God. At this moment in time, I don't know how I would rise in the morning if I did not have this gift that I acknowledge as faith. I honor the light that resides within me, and I am grateful for the moments when I am given line of sight to that light residing within the people around me. For you, this source may come in any form.

Take a moment here to pause and reflect on your own experience of the Universal Call.

A UNIVERSAL RACE

The nine Points of the Enneagram illuminate the inner workings of our individual and collective humanity. As human beings we all have basic needs and experience a variety of emotions, but fear is behind so much of what divides us as a species and keeps us in a sleep state of disconnection. As stated earlier, we all belong to one universal race called "human"; however, we have managed to buy into a whole plethora of dividing factions and surface differences to use as justification for who gives and who receives. This bias-based way of functioning affects everything in our lives from who gets to go to the front of the line to who can't even enter the building. Who lives and who dies. Ultimately, who has freedom and who does not. So much of this has had such a long and successful run because we, as a collective global society, have allowed it.

When I began writing, I was at home taking shelter from the wildfires in California. The massive blaze engulfed the West Coast; people were being evacuated from their communities to ensure their safety, even amid a global pandemic. Now, seasons have come and gone, and yet the pandemic persists. I still wear a mask when I leave my home: initially as a requirement of the COVID-19 pandemic and additionally for protection from the poor air quality due to the ash that fell upon the San Joaquin Valley. I must admit that the physical phenomenon of donning a mask before I can walk out my front door gives me pause for much reflection. It has opened me up to the awareness of another awakening. This awakening was not unexpected, and it is still painful. I feel the physical separation from friends and family, and it is difficult to bear, a feeling shared by most of us regardless of our differences. Perhaps the silver lining in this global unrest will be a greater appreciation for human connection, and ultimately racial justice and social equity will emerge as a priority. And yet another awakening was lingering on the horizon. Once again, not unexpected, but this time it was too painful to bear. It arrived in the form of George Floyd.

When George Floyd was murdered, it happened in full view of anyone with access to any form of technology that allows for the streaming of events in real time or playback. We collectively experienced an unprecedented moment. It was not an unprecedented action. The fact that we were given a front-row seat to the last 9 minutes and 29 seconds of George Floyd's life was shocking, insane, and unbearable. The next day many of us woke up in the midst of what I call the reaction-resistance-response mode. There is no question that the murder of George Floyd administered a jolt to the nervous systems of people around the globe. Many people could not describe their feelings about what they witnessed; however, I noticed a pattern beginning to emerge.

Shock
REACTION
"WHAT IS THE WORLD COMING TO?"
"THIS CAN'T BE HAPPENING."
"HOW COULD THIS HAPPEN?"

Denial
RESISTANCE
"THERE IS MORE TO THIS STORY."
"THIS CAN'T BE REAL."
"SHOW ME THE PROOF."

Action
RESPONSE
"HOW CAN I MAKE A DIFFERENCE?"
"WHAT CAN I DO?"
"WHAT SHOULD I DO?"

REACTION

My phone was blowing up with texts and e-mails from people all around the world. Most of them did not know what to say. They simply wanted to share their concerns and extend some level of connection to the pain that they knew I must be feeling as a Black-bodied person. Most were White-bodied, many were Brown-bodied, all were shocked and feeling helpless and disturbed by what they had witnessed. Many were waking up to the inequity of care and compassion that gets extended to bodies of color. There were questions asked, and there was also a holding of sacred space for and with me. I was having a strong reaction, which was the collective exhaustion of my people. *Another Black body down. Gone. Forever. When will it end? Will it ever end?*

RESISTANCE

Shortly thereafter, and I mean very shortly, came the *haters*, and the belief that this man deserved to be treated as less than human began to emerge. Justifications of every variety were posted on social media. I quietly and carefully hid the posts that made it to my daily feed with a heavy heart. I recognized that this was not the time for me to fight the resistance. I was hurting and this heinous act of violation of a Black body had created a deep rupture in my being. I found myself going numb to the onslaught of hatred that began to gain momentum as a form of celebration of this man's murder.

RESPONSE

Different forms of activation of Allies started popping up around the world. Requests for resources for the White-bodied people to educate themselves became a daily occurrence. Copies of Robin DiAngelo's *White Fragility*, Resmaa Menakem's *My Grandmother's Hands,* Ibram X. Kendi's *How to Be an Antiracist*, and Ijeoma Oluo's *So You Want to Talk About Race* became bestsellers literally overnight. Documentaries were released. Anti-racism groups began forming online. Personally, I was spending 12 to 14 hours in front of my computer on Zoom facilitating group discussions about race and coaching CEOs and leadership teams, along with facilitating healing humanity seminars and workshops. I tried to keep the momentum going in this moment of possibility. The human attention span is short.

Fast forward to January 6, 2021. *This was also a response.*

INDIGNITIES AND OTHERNESS

I have witnessed this pattern of reaction-resistance-response for as long as I can remember. Each time I am reminded of the mask metaphor: I have worn a mask all my life, and I am beyond ready to take it off. It is not possible to do this until I know that I will be safe and accepted exactly as I am. As I contemplate this metaphor, I recall how the Enneagram has helped me to be present to my own woundedness and to do the healing work that allows me to breathe. An internal and external response. We all have a right to breathe, to take air into our lungs. This is a right that was taken away from George Floyd, with the whole world watching. *The simple right to breathe.*

To be a Black American is to live with a sense of isolation and perpetual otherness—the extreme opposite of oneness. The pandemic did nothing more to us than racism had already accomplished. COVID took our lives at a disproportionate rate. It exposed us to more risk, even as it claimed our bodies for the grave and left us to work often unprotected from the virus. It took jobs away from us disproportionately. It held the world captive to witness the inhumane murder of George Floyd. Another destroyed Black body shook us to our core and the world cried out for justice . . . even as the murders continued. I would be remiss if I did not call out that there are many compelling reasons to take a close look at racism. So much of othering stems from this system of oppression that has made it easier—dare I say "normal"—for the successful marginalization of individuals belonging to groups that do not fit the descriptors of the dominant cultural norms in every society.

The daily indignities that create wounds of racial injustice and othering are ubiquitous. I can only share some of them with you in this book, since it would be impossible to share all of them, and honestly, it would be too painful to relive. When I was a practicing psychotherapist, I would help people understand how trauma lives on in the body and how to heal those wounds. Addressing the collective wounds of people pushed to the margins is a work in progress. I understand and respect the process of doing this inner work. I too am on this path. It is not the quick fix or a "just manifest joy and you will be fine" that we often hear in podcasts. This is deep work that requires consistent heavy lifting. It would be easier if the violence and the hatred that is so prolific did not exist. But it does. So every day we take steps toward healing. And every day we are retraumatized. But we must persist.

In retrospect, we have *all* been living in a state of isolation, in one way or another, for centuries. Most people—people of color and White people alike—have avoided tough conversations and right action for as long as I have been alive. My generation, the baby boomers, and the generations that came before me would give a resounding chorus of affirmation to this reality. However, by the very nature of this disconnection, we have collectively perpetuated a destructive man-made social construct that has fostered our separation and isolation. It is our *connection* to our humanity that strengthens us, restores us, and bridges the chasm of our differences. Systemic racism, marginalization, and othering accomplishes the exact opposite. In order to connect to one another we might heed the wisdom of Socrates to "first know thyself."

Pause here and reflect on the condition of your connection to humanity. Who wears a mask that cannot be removed? Is it you or others around you?

FACE IT TO CHANGE IT

We know racism is the foundation we stand on to justify othering in all of its ugly forms: sexism, homophobia, transphobia, xenophobia, ableism, classism, religious discrimination, ageism, national origin discrimination, socioeconomical inequities, and so on. So in order to face an age-old adversary that has infected every corner of our culture, we need a plan, a guide that leads us through challenging times. Something more than a wish and a flurry of temporary activism—we need a miracle. The kind of miracle that emerges from faith, trust, and truth. The mere recognition that there is more that unites us than divides us is a first step toward bridging the divide. When we take the time to try to understand one another, it's easy to discover we are not so different after all. We may occupy different perches in a hierarchical societal structure where our individual perspectives show us different views of the same dilemmas. However, the societal structure of systemic racism and the flourishing of othering has set us all up to fail. We were socialized into a system of beliefs that perpetuated and supported racism and othering. We were taught and conditioned to believe that White-bodied humans hold more value than people of color. Many people were taught that heterosexual people are "normal" and anyone who does not fit into that category is "abnormal." Some of us were also given the message that people with disabilities were "less than" and consequently, we showed them less respect. Even in the realm of class and social standing, we harbor messages of value based on where a person resides in the social hierarchy.

This phenomenon exists throughout all the dimensions of our diversity in some form or another. These messages appeared everywhere from the time we were born. Whether you are Black, Brown, White, Asian, male, female, nonbinary, queer, Christian, Jewish, Muslim, a person with a disability, socioeconomically disadvantaged, or any form of "other," you may have been taught things that were less than kind, useful, or true about people whose bodies, ethnicities, cultures, or values appear different from yours. You may even have been taught to devalue your own body based on the way it shows up in this world. Some of us share points of intersectionality that affect our perceived worth on multiple levels. Our different vantage points on issues that are vital to our survival may appear insurmountable. I assure you they are not. If we choose to move forward, we all have some things to unlearn and we must reeducate ourselves.

Much like an infection that requires treatment before it enters the bloodstream, we will have to inspect our own internal wounds and address them if we expect to survive. Find out where the wound is located in your being and begin the healing process. Cleanse, disinfect, and apply a clean bandage, and be patient with the healing process. Systemic racism and othering has inflicted wounds upon all humans, regardless of how your body shows up in the world. We have seen the violence leading to death and destruction to the bodies of the Love Warriors among us. It will be the acceptance of our own flaws and differences that ultimately changes our future and leads us forward.

In a global society, we must ensure that the trajectory of our new path forward is aligned with unconditional respect for all of humanity. To thrive and prevail during these challenging times is to allow ourselves to learn from one another through our collective connection. In order to accomplish this, our differences must be carefully brought to the surface, acknowledged, and respected as valuable aspects of our human diversity. This process is a challenge we must face together with love, compassion, and connection. These words from the distinguished Black author James Baldwin remind all of us to be present to and with our challenges: "Not everything that is faced can be changed, but nothing can be changed until it's faced." This is where the Enneagram presents as a powerful guide for personal, individual, and collective transformation.

What do you need to surface and explore to experience a shift in your own being?

Chapter 3

WHAT IS THE ENNEAGRAM?

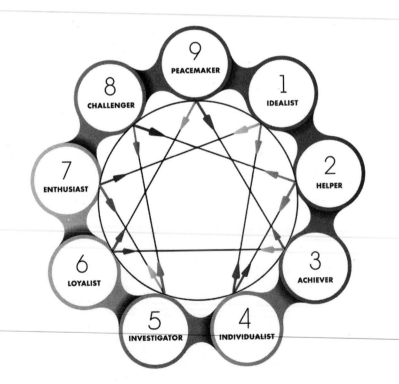

THE SYMBOL/TYPOLOGY

The Enneagram is an archetypal personality system that combines modern psychological practices with a deep foundation in ancient traditions, religions, cultures, and spiritual practices. It is a model of the human psyche taught as a typology of nine Points and personality types. These Points are given names that are reflective of the energy of nine different types. The Enneagram is inclusive and connects people across the many aspects of our humanity that are commonly used to divide us. Stemming from the Greek words *ennea* (nine) and *grammos* (a written symbol/map), the nine-pointed symbol has a fascinating history that can be traced all the way back to the sacred geometry of Pythagorean mathematics. It is important to note that while the symbol has rich historical origins, the modern use of the Enneagram as an archetypal personality system is more easily identifiable. This system traces back to the psychospiritual teacher Óscar Ichazo from the 1950s and the Chilean psychiatrist Claudio Naranjo in the 1970s. Naranjo's work was influenced by the earlier teachings of George Gurdjieff and the Fourth Way tradition.

The Enneagram is a model of the human psyche, and when applied as a way of doing our inner work it accelerates a cognitive shift into mindfulness at an individual level. This inner work uncovers the focus and patterns of behavior that subconsciously drive and motivate us to act in certain ways. In making these patterns and motivations conscious, the individual is able to transcend barriers and challenges to create deep and sustainable change in themselves and in their environment. By doing this work, we uncover the answers to many different challenges—answers that we didn't know were possible. The Enneagram is a useful tool to engage with as you begin the process of doing your inner work. As we look at any man-made construct, we can utilize the power and wisdom of the Enneagram to deconstruct systems that have been created from our egoic-driven patterns of behavior.

HOW IT WORKS

Below are the various components of the Enneagram. Later on we will explore how each of these components manifests within the Enneagram energies depending on a myriad of factors.

POINT/TYPE

Energy exists everywhere. Our words have a certain energy, as do our attitudes, behaviors, and beliefs. There are distinct energies at each of the nine Points of the Enneagram. When we talk about Enneagram Point/type, we are referring to the place on the Enneagram where you embody the strongest energy, but remember we have access to all nine Points. When you explore all nine Points, you may feel a connection to many of them; however, the energy at one of the Points will be your dominant energy or what is referred to in Enneagram teaching as type. Sometimes when the word *type* is used, resistance arises and people feel like they are being put in a box. I have had many clients and students who use their identification with a certain type as an excuse for bad behavior. "Don't be mad, you know I'm a Seven!" "I'm not moody, I'm a Four!" or "I'm not being critical, you know I am a One!" I have listened to that long enough to choose to be mindful of my language when teaching. There is something freeing about identification with *Point* versus *type*, though it is important to understand why both terms are useful. As a person who stands at Enneagram Point One, I feel a certain freedom to move around to the other Points and to actually have an experience of the different energies. Just as we make choices about many things that do or do not work for us, you are free to think of yourself as a particular type or as standing at a particular Point from which you lead or start. Do what works for you while you are finding your way on this journey. Those of us who write about or teach the Enneagram are here as your guides and we cannot determine your type or Point. That is part of your journey, and we are simply here to walk beside you as you explore a powerful way to do your inner work. This book in particular should serve as a guide to dive into the inner work necessary to move into a space where you are able to heal yourself and thus help heal humanity.

Keep in mind that we start at Point Eight and continue clockwise through the Enneagram map in order to address the Points in each Center as a group instead of going in numerical order. The order is Eight-Nine-One-Two-Three-Four-Five-Six-Seven.

INSTINCTS

There is another component of the Enneagram that will not be examined in this book known as the "Instincts," sometimes referred to as "Subtypes," within each Enneagram energy: Self-Preservation, Social, and Sexual or One-on-One. The exploration of the instincts requires a much deeper exploration into the intricacies of how each Point can manifest differently. Using the three different instincts within each Enneagram energy produces twenty-seven unique "Instinctual Variants"; when we combine the wings into the equation we are presented with fifty-four unique variations within the Enneagram. As you can see, this information would require many more pages, and as such we intend to concentrate on the nine main Enneagram energies. The inner work that may develop after reading this book may help you to discover your instinct with your dominant Point, but for now we will focus on the basic mechanics of the Enneagram as outlined in the next section.

CENTERS OF INTELLIGENCE

The Enneagram is composed of three centers: Body, Heart, and Head. Sometimes these centers, or triads, are referred to as Body/Instinctive, Heart/Feeling, and Head/Thinking. Each center has a connection to particular emotions: Body is connected to anger and rage, Heart is connected to shame and guilt, and Head is connected to fear and anxiety. Points Eight, Nine, and One reside within the Body Center. Points Two, Three, and Four reside within the Heart Center. And finally, Points Five, Six, and Seven reside within the Head Center. If you are still in the early stages of your Enneagram journey and are trying to determine your type or Point, exploring the centers may help you find where you land on the Enneagram map. It is important to remember that we are beings composed of all three centers and have the ability to access our Body, Heart, and Head Centers at any given moment. We will explore each of the centers later in the book and examine how we must align our Body, Heart, and Head Centers to activate as engaged Allies and Advocates.

BASIC FEAR

Each Point has a basic fear. Later in the book, when we describe the basic fears for each Point, take note of what comes up for you. If you have a strong response to a specific basic fear, it might be worth exploring regardless of where you fall on the Enneagram map. The basic fear is how we rationalize what we do, how we feel, and how we navigate obstacles throughout our lives. In some cases, the basic fear directly opposes our basic desire, and for some it is how we avoid showing up authentically as our true self. While we all have universal fears, there are specific fears that create patterns of behavior associated with each Point.

BASIC DESIRE

Many people who challenge this particular aspect of the Enneagram argue that "we all want to be happy" or "we all want to be loved." While this may be true, for each of us the desire to be loved or to be happy has conditions. For example, as a human who stands at Point One, my basic desire is being good, doing the right thing. Being happy and being loved comes with the conditions of being good and doing the right thing. Determining the basic desire is a key step in finding your dominant energy on the Enneagram map. Reflecting on your life as you have experienced it thus far, you can begin to look at some of the moments that you found to be memorable. Explore the emotions that you experienced and what was happening for you at a deeper level. You may be able to surface some unexplored patterns, answers, or even a few unhealed wounds.

CORE MOTIVATION

When the basic desire and the basic fear come together in the background of our functionality, we have the core motivation. These two elements of our way of being in the world are constantly challenging us to get what we most desire at any given moment while avoiding what we fear will cause our own demise. The internal drive, the reason you wake up in the morning, how you navigate life—however you refer to this "thing" that gets you going or stops you in your tracks—is your core motivation. It is the factor that drives most of your decisions, consciously or subconsciously, and it is how your personality navigates life. The core motivation is often referred to as being simply the basic desire; however, as it is usually compensation for the core fear, these two are the essential elements that drive your engine.

WINGS

On either side of your dominant Enneagram Point, there are two Points referred to as "wings." For instance, Point One has easy access to the energies of the Nine and Two wings. Point Two has access to One and Three, Three to Two and Four, etc. This is one of the many reasons that two people who share the same dominant Point can have different ways of showing up. My husband and quite a few relatives are Nines. Many of their behaviors are similar, but just as many are different. As the Enneagram begins to pique

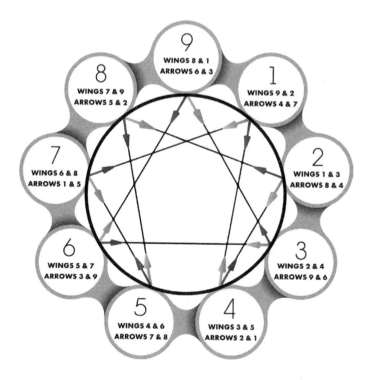

your interest, you learn more about these concepts. It's important to remember that this is not a cookie-cutter system but rather a highly evolved complex schematic that still respects the uniqueness of the individual, nature, nurture, parental overlay, and a multitude of factors to name a few. The energy of your wings can also enable some Points to access the other centers despite having no direct arrows. As you begin to read and engage in the inner work, explore the Points that reside on either side of your dominant Enneagram Point; you may find the information useful in your search for alignment of your three Centers of Intelligence.

ARROWS

The Enneagram lines and arrows, also referred to as the stress and security Points or directions of stress and growth, connect the Points across the map. Many Enneagram practitioners use the arrows as one-way streets during stress and growth, leaning into the perspective that you either go one way or the other. Up or down. Stress or growth. There is an expanded perspective on this as we gain recognition that the Enneagram offers us the gift of fluidity. We do not have to get stuck moving in one direction with the belief that we only have access to the low side of our stress Point or the high side of our growth Point.

There are multiple ways of using the lines and arrows when we begin to see them as connections to pick up specific qualities at specific times. For instance, some practitioners believe during times of conflict and stress, a One will move to the unhealthy energy of Four and become moody, withdrawn, hypercritical, and irrational. In the same context, during moments of growth and security, a One will move to the healthy energy of Seven, becoming lighthearted, spontaneous, less rigid, and flexible. These are the "one-way streets." In contrast, we have more fluidity in movement with the arrows. For instance, a One has the ability to move back and forth between the healthy and unhealthy energies of Points Seven and Four as they experience both stress and growth. In the IDEA space, we believe it is important to use the arrows as "access to the gifts" of each Point— we move freely between these connections, picking up both positive and negative energies. There are positive qualities to pick up during times of stress and many of these qualities can serve as a catalyst for growth and help us find our virtue. The energy we pick up from our lines or arrows can also facilitate the movement to other Points when needed—especially for the Points that face the chasm between centers. We dive into this phenomenon in later chapters.

LEVELS OF ACTIVATION
(ACTIVE OTHERING—PASSIVE OTHERING—ADVOCACY)

In IDEA work, we combine the arrows and wings with the levels of development outlined by Don Riso and Russ Hudson, two beloved Enneagram patriarchs, to illustrate the levels of activation. This new way of navigating the Enneagram allows for all of us to move freely within the different Enneagram energies in order to activate as an Ally or Advocate for all of humanity. Instead of using the traditional method of movement with the arrows, we believe that people have an opportunity to access the gifts from all Points, especially within the connected energies for their dominant Point to move through the passion/blind spot/suffering, fixation/trap/pattern of behavior/ constriction, and access the virtue/gift/expansion. Later on you will have the opportunity to explore the bonds to different Points and discover the positive and negative aspects of each connection.

PASSION/BLIND SPOT/WAYS WE SUFFER

Each Point holds a specific passion, sometimes aligned to the concept of the deadly sins. In their book *The Wisdom of the Enneagram*, Don Riso and Russ Hudson explain the passion as "the root of our imbalance and the way we become trapped in ego."

The passions represent the nine main ways that we lose our center and we become more susceptible to the distortions of personality and disoriented from reality. It is an essential part of who we are, and yet we try to reject rather than respect the power of this part of our being. The rejection, or lack of acknowledgment, of the passions can leave us paralyzed in a toxic pattern of behavior that distorts our true selves. While our passion is ever present, it does not need to control our actions, behaviors, and beliefs in a negative way. Instead we invite you to examine your passion and use it as a warning system to recognize when your actions, behaviors, and beliefs are setting you up to become trapped in your fixation.

FIXATION/TRAP/PATTERN OF BEHAVIOR/CONSTRICTION

We all have a way of becoming trapped in our personality, which can be demonstrated through the fixation. These "traps" are mental blocks we hold on to when attempting to justify our reality and the subsequent actions we take, beliefs we hold, and emotions we feel. The fixation of personality is a distortion of our true selves and a tricky obstacle to overcome.

VIRTUE/OUR GIFT TO HUMANITY/EXPANSION

The honoring of our true selves and who we are meant to be develops when we land in our virtue. These specific characteristics can be expressed through the emotional awareness of the authentic self: letting go of ego, self-deception, and emotional vices. When we access our virtue, we become selfless and altruistic in our actions, feelings, and beliefs. A deep dive into the inner work is a key step in accessing the virtue at each Point.

The passion can be used as a wake-up call to remove yourself from the trap of your fixation. By acknowledging both the passion and fixation, we are able to uncover the path to our virtue, where we can reconnect to our own humanity and begin the healing process. When we touch the passion of our Enneagram energy in order to move through our fixation and land in our virtue, we make the journey from active to passive othering and finally to Advocacy.

LEVELS OF DEVELOPMENT/LEVELS OF HEALTH/
FLUIDITY OF MOVEMENT

The levels of development, created by Don Riso and Russ Hudson, demonstrate the varying degrees of how each Point can show up in the world. "Unhealthy," "average," and "healthy" refer to the levels of development and the overall state of a person's ability to function. The energy at each Point can show up *very* differently depending on how healthy or unhealthy the individual happens to be; this is a common reason why so many people mistype or feel uncomfortable at their dominant Point. The Enneagram Institute, founded by Riso and Hudson, perfectly sums up this concept:

> *The Levels of Development provide a framework for seeing how all of the different traits that comprise each type fit into a large whole; they are a way of conceptualizing the underlying "skeletal" structure of each type. . . . Further, with the Levels a dynamic element is introduced that reflects the changing nature of the personality patterns themselves. You have probably noticed that people change constantly—sometimes they are clearer, freer, more grounded, and emotionally available, while at other times they are more anxious, resistant, reactive, emotionally volatile, and less free. Understanding the Levels makes it clear that when people change states within their personality, they are shifting within the spectrum of motivations, traits, and defenses that make up their personality type.*

THINGS TO REMEMBER

- There are nine Points on the Enneagram map. We have access to all of the Points, but we lead with one dominant energy. The numbers are not a scale, meaning no Point is better or worse than any of the other Points.

- No Point or type is inherently gendered or dependent on dimensions of diversity (perceived race, socioeconomic status, education, age, religion, etc.). While the descriptions and energies of the Points are universal and are not dependent on certain identifying factors, it is important to note the way an Enneagram energy manifests can vary based on cultural or environmental influences, or psychological well-being. For instance, some cultures have certain gender roles or religious influences that color the Enneagram energy, but these factors do not fundamentally change a person's dominant Enneagram Point.

- Your dominant Enneagram Point does not change throughout your life or shift based on home or work life. You are born into your Point or type and your experiences adjust how you navigate life, access your wing energy, travel with the arrows, and drop into the levels of development.

- No one can tell you where you stand on the Enneagram map. You find your place by reading, researching, and exploring all aspects of all nine Points. Tests can help you narrow down the Points and you may find your Point or type by a process of elimination. Tests are not always the defining factor of where you stand on the Enneagram map and the quality of the tests matters.

- Many people mistype and thus spend years trying to find where they stand on the Enneagram map, or try to fit themselves into whatever they want their dominant energy to be. Not every aspect of the Point may apply or appeal to you; this does not mean you are mistyping. You may mistype, but there is wisdom in learning why you mistyped and what it means to connect to a certain energy that may not be your dominant Point within the Enneagram. Explore the core motivations and basic fears of the Enneagram Points to help you dive into the complexities of your own personality. The process of discovering where you fit within the Enneagram is a journey, not a destination.

ENNEAGRAM REFERENCE SHEET

POINT	MOTIVATION	FEAR	PASSION	FIXATION	VIRTUE
BODY CENTER: Anger and Rage					
8	In control and strong, able to protect self and others	Harmed or controlled by others, vulnerable or weak	Lust	Vengeance	Innocence
9	At peace and in harmony, able to have inner stability	Experience loss or separation, deal with conflict or change, have inner peace disrupted	Sloth	Indolence	Action
1	Good and virtuous, have integrity, do the "right thing"	Wrong, corrupt, unethical, cause harm to others, make mistakes	Anger	Resentment	Serenity
HEART CENTER: Shame and Guilt					
2	Loved and wanted, needed by others	Unlovable, unwanted, unneeded by others	Pride	Flattery	Humility
3	Valuable and successful, impressive to others	Worthless, a failure, not good enough, seen as unimpressive	Deceit	Vanity	Truthfulness
4	Authentic and unique, true to self and inner experience	Without a unique identity, ordinary and mundane	Envy	Melancholy	Equanimity
HEAD CENTER: Fear and Anxiety					
5	Competent and knowledgeable, capable in any situation	Useless, incapable, uninformed, depleted of resources	Avarice	Stinginess	Nonattachment
6	Secure and safe, have a plan and stability	Without guidance, security, and support, uncertain of things	Fear	Cowardice	Courage
7	Happy and content, free to choose, keep their options open	Deprived and in pain, have freedom of choice taken away	Gluttony	Planning	Sobriety

BODY CENTER 8-9-1

Eight: The Challenger
The Powerful, Dominating Type

Motivation: to protect oneself, to be in control, to be strong

Fear: to be harmed or controlled by others, to feel weak or vulnerable

Passion: Lust

Fixation: Vengeance

Virtue: Innocence

Words associated with Eight:
authoritative, hardworking, strong-willed, confrontational, forceful, passionate, outspoken, protective, abundant energy, persistent, maintain power, independent, industrious, defensive, combative, harsh, rageful, egocentric, boastful, vengeful, demonstrative

Nine: The Peacemaker
The Easygoing, Self-Effacing Type

Motivation: to be at peace, to have harmony and inner stability

Fear: to have loss or separation, to deal with conflict or change, to have their inner peace disrupted

Passion: Sloth

Fixation: Indolence

Virtue: Action

Words associated with Nine:
calm, quiet, easygoing, accepting, supportive, "numbing out," accommodating, wallflower, dependable, routine, stable, hardworking, pragmatic, disengaged, emotionally indolent, indifferent, angry, complacent, stubborn, dissociation, apathetic, repressed rage

One: The Idealist
The Rational, Idealistic Type

Motivation: to have integrity, to be good and virtuous, to do the "right thing"

Fear: to be wrong or make a mistake, to be corrupt or unethical, to cause harm

Passion: Anger

Fixation: Resentment

Virtue: Serenity

Words associated with One:
principled, organized, ethical, crusader, fastidious, noble, fair, objective, "sense of mission," practical action, highly critical, impatient, repressed, angry, judgmental, controlling, rigid, puritanical, emotionally constricted, scolding, abrasive, punitive

HEART CENTER 2-3-4

Two: The Helper
The Loving, Interpersonal Type

Motivation: to be loved and needed

Fear: to be unlovable and unwanted or not needed

Passion: Pride

Fixation: Flattery

Virtue: Humility

Words associated with Two:
unconditional love, helpful, caring, generous, considerate, reliable, compassionate, empathetic, seductive, intrusive, possessive, seek validation, angry, resentful, hurt, manipulative, deceitful, emotional distortion, domineering, coercive, patronizing

Three: The Achiever
The Confident, Success-Oriented Type

Motivation: to be valuable, desirable, successful

Fear: to be worthless, a failure, not good enough, to be of no value, to not be seen as impressive

Passion: Deceit

Fixation: Vanity

Virtue: Truthfulness

Words associated with Three:
hardworking, dedicated, driven, ambitious, resourceful, impressive, motivated, successful, distinguished, pragmatic, opportunistic, narcissistic, egocentric, attention-seeking, deceitful, "impostor complex," seek validation, social climber, arrogant, devious, self-absorbed, vindictive

Four: The Individualist
The Sensitive, Introspective Type

Motivation: to be unique, true to self and inner experience, to be authentically themselves

Fear: to be without a unique identity, to be ordinary, to be mundane

Passion: Envy

Fixation: Melancholy

Virtue: Equanimity

Words associated with Four:
creative, emotional, empathetic, connected, expressive, deep, artistic, romantic, unique, authentic, eccentric, poetic, judgmental, moody, self-conscious, tormented, dark, depressive, angry, lost, shame, self-destructive, hopeless, despair, macabre, self-absorbed, lost in fantasy, emotionally distorted

HEAD CENTER 5-6-7

Five: The Investigator
The Intense, Cerebral Type

Motivation: to be competent and knowledgeable, to be capable in any situation

Fear: to be useless, uninformed, and incapable, depleted of resources

Passion: Avarice

Fixation: Stinginess

Virtue: Nonattachment

Words associated with Five:
intelligent, cerebral, wise, well-rounded, innovative, eccentric, open-minded, pioneering, complex, perceptive, independent, inventive, visionary, competent, isolated, withdrawn, antagonistic, cynical, argumentative, intellectually arrogant, phobic, reclusive

Six: The Loyalist
The Committed, Security-Oriented Type

Motivation: to be secure and safe, to have certainty

Fear: to be without guidance, security, and support; to be uncertain of things

Passion: Fear

Fixation: Cowardice

Virtue: Courage

Words associated with Six:
loyal, reliable, security-oriented, revolutionary, innovative, structured, hardworking, persevering, contradictory, dependent, indecisive, defensive, reactive, fearful, anxious, insecure, unpredictable, stubborn, suspicious, panicked, paranoid, highly divisive

Seven: The Enthusiast
The Busy, Fun-Loving Type

Motivation: to be happy and content, to be free to choose

Fear: to be deprived and in pain, to miss out on something, to not have freedom of choice, to feel trapped

Passion: Gluttony

Fixation: Planning

Virtue: Sobriety

Words associated with Seven:
enthusiastic, curious, joyful, optimistic, adventurous, fast learners, humorous, lighthearted, bold, vivacious, spontaneous, scattered, self-centered, narcissistic, insensitive, impulsive, erratic, moody, panic-stricken, denial, avoidance, coldhearted, jaded, offensive, detached

If this is your first foray into Enneagram, there are unlimited resources available on the study of the Enneagram and the different ways of using its wisdom in relationships, business, spiritual growth, teaching, and many other applications. If you have previous knowledge of the Enneagram, this section can serve as an easy reference guide of the basics.

Chapter 4

THE IMPORTANCE OF
INNER WORK

I define inner work as the process of shutting down the external noise, lowering the volume of the unnecessary chatter in your head, and making the choice to go inward into unexplored places of your inner self. Inner work is psychological and spiritual in nature; it is a process where you learn to open your mind, expand your heart, and experience your true self at a soul level.

IDEA work is not sustainable without having an ongoing relationship with and dedicated practice for "doing the work." You need to surface your inherent biases, internal wounds, and trauma to build the capacity to go through the fire without being consumed. Inner work reveals who you were created to be—sometimes referred to as your *higher self* or *authentic self*. Through inner work you begin to uncover the path to self-healing, an integral step toward collectively healing all of humanity. This process is often overlooked on the conventional path of IDEA work. We are taught to approach it from a headspace by reading books and articles, attending workshops, and collecting new language and tools. This process is inadequate because it does not allow us to deepen the practice of observing our own way of behaving in the world. It is, however, the methodology that we have collectively embraced to educate ourselves. The deficiencies in this approach have left us with a lack of understanding in activism and advocacy, which creates burnout, frustration, and hopelessness.

Our world is full of people taking action, protesting, changing laws, connecting to marginalized communities, getting out there and trying to make a difference. If you want to see this work through and help to make the world a safer, kinder, and more equitable place, cultivate a way to take your inner work and spiritual practice to a deeper level. This is why I use the Enneagram to help me remain present, openhearted, and open-minded. Without my inner work and daily spiritual practice, the challenge feels overwhelming and hopeless. Everyone is free to choose the path that is best suited to helping them become a Love Warrior, Ally, and Advocate. For those of you who have a spiritual path or are cultivating an inner work practice that deepens the connection to a source of power greater than your own, stay the course.

There are teachers, therapists, coaches, and counselors learning about diversity and inclusion who still have unexplored inherent biases, unhealed internal trauma, and psychopathology. If we truly intend to repair the divides our world currently faces, we must start with ourselves. The Enneagram provides a detailed guide for your inner work and allows you to move out of the singular occupation of only your headspace. You can learn how to gain access to the most important part of your being by opening your heart space. This is what ultimately creates the divine alchemy in this work to activate your body to show up as designated Allies and Advocates.

In order to begin the activation process as an Ally or Advocate, work on becoming a person who consistently shows up for people across differences. Let's look at some basic steps to begin your work.

- What motivates you to engage in this work?

- Explore the barriers that prevent you from engaging in the work or remaining present. What stops you?

- What is the fear behind your inaction, and what is the root cause of that fear?

Love Warriors reside physically and psychologically in the margins of society based on any dimension of our diversity. We are the recipients of the bias and consistent indignities from our siblings born into the automatic advantage or positional power of what is considered to be normal or "better than" in every culture. While the oppressor must bear the full weight of the responsibility to end oppression, as Love Warriors we are not powerless. Just as we choose not to accept disempowering labels such as "minority," we must take our personal power back and use our positional power to know and bring justice and peace to every perch that we occupy.

Let's look at some basic steps to your work in order to begin the activation process as a Love Warrior:

- Begin to explore your early messages about your own self-worth.

- Start to familiarize yourself with what allows you to feel connected to love.

- Ask yourself: what is the outcome you want to achieve as a Love Warrior?

Inner work provides you with the opportunity to unearth the trauma that keeps you in a state of constriction. Much like a small child in the fetal position, unacknowledged trauma constrains your energy and prevents you from movement toward full and free expansion. As you progress with your inner work, you are then able to address and heal the internal wounds that have fostered either a lack of self-worth and hope or the creation of implicit biases and feelings of overwhelming exhaustion that created obstacles along the path of reconnecting to humanity.

These are such crucial elements of the work that when you bypass or skip over them, false allyship or hollow activism can manifest. When you neglect your inner work, despite spending endless hours reading books, studying techniques, or attending workshops, you will fail to activate. You may become very well versed in all the diversity-related "-isms." You may even have the right words and a bird's-eye view of the issues, but when it comes down to it, you fail to activate and take action because you bypassed the real work that needed to be done. This is when you look in the mirror and ask yourself, "Do I really want to be a part of the solution?" If the answer is yes, then begin with the basic inquiry for Allies, Advocates, and Love Warriors. Remember: anger, fear, guilt, and shame are paralytics. They freeze you in your tracks and will always exude a strong energy to keep you where you may be residing right now, inside your comfort zone. There is no growth inside your comfort zone and definitely little hope for leaving this world in a better place for future generations.

Examine your thoughts, feelings, intuitive responses, and reactions as we define the path of IDEA that brings the work of becoming an Advocate into sharp focus. One of the most important outcomes of doing your inner work with the Enneagram as a road map and guide is moving away from helplessness and toward hope. The only actions, attitudes, behaviors, and responses we can truly control or take responsibility for are our own. Becoming an Ally and Advocate does not allow you to stay inside your comfort zone. The work of becoming an Advocate is not always popular, openly welcomed, or accepted by all. Initiating uncomfortable conversations is probably not on your top 10 list of favorite things to do.

We need to understand the guidance of our basic desire, the courage to face and understand our basic fear, and the moral strength to step into the virtue required to continue the work. Friendships may already be tense and strained, families divided, and communities have assumed polarizing positions. However, if we stay on the path, we can finally begin to navigate through the landscape of healing humanity's many divides. The goal of this journey is to manifest the reality of being "good people": taking your place in the evolution of humanity to step up and become part of the solution. The integrity of this substantive experience will enhance your personal experiences and expand your individual and collective knowledge. If you are willing to go into uncharted territory, be mindful that not all well-intentioned people immediately reap the benefits of their good intentions. As Malcolm Gladwell says, "researchers have settled on what they believe is the magic number for true expertise: ten thousand hours."

OVERCOMING BIASES

I want to bring this section of the book specifically to the attention of everyone who falls into the passive othering/average levels of development. While you may not like some of the things that are changing or agree with the way that change is coming about, taking no action *is* action. Our collective biases will destroy our cultures, countries, and ultimately our planet. Unfortunately, if there is no movement among the passive othering/average levels of development—where most of humanity stands at every point of the Enneagram—we face unprecedented erosion of our professed values. We are the sum of our individual and collective experiences, and we spend our lives trying to resolve things that happened to us, for better or worse.

When you think about this world that we are living in today, some of what is happening right in front of our eyes is frightening. I see it as hurt people hurting *other* people. We all have our biases, and if you think you are the exception to that rule, I'd love to meet you. Our biases, unfortunately, are too numerous to name. If you are curious about your implicit biases, I recommend that you go online and take the Harvard Implicit Association Test. It's free and you can test yourself on more categories of bias than you have time to spend on that task. Try testing to learn more about the biases you have about people who are categorized as different from you. The most liberal humans are often shocked by this exploration. While I did say that it is free, I failed to mention that it just might ruin your day. This is a good place to begin some inner work with respect to where and how we picked up much of our implicit bias.

We receive messages from some very well-intentioned people from the time that we draw our first breath of air about who is good, who is bad, who is right, and who is wrong. These messages come from parents, family members, religious and spiritual leaders, educators, colleagues, media sources, peers, and pundits. In a 21st-century world, we now have social media that tells us who to respect and who to knock down from the pedestals that we placed them on based on a "cancel culture." All of the aforementioned sources influenced the lens through which you see, perceive, and receive the world. We spend our lives being preprogrammed with the values, attitudes, behaviors, and beliefs from the people in our environment. Unfortunately, when you leave your family of origin, the messages that no longer serve you or the rest of humanity go right along with you.

When I began studying the Enneagram, I could see for the first time the rigidity at Point One of my judgments about certain topics. Being raised Catholic and having been taught that "it was the one true religion" kept me out of places of worship that were unfamiliar to me. The nuns and priests really hammered that one in good and tight. My inner work with the Enneagram helped me to get out of the grip of my binary thinking. I began to realize that everything is not right or wrong, good or bad. Some things just *are*. They don't require judgment. Many concepts that I struggled with turned out to be both/and: challenging and true; complicated and acceptable; Christmas and Hanukkah; male, female, and nonbinary; Black, White, Brown, Asian, and multiracial. What has been your pattern of behavior around your choices? Rigid or flexible? Exclusive or inclusive? Expansive or constrictive? Your historical path around choices is a key indicator about your beliefs and behaviors. What do your choices about people tell you? There is a lot to learn about who you are and how you are as it pertains to the people you select (include) or discard (exclude). The examination of the cast of characters that inhabit your world may lead you to conclude that your default position in choosing people is *sameness*.

If your world is fairly monolithic, it won't matter to you until something or someone pops up and forces the circumstance of reaching deep within to become more inclusive. If this circumstance is/was difficult for you, it's time to learn a few things about yourself first, and then you can learn about others. If you live your life as an inclusive person, just keep applying what you've learned to increase your comfort zone. Inclusive behaviors promote growth by definition or "adding to"; exclusive behaviors promote stagnation or "keeping out." Rejecting, shutting down, and keeping out are all examples of active negative behaviors. Many people have become masters of this process. If you find that your world is pretty monolithic, open yourself up to learning a new way of moving through your life. Check your contact list.

Look at who is present in the environment where you work and socialize and then expand your circle of acquaintances so you cultivate authentic relationships across differences.

Every Enneagram Point (more on this in Part 2) teaches you what you look like on the high side of your type, or dominant Point, as well as what you look like at the average and low side. I teach this as Advocacy, passive othering, and active othering, respectively. When you have interactions with people across differences, allow yourself to notice whether or not you perceive any discomfort. If you do recognize an internal shift, it may take the form of constriction or expansion. Allow yourself to become familiar with your own responses and reactions. Remember that energy can be felt and received without a single word being spoken. If you are triggered by differences and your response is a pulling inward or constriction of your energy, I recommend that you first explore the reason behind this reaction. Allow yourself to breathe and acknowledge the inner work that needs to be done. Our biases are linked to the stereotypes that we were all downloaded with from day one. They are etched into the very fiber of our being, and while we can't necessarily snap our fingers and make them go away, we can learn to notice and manage our reactions. Remember, we did not ask to receive any of these stereotypes and biases. They were freely expressed, all prepackaged and gifted to us by an ego-driven and personality-fixated world that often views people as objects.

In my belief system, when I notice my reaction across differences toward the people who are deeply entrenched in the distortion of defending and perpetuating oppression, I have to dig deep. It is in these moments that I experience God's love and compassion, and I have learned that I need a healing dose of kindness to balance out the anger and the pain. I steady myself under the weight of the recognition that while there are many people in the world who experience life through a similar lens to mine, there are many more who are living their lives and having an entirely different experience. After I have steadied myself to breathe another day, I get busy looking to see how kindness will manifest. Not ordinary everyday kindness. That's too simple. I need radical kinetic kindness.

Kinetic is a self-generated energy in motion; kindness is the quality of being warmhearted, considerate, humane, and sympathetic. Kinetic kindness in complete synchronicity is a winning combination. It is a leap from connecting your new learning and positive intention to transformational action. This is kindness in motion, and the greater the frequency, the better the outcome. Kinetic kindness and selfless service are no longer an integral part of our innovative society. Organizational cultures are challenging and competitive. Neighbors are not as connected, thus creating a more apathetic version of neighborhoods from the past. We are pleased but surprised when we receive excellent customer service. Most people have learned to suit up for the battle we expect to face to get something fixed, changed, returned, or resolved.

Sadly, the Love Warriors have to contend with the consistent indignities that are ubiquitous, whether we are hailing a cab, waiting to be seated in a restaurant, or exchanging an item at a local store.

"What can I do for you today to make your time here just a little better?" Does anyone hear these words anymore? If you follow that up with kinetic kindness (action), then our interactions are functioning at their highest level. This is as it should be, and it can and should become the norm. This is what it feels like to actually have interactions that demonstrate that we respect one another as intentionally connected human beings.

People who are valued and feel welcome, accepted, and included will shift the culture as we manage our implicit biases and work together as Love Warriors, Allies, and Advocates. You can be the spark that ignites the flame. And together we can create the momentum and encourage others to show up, step out of the shadows, and get busy everywhere doing everything possible to change our world—for the better.

However, to do this we must broaden our thought process, open our hearts, and engage our bodies in actions to make a difference. Connecting our three centers (Body, Heart, and Head) to wake up and be present gives the phrase "If You See Something, Say Something" a whole new meaning. Bias comes in many forms, but we can get this runaway train back on track. We need to allow it to be okay again to be a caring human being. One of my favorite Mother Teresa quotes is "It is easy to love the people far away. It is not always easy to love the people close to us. . . . Bring love into your home for this is where our love for each other must start." Doing your inner work using the framework and archetypes of the Enneagram is holding up a mirror that will reveal your true self.

BALANCED MESSAGES

There are many ways in which we are taught to navigate life; some of us are conditioned to view the world through a lens of anger, shame, and fear, and others through a lens of love, connection, and compassion. One of the defining factors that affects the way you navigate as an adult and the way you manage the wounds of your past is how early you received a *balanced message*. Whether acquired consciously or subconsciously, this message colors the lens through which all of your actions, beliefs, and behaviors are filtered through and projected out into the world. When we use the term *balanced message*, we are referring to all of the early influences that impact how you categorize and value certain people, characteristics, or dimensions of diversity. A balanced message is one in which common stereotypes and biases are challenged or addressed in a positive manner to find common ground or gain new perspective.

The younger you were when you received a balanced message about values and honoring dimensions of diversity, the more likely you are to have a positive experience later on during internal or external conflict around addressing biases and stereotypes. Adapting to new ways of navigating the human experience is easier when we are taught to evolve our approaches at an early age. Overcoming these internal biases is much more difficult to break free from for those who experience this message later in life or for those who are unfortunate enough to *never* experience equity through a balanced message. The cycle of anger, shame, blame, guilt, and fear is a constant way of being for some; unconsciously reverting to a default of "justified" behaviors based on unhealthy early messages and influences. If you experience bias, bigotry, or harmful actions (physical or psychological) inflicted upon you or people that you are connected to, this negative experience can create a mental and somatic blueprint that activates when you navigate all future interactions in similar situations with similar groups of people.

The biased actions, when experienced, create even more internal biases projected toward those you feel have wronged you in some way. This is a difficult cycle to break, but it is not impossible. We are all somewhat wounded in one way or another, sometimes as a result of our past experiences, present circumstances, or our childhood. This is an unavoidable fact of life. Every single person within our human race has experienced some sort of trauma, whether deeply painful or relatively mild; depending on multiple factors, they either retain these wounds and project them outward or address the wounds and heal accordingly. Many of us carry wounds from our past and attempt to address, accept, and heal, or reject, deny, and unconsciously reinforce them in our own individual way. The longer the trauma exists unaddressed, unresolved, or even reinforced, the deeper it roots itself in our being.

So it is reasonable to assume that an adult who feels the need to demonize another based on a dimension of their diversity that is beyond their control—perceived race, gender and sexual identity, socioeconomic status, or cultural background—is likely a hurt individual projecting their own pain onto others and acting out of anger, shame, or fear. This is never an excuse for destructive or problematic behaviors and actions. Instead, it is an invitation to consider another perspective and maintain an open heart to explore a more compassionate approach for reconnecting across differences.

Have you ever considered that someone who is attacking another for their political views, skin color, perceived race, gender, or sexual identity may have some deep, unexplored wounds of their own? Have you considered that your experiences of being Love Warriors have prevented you from seeing the humanity in another person beyond their projected persona?

THE HIERARCHY OF VALUE

As we look into the social construct of race, the hierarchy of value placed on dimensions of diversity, the fallout of our learned behaviors, and our early influences, one can only begin to question how our collective community created these divides—and then somehow accepted them as the social norm.

In a way, we were all set up. Set up to believe in the othering of our people and in creating divisions where there should have been connections. Whether you grew up in a privileged community or a marginalized one, we have all been steeped in a culture of categorizing and placing stereotypes on people as a way of justifying our actions or beliefs. In our early days, we were taught lessons about our history and culture from polarized textbooks and out-of-date curriculum (a practice that still exists today, e.g., the debate on teaching critical race theory and human health sciences in regard to gender and sexual diversity). At the same time, our families equipped us with a set of values, messages, and belief systems that may have furthered our unconscious or implicit biases. These early influences make up the foundation for the justification of what data we select and for the meaning we add to said data. Additionally, our experiences throughout our lives influence how we make sense of chaos and the unknown. We will explore these processes in depth later, but first let's consider the following scenario: if your education was lacking in truthful depictions of our history and your family happened to be monolithic, you may have an entirely different truth or reality compared to someone whose education was more historically factual or inclusive or whose family may have been more culturally diverse. This is not to say one experience was right and one was wrong, or one was better or worse than the other. The experiences are different. And these differences sometimes cause conflict later on in life if left unexplored. Living your life from one perspective deprives you of a beautiful opportunity to connect to humanity through developing an appreciation for different experiences. It will be these experiences that allow for the cultivation of generosity, community, and compassion. One of the major dividing experiences we currently face involves the way in which we were taught about systemic racism and the process of othering.

A FLAWED HISTORICAL CONTEXT

The revolving door of racism and othering is perpetuated by our early influences and fueled by our implicit biases. This system and our learned behaviors are not easily changed or consciously addressed. One must be mindful of when and how we look into our actions and uncover the root cause of why we established them in the first place. Most of the time we are not given the opportunity to step back and explore our implicit biases; our society is on autopilot, living each day without having to wake up to the real world, let alone to the reality of how flawed and engineered our existence has become.

The baby boomer generation is a prime example of this phenomenon. The parents of this generation passed on messages rooted in the Jim Crow Era and the Great Depression laced with a wartime mentality and the mainstream devaluing of specific groups of people. And despite living through the civil rights movement, baby boomers in both privileged and marginalized communities accepted and justified the reality that to succeed certain people must work twice as hard for half as much and persistently prove that they had any value and worth. The culture was different from what we know now as "civil"; people considered "other"—people of color, women, members of the gender and sexual diversity community, immigrants, Indigenous peoples, the socioeconomically disadvantaged, people with disabilities—were fighting daily for basic human rights. Rights that should have been inherent and equal were in the hands of the people who represented the polar opposite of whom these rights directly affected. Unfortunately, we are still fighting the same battles; we just have a new set of guidelines for navigating these challenges.

As time passed and baby boomers began families of their own, the messages they received as children were naturally passed on, filtered through their collective generational experience. These messages, cultivated around the end of World War II, were rooted in "traditional American values" and "the American Dream" and bolstered by a set of generational disciplines: success, work ethic, competitiveness, pride, and self-reliance. These messages were also influenced and distorted based on the individual's dimensions of diversity. Americans of color and those considered "other" had a very different experience growing up during the civil rights movement in comparison to the experience of those who already had these basic human rights. This is not to say there were not White-bodied Americans who experienced discrimination, prejudice, and disenfranchisement during these times; many people were subjected to a myriad of unfair practices and policies. One difference for White-bodied Love Warriors was and is that they could and can still claim their Whiteness. This mentality increases the divide between marginalized groups as socioeconomically disadvantaged White-bodied individuals or otherwise "other" could revert to an unhealthy mindset of "at least I'm not Black." This way of thinking prevented disadvantaged Whites and disadvantaged Blacks from sharing their concerns about being Love Warriors and these divisions became a hotbed for hatred. Add any element of intersectionality and these divisions grew exponentially.

THE ROOT OF OTHERING

If we consider racism the root of othering in our world from which all other "isms" and divisions begin to flow, we can easily visualize and demonstrate how this social construct led to so many disconnects. As we've discussed, we all learned that we had a place in society and a certain way we had to navigate in order to survive. In general, White people and people of color had very different experiences of finding their place in society. If we add the intersectionality of being "other"—for instance female, nonbinary, gay, poor, or a person with a disability—these experiences veer off in distinct tangents, each tangent with its own disadvantages and challenges to face. But the underlying devaluing of certain people and the lasting effects of creating these inequities can usually be traced back to how racism paved the first destructive path of othering within the modernized human race. Our society collectively learned that it was acceptable to categorize people, to give certain groups advantages and withhold opportunities from those who did not reside within the dominant "majority," and to penalize people for factors beyond their control. As a direct result, the people with power— from the beginning—put systems, practices, and policies in place to not only protect their own power but to control and limit the power of those they felt were inferior or less than at a human level. As we explored at the beginning of this book, race is a man-made social construct, which Robert Wald Sussman reaffirmed in *The Myth of Race:*

> *"What many people do not realize is that this racial structure is not based on reality. Anthropologists have shown for many years now that there is no biological reality to human race.... There is no inherent relationship between intelligence, law abidingness, or economic practices and race, just as there is no relationship between nose size, height, blood group, or skin color and any set of complex human behaviors. However, over the past 500 years, we have been taught by an informal mutually reinforcing con-sortium of intellectuals, politicians, statesmen, business and economic leaders and their books that human racial biology is real and that certain races are biologically better than others. These teachings have led to major injustices to Jews and non-Christians during the Spanish Inquisition; to [B]lacks, Native Americans, and others during colonial times; to African Americans during slavery and [R]econstruction; to Jews and other Europeans during the reign of the Nazis in Germany; and to groups from Latin America and the Middle East, among others, during modern political times."*

To understand the depth of division within our society and how it man-ifests, it is imperative to start at the beginning and pull out this toxic weed by the very root from which it has sprouted. We were taught at a very young age the difference between right and wrong, good and evil, what held value and what did not, and in some cases, what was considered acceptable or un-acceptable. As we've discussed, this concept, combined with life experiences and our learned behaviors, allows us to explore how the early messages and early influences ultimately shaped how we show up in the world.

The practice of using past experiences and learned behaviors to inform our actions and beliefs has existed since the beginning of our collective history as a human race. The primal instinct for the human brain to make sense out of a chaotic world began as an evolutionary response for survival. We are presented with all of the available data, we select certain data and begin to attach meaning as a way of justifying our beliefs or preconceived assumptions. This cycle is self-perpetuating if left uninterrupted, and it fundamentally affects the way in which we are able to process new data. In an attempt to avoid a state of cognitive dissonance or unfamiliar experiences, which may cause us harm, most people employ the practice of making assumptions based on learned behavior. It is an evolutionary trait we all share, dating back millions of years; for instance, our early human ancestors avoided foods that made them ill or proved fatal. To prevent the same fate from befalling others within their tribes, they would pass on the knowledge of avoiding anything that resembled these poisonous foods, thus ensuring the survival of their community.

We can illustrate this concept by considering the act of foraging for berries by our early ancestors; blueberries are a delicious ingredient we now use in pancakes and pies, while Belladonna berries, also known as deadly nightshade, are widely recognized as one of the most toxic plants in the world. Both berries have a similar appearance and can easily be mistaken for one another even though they belong to very different classifications within plant taxonomy. So in theory, it would be safe to assume that at some point our species developed an aversion to the deadly Belladonna plant through knowledge passed on by our ancestors. At the same time, we embraced blueberries as a healthy addition to our diets based on the simple fact that we were told it was acceptable, desirable, and valued. While this is an overly simplistic explanation of a much deeper concept, the origins of attaching our own meaning to external data are clearly present even in our earliest history as a species. It was, and remains, a way of protecting ourselves from things we don't quite understand, or a way of avoiding learning more about something out of fear. This principle can also be observed in regard to groups of people living and traveling together, and protecting their culture from outsiders. There is a phenomenon that occurs around assumed similarities and assumed differences; a tendency to feel more comfortable in a room full of people that look like you. This is known as affinity bias. When we go beneath the surface we find that our assumptions and biases create the perfect storm for exclusion of people who do not share the same or similar external dimensions of diversity.

And so here we are, as a divided community with the accepted reality that certain people are valued more than others; value based on assumed race, skin color, gender and sexual diversity, socioeconomic status, and a myriad of other categorizing factors. We accepted this reality based on the information our ancestors passed down to us regarding value within the social hierarchy: messages passed down from generation to generation for centuries. The devaluing of individuals by the dominant and advantaged groups has been a source of fear, violence, and division for so many years. For us to address these inequities, the hardships experienced by marginalized communities, and the process of creating space to bring people back from the margins, we must first look at ourselves. How did we establish our values, where did we pick up these behaviors or beliefs, and what biases and stereotypes did we adopt throughout our lives?

We are all inhabiting this planet together and no one is leaving any time soon, so resolving our differences and building bridges across the divisions is crucial to our quality of life. It is clear that we have a great deal of work to do to make sure that this planet remains inhabitable and sustainable. The pandemic may have taken many of our friends and family and changed so much of what we consider normal; however, if we remain present, there are some valuable lessons that will be revealed for all of us. We are all here together and most of us have the capacity to learn how to treat one another. We begin by learning how to unravel our own internal wounds, address our implicit biases, and reconnect to our authentic selves. This is where our inner work begins.

MECHANISMS FOR CHANGE

Over the years we have facilitated various workshops and programs for people who maintain placement at all levels of the diversity spectrum. Regardless of how their bodies show up in the world, participants learn to engage in the inner work necessary to move beyond saying, "I am not biased/prejudiced/racist/etc. . . ." to actively showing up as authentic Allies and Advocates for all of humanity. This work includes White-bodied people seeking authentic connection through addressing their implicit biases and uncovering how they have consciously or unconsciously contributed to systemic oppression.

The work also includes the humans who fall into the category of "other," a.k.a. Love Warriors, addressing and healing their wounds and the biases they have developed in order to find a way to truth, trust, and connection. The work provides everyone an opportunity to uncover a path back to honoring our collective humanity.

Much of our work explores the invasive roots of systemic racism as a metaphorical tree and follows the branches of othering as they extend their twisted branches throughout our humanity. We study the symbolic branches as they become interwoven across our communities and we begin to address the inequities of power, privilege, and position. Human beings who are disallowed basic fundamental freedom to move freely through the world unencumbered by constant obstacles live with the constant inquiry of whether or not we belong in the space that we occupy. We are all members of a human family, but we exist in a divided and socially constructed hierarchy based on a wide variety of categorizing factors: perceived race, gender and sexual diversity, religion and spirituality, family, socioeconomic status, career path, education, geographical location, hobbies, relationships, age, and more.

UPDATE THE GOLDEN RULE

Most of us grew up learning that the Golden Rule was a respectful way to navigate relationships—*treat people the way you want to be treated*. However, as we evolved and the world changed around us, we also expanded beyond the scope of this Golden Rule. We are faced with the challenges that come from a continuously diversifying society, and we must learn how to focus on the facets and choices of what is being valued or held from an unfamiliar perspective to understand people across differences. In order to redirect the lens and honor the humanity of each individual, we aligned the Golden Rule with the Platinum Rule—*treat people the way **they** want to be treated.*

When communities, workplaces, and our sectors of socialization were completely monolithic (or so some people thought) the Golden Rule worked out fairly well for most. Now we live in an openly diverse society where we do not all come from the same background, may not share identical values, and have different ways of navigating through the world. The Platinum Rule is directly opposed to the widely accepted Golden Rule, and the distinction is an important element of maintaining a healthy and compassionate approach to connecting across differences. This approach allows us to expand our comfort zones by developing our capacity for discernment and connection. To apply the Platinum Rule, we must learn about differences and move away from being locked into binary and dualistic thinking. Our differences can be a cause for growth and celebration versus stagnation and irritation. The Platinum Rule does not assume sameness but rather that we pause, breathe, and prepare ourselves to learn something new through a compassionate and respectful approach to different perspectives. By aligning the intended outcome of the Golden Rule with the Platinum Rule, we developed new mechanisms for change and connected the Enneagram with inclusion, diversity, equity, and anti-racism strategies.

THE HUMANITY MOSAIC

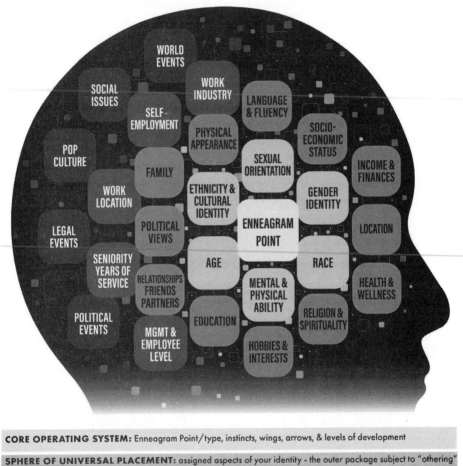

CORE OPERATING SYSTEM: Enneagram Point/type, instincts, wings, arrows, & levels of development

SPHERE OF UNIVERSAL PLACEMENT: assigned aspects of your identity - the outer package subject to "othering"
Ethnicity & Cultural Identity, Sexual Orientation, Gender Identity, Race, Mental & Physical Ability, Age

SPHERE OF ACCESS & OPPORTUNITY: characteristics some people get to choose & others do not
Physical Appearance, Language & Fluency, Socioeconomic Status, Income & Finances, Location, Health & Wellness, Religion & Spirituality, Hobbies & Interests, Education, Relationships Friends & Partners, Political Views, Family

SPHERE OF POWER & PURPOSE: what you do based on access & opportunity
Work Industry, Self-Employment, Work Location, Seniority/Years Of Service, Management & Employee Level

SPHERE OF PASSION & POSITION: major events & historical milestones that shape your experience
World Events, Social Issues, Pop Culture, Legal Events, Political Events

In our exploration of the dimensions of diversity, we developed a mechanism that we refer to as the *Humanity Mosaic*. The Humanity Mosaic challenges individuals to transcend the superficial inquiry of visible diversity and explore deeper into the intricacies of individual identity and their inherent value. This process shines a light on the multifaceted aspects of people's self-identification and provides an opportunity for a rich and enlightening dialogue. The entire process highlights how each Enneagram energy navigates through the world from different lenses. We navigate through and beyond the ring of assigned identification/universal placement, delving into its effect on access, opportunity, and influence. Taking our dominant Enneagram energy experiences into account, we look at how we place value on all of the dimensions of diversity.

The inner work requires us to look at the things we do not have the ability to control and invites us into the deeper inquiry of what we hold sacred and subsequently what may be completely outside of our peripheral vision. Exploring these unconscious connections and blind spots extends into how we accept and navigate the scourge of systemic racism and perpetuate the destructive practice of othering. This process addresses many of the "isms" and inherent biases that we have accumulated and continue to act upon consciously or unconsciously.

CORE OPERATING SYSTEM

At the heart of our individual mosaics rests our *core operating system—* our Enneagram Point/type, the Centers of Intelligence, instincts, wings, arrows, and levels of development. Our Enneagram energy is established at birth, and though it does not change from Point to Point, it can be affected throughout our lives.

SPHERE OF UNIVERSAL PLACEMENT

The next level is the *sphere of universal placement*, or our internal dimensions of diversity. These are the things that we are born with and that we generally do not have control over. While there is some debate as to which dimensions can be changed or chosen after birth, specifically gender and sexual diversity, this level is composed of "automatic" aspects of your identity, aspects that you did not choose at birth. The level at which any of these aspects of our identity can be changed or controlled continues to be debated as we evolve as a species. In short, this is the outer package that is subject to othering.

SPHERE OF ACCESS AND OPPORTUNITY

The next level is the *sphere of access and opportunity*, a narrow or broad spectrum of possibilities that some people have the ability to control and some people do not. This is the level most people assume can be changed if a person so wishes. This thought process is a key element in how people assign stereotypes and assumptions based on the aspects that reside in this level of the Humanity Mosaic. The group is composed of factors like education, physical appearance, language and fluency, socioeconomic status, income and finances, location, health and wellness, and so on. What many people do not have line of sight to is that this level depends on many factors related to your access to opportunity:

- Do you have the ability to move from your location if it is deemed undesirable?

- How much can you or your parents afford to ensure a quality education?

- Do you have health insurance or access to a doctor should an emergency arise?

- Are you able to sustain a savings account to ensure future financial stability?

- Is your religion or spirituality a foundational aspect of how you were raised, and did you have the opportunity to experience other religions, traditions, and methods of worship?

This is the level where we begin to see othering take effect and witness the disparities that arise based on a person's Humanity Mosaic: systemic racism; gender and sexual discrimination; socioeconomic disparities; religious persecution; physical, mental, and nonvisible disability discrimination; spatial inequities; and so on.

SPHERE OF POWER AND PURPOSE

The next level is the *sphere of power and purpose* and is composed of a person's career path and all accompanying factors. This level is dependent on a person's access to opportunity and can be affected by systemic inequities: gender pay gap, resume discrimination, location access, educational disparities, and so on.

SPHERE OF PASSION AND POSITION

The final level is the *sphere of passion and position;* it is the generational impact on a person's mosaic. Often overlooked, this level shapes the perspective of people of a specific era and can create generational gaps between individuals based on the events and issues during that time. For example, consider the effects on a generation after experiencing the civil rights movement, the Vietnam War, cell phones, the Internet, 9/11, the Black Lives Matter movement, and other historical circumstances. These elements have a profound impact on people and may not translate across generations.

HOW TO APPLY THE HUMANITY MOSAIC

A baseline exercise we employ is to invite participants to choose 3 out of the 29 mosaic tiles representing the individual dimensions of diversity. These individual tiles represent their identity. We encourage them to select the dimensions that are most important to their self-identification and explain that without those three selections plus their dominant Enneagram energy, they would not be recognizable as authentically themselves. Each participant is asked to share what three dimensions of their diversity they chose and explain the reasoning behind their selections.

The selection process evolves as participants dive deeper into the inner work. More often than not, the individuals draw from their value and belief system, and their decisions are reflective of the core motivation and basic fear of their dominant Enneagram energy.

The process is then deepened by allowing individuals to explore how their choices compare with people of similar backgrounds and Enneagram energies, and then later across differences. The Humanity Mosaic challenges us to explore the choices of what is being held or valued in different ways across the dimensions of diversity and invites us to uncover our early influences and messages from the perspective of our dominant Enneagram energy.

To illustrate how this process works within the Enneagram, we will demonstrate how our Points navigate the Humanity Mosaic.

Dr. Deborah Egerton (Dr. E)
Self-identification: Enneagram One, BIPOC, Female

As an Enneagram One, I value goodness, integrity, and doing the right thing even if it involves conceding something of personal value. For me personally, honoring the dignity of every human being is the way that I choose to move through the world. I believe that who I am when no one is watching should be who I am when there is an audience. I don't want to be a version of myself. I want to be my true authentic self.

I selected race as my first choice. When I look at myself from the inside out, I see the manifestation of my ancestry, my people, and all that I bring from within me into the world. I am a Love Warrior. I believe that my African American body and the bodies of all members of my collective family must be defended and protected from further harm, now and in the future. My approach to this war (and it is a war) is to harness the power of love and activate Love Warriors around the globe to become the embodiment of love, and change how we choose to be in community with one another. Only love can drive out the darkness of racism and othering.

My second choice is gender. I am a woman. I am a Black woman. I am a matriarch, a mentor, and a mystic. The assignment at birth of my gender as female is aligned with who I am and how I show up in the world. I am aware my gift of the maternal instinct, as defined by societal norms, does not encompass all that I bring into the world, particularly as a Black woman.

I feel the earth tremble just a bit at times when I lean into my power. Black women have taken on the role of matriarchs for the survival of our people. I lead with love, nurture with kindness, and embrace all parts of my feminine being. I define my womanity from the inside out. I experience my strength in my body, my courage in my heart, and the wisdom in my head. All these attributes are embodied in my female form. My heart opens easily, and my emotions are readily accessible. Society allows for this if you are a woman. I am in touch with the strongest aspect of my energy, which is my creative life force. My inner work allows me to plug in to the full experience of being a woman and not to let that be defined by rigid cultural and societal structures.

My third choice is my religion/spirituality. I will admit to having many struggles with dogmatic religion. I was raised as a Catholic and still find comfort in the silence of an often-empty Catholic church, the rituals of the Mass, and the sacrament of Communion. When fortunate enough to have a priest step into the pulpit who preaches a message of love and compassion, I feel that something inside me is nourished, and I can take that spiritual food to nourish my soul for another week. My spirituality extends far beyond a Sunday Mass. It is my connection to Spirit that sustains me moment to moment, breath by breath. I rely not on what I cannot see, but rather what I can feel, experience, and receive from the loving source that I know to be God. I am guided, protected, and called to serve in a way that is beyond my comprehension, and I trust without knowing how or why. My faith gets me out of bed in the morning and allows me to step into my purpose here on Earth.

Lisi Mohandessi, co-author and graphic artist (Lisi)
Self-identification: Enneagram Two, Person of Color, Female
As an Enneagram Two, I value kindness, connection, and service above all else. My choices within the Enneagram align with my ability to maintain and fulfill my core motivation of being loved

and needed by others and directly opposes my core fear of being unlovable or unneeded.

I selected family as my top priority; my family is truly everything to me. They provide support and a foundation for love and kindness. I was taught at a very early age to treat people as if they were part of my own family. My main objective in life stemmed from a lesson I was taught by my mother and father: be kind, do no harm, and help out when you can. I am sure there were many lessons I learned early on, but as an Enneagram Two, I clearly held on to the values that aligned with my core personality. My parents faced many challenges at a young age, as they were an interracial couple living in the Deep South during the '70s and '80s. They encountered many unkind people and challenges to their connections, but through it all they held on to love and kindness and passed these values on to my siblings and me. My mother and father worked hard for us to have a stable home, a great education, and access to opportunities. I learned early on that if you worked hard, went to school, and took advantage of the opportunities presented to you that you could provide for yourself and your family, and live in a space of love and connection. You could continue to spread love and kindness through opportunities many take for granted or are unable to access.

This brings me to my second choice: socioeconomic status. This choice felt narcissistic and conceited as an Enneagram Two; however, I explored what my socioeconomic status really meant for me. My access to education, financial stability, and opportunities to advance my career meant that I could share my status with others, bring people back in from the margin by fighting for causes, provide financial support to charities and shelters, educate myself further on how to better serve my community, and create the opportunity to pursue the things that were important to me. I do not consider my socioeconomic status a source for wealth or social status, rather it serves as the opportunity to give back and share the resources with others. I am grateful for my access to opportunity and my privilege as an educated woman from a stable family.

My final selection is work industry. I'll be candid in admitting this one changes from time to time depending on what I am dealing with in life. For a while now, I have felt a strong connection to work industry, as this has been the focus of my life for the past few years. Working with Dr. Egerton and the Enneagram to bring awareness to social justice and othering has presented me with many opportunities not only to fulfill a need of another human but to also bring my core values out into the world. We work to help others through healing their internal wounds so that they can move forward and spread love, light, and kindness. To me this is the epitome of Two energy: be kind, help others, do no harm, show compassion, and share love and light.

———————

The next step to deepen the process is looking at what is being chosen, held, and valued by someone whose Humanity Mosaic may differ from yours.

- This process is completed in dyads and allows participants to connect and remain present in a safe space. The partnership creates an environment where opposing perspectives are brought forth and appreciated on a deeper level with respect and dignity.

- Each person is allowed space to explore their self-identification and the value placed on a specific area within the Humanity Mosaic. The listener is provided with an opportunity to gain a new perspective on an area that may have previously been a blind spot.

- The roles are then reversed, and the process continues. The last choice of each individual is discussed and explored, which may bring forth some unconscious biases and hidden stereotypes.

- The conversation with someone whose first choice is your last choice can be extremely rich and enlightening.

Dr. E

My areas of passive consideration are located in the sphere of power and purpose *and revolve around the importance of a person's career path as an employee. While I recognize that during my life I have learned how important it can be to be flexible and be willing to reinvent myself when necessary, I am also aware that I have never entertained the notion that I would stay in one job for my entire life. I feel that the spirit of entrepreneurship is something that is hardwired into my DNA. When I was an employee and assigned certain duties under my job description, I always reengineered my job description based on "other duties as assigned." Because of this exercise that has been described here, I can now understand and respect why someone would choose to grow where they are planted and rise up and through a system that becomes familiar and beloved. My Enneagram One lens is always scanning for things that can be improved or perfected. The change of venue and change of pace and face give me more opportunities to see and work with the flaws in a system. There is no mystery here for me when I think about my affinity for diversity and working. Fighting for the Love Warriors. I want and seem to need to fix things wherever I can find them. I teach the people to fish, so to speak, so that they can sustain the effort after I move on. I am also a strong proponent of "power with" versus "power over," which is something that I have been able to exercise more easily as an entrepreneur.*

Lisi

There are a few aspects within the Humanity Mosaic that I feel little to no connection with. However, one area stands out time and time again: pop culture within the sphere of passion and position *or the generational impact. Admittedly, I am not a fan of social media or the many facets of the so-called millennial life. I have witnessed the harmful impacts of Facebook and Twitter and the persistent flooding of oversharing and toxicity that follows. In my experience, people utilize these platforms to spew hatred, division, and biased practices, all while hiding behind a screen and avoiding the responsibility that comes with propagating these destructive messages. The community aspect and cute animal videos seem few and far between the messages of polarizing political rants, false information, and intentional jabs at humanity. The disconnection these outlets can foster is truly astonishing. For me, this is a lost opportunity to use these platforms for good and for reconnection. We have collectively tarnished a resource intended to bring people together, and instead use it as a tool for dividing ourselves and justifying our biased beliefs with like-minded individuals. As a Two, this hurts me to my core and leaves me feeling disheartened at the lack of kindness, compassion, and connection within our human family. I was taught "if you don't have anything nice to say, don't say anything at all." And so I find myself judging and forcing stereotypes on people who focus on followers and likes, or people who use social media platforms as methods of communicating messages that I deem irresponsible, polarizing, or antagonistic. I often have to stop myself and remember that my lack of appreciation for the social media aspect of my generation's collective pop culture does not give me permission to judge, criticize, or place blame on other humans.*

CONNECTING THE DOTS OF INNER WORK

Uncovering the origins of your value system opens the door to developing compassion for yourself and others. A key step in the process is acknowledging that you are not responsible for the early messages you received or for the implicit biases with which you were imbued. However, once acknowledged, you are responsible for uncovering the biases in a healthy way and engaging in the inner work necessary to move from judgment and division and into empathy and connection. It is important to remember that you are not to blame for the people who formed your early experiences; we didn't ask to have biased parents, teachers, or family, and they probably didn't ask for it either in regard to their parents, teachers, and family. This is not to say all parents or early influencers were bigots who passed on racist, sexist, homophobic, or biased messages—but the values inhered were usually formed in a separate era with different collective values and an unconnected culture. Things were different. They grew up with certain messages about who had more societal value, who had the power to make the rules, whose bodies were or were not worthy of love, and who could or could not improve their situation—and it is vital to recognize that these messages are not in line with a world where we are trying to reconnect across our differences. For the most part, our parents, teachers, and families encouraged us to be decent humans, to work hard, to provide for our families, and to try not to be sociopaths. But the values we hold on to, and especially the ones that shape our ethos, are hidden in the crevasses and corners of the beliefs, words, and actions of our early influences. These values became our implicit biases, whether we asked for it or not. We then shaped our own belief systems around these learned messages and early influences and, more often than not, passed them on to the next generation. The ultimate challenge here is that most of us get these messages packed up for us . . . *not by us.* We are given these biases and we carry them out into our adult life. Sadly, many of us never unpack this baggage. What we do not surface will not be explored. Without the deep exploration of what we are bringing forward into our adult lives, we will either pass on bias or grace, never knowing the difference between the two. It seems like a self-perpetuating cycle. We can stop the destructive wheel from spinning by:

- choosing to do our inner work,

- examining the baggage that came preprogrammed with bias,

- exploring the decision matrix that we employ for making our choices about groups of people, and

- noticing whether our preprogramming leans toward compassion or persecution.

CHALLENGE YOUR INNER VOICE

Many people on the journey to becoming Allies and Advocates for the collective healing of humanity are surprised or triggered into a state of denial when they begin to uncover their unexplored internal wounds. The constant momentum of life prevents many of us from waking up to the red flags in our own behavior and actions. This is true for all people, no matter their individual diversity: Black, White, Brown, Asian, Indigenous, male, female, nonbinary, trans, straight, gay, rich, poor, educated, uneducated, young, or old. Everyone experiences a moment of disbelief when they uncover an unconscious bias. It is the equivalent of discovering you've been lied to your whole life, except the person lying to you ... is you. It's that little voice inside your head whispering judgment, hatred, or hostility toward another human being. We all have that little voice; sometimes it helps us process new information and consider different perspectives with compassion and integrity, and other times it pushes us into fear, anger, and shame.

To illustrate this concept, let's consider a few commonly known stereotypes that have plagued our culture for years.

Scenario One: The little voice might say, "What a lazy human, using food stamps to buy milk ... maybe if they just got a job ... " Pause right here. Take a breath. *What do you really know about this situation? Why are you automatically assuming this person must be lazy? Do you actually know that they don't have a job from the mere fact that they are using food stamps? Are you maybe placing some unfair or harsh stereotypes on this person? Is it possible that they are living paycheck to paycheck due to external factors beyond their control? Have you considered that they are struggling to feed their family and simply trying their best to survive, just like you?*

Scenario Two: The little voice might say, "I don't get this whole 'trans' thing. Male or female, there are only two genders. You don't get to pick what you want to be." Pause right here. Take a breath. *Why are you invested in another person's gender identity? How does a person's gender affect you in any way? Is it possible that you do not have all of the information that encompasses the vast world of gender and sexual diversity? Have you considered that this person has a strong connection to their gender or sexual identity and your* *opinion is a direct attack on their existence as a human being? Are you accessing your capacity for compassion and empathy, or are you denying yourself the opportunity to honor your humanity and the humanity in others?*

Scenario Three: The little voice might say, "You can't trust that police officer; they are White and therefore racist." Pause right here. Take a breath. *Isn't it unfair to assume that, since they are police, they are automatically racist? And isn't it also unfair to assume since they are White they are automatically racist? Is it possible that the collective experiences between law enforcement and people of color may have distorted your ability to navigate this particular situation with an unbiased and rational approach? Can you give this person a chance to show their true self before you react with judgment and fear? How does applying this generalization to an entire profession and all White-bodied people help you address your biases? Remember: the crisis faced by people of color and law enforcement cannot be addressed, improved, or healed when you begin from a space of bias, mistrust, and hopelessness.*

- Take a moment to consider a new perspective.

- Breathe and find presence in this space.

- You are viewing someone as an object, thus dehumanizing them.

- Take a look at this person and study them.

- Put yourself in their shoes and switch places.

- Consider that you could have been born into their body instead of the body you occupy right now.

The unconscious pattern of toxic thoughts and the justifications we make for holding on to them is not only hurting humanity, it is preventing us from addressing the real problems. We all have internal unhealed wounds that affect how we navigate the world and the divisions we face as a society. Until we can stop the little voices in our heads and address the stereotypes and beliefs that continue to impede our path to healing, we cannot reconnect as a human race. Find your internal wounds. Acknowledge and challenge your inner voice. Uncover and address the messages you've been holding on to. Pause and take another breath. Begin by asking yourself: *Are they true? Do they prevent me from seeing a person as a person and instead do I view them as an object? How do the implicit biases I have prevent me from healing? Am I willing to challenge what I think I believe and begin to see things from a more compassionate and empathetic perspective?*

It is vital to not only begin the process of addressing our internal wounds but also to persevere through all of the challenges we may encounter. This work requires persistent presence and intentional reflection; you don't just fall into authentic Allyship and Advocacy, and you certainly won't be able to miraculously heal the trauma you've been holding if you remain angry and fearful on the margins of society. The journey is just as important as the destination, which is an essential lesson we sometimes forget. As long as we are trying to do better and be better, we are moving toward Allyship, Advocacy, and healing through reconnection. The moment you fall back into toxic patterns of bias and bigotry and avoid stepping into the light, you lose your footing on the path toward healing. It is a constant battle ladened with challenges, but with presence, compassion, and empathy, we are all entirely capable of remaining receptive to light, love, and Advocacy.

In order to remain activated as an Advocate, it is important to remain engaged in ongoing work that takes you out of the pages of a book and into conversations. Building authentic relationships and being in community with people who are also on the journey of Allyship, Advocacy, and healing are essential.

We provide ongoing workshops and have created communities of engaged Allies and Advocates from all walks of life, who learn how to practice and remain on the path toward healing humanity. The closing section of this book provides resources and information to continue the work.

Part II

THE
INNER WORK

Chapter 5

THE DEFENDERS—
BODY CENTER:
8-9-1

The Body Center, or Instinctive Triad, is home to Points Eight, Nine, and One. These three energies have a gut wisdom, a feeling in their bodies during times of conflict, chaos, or just in their daily lives. This group is centered around action, affecting the world or their environments in order to avoid being affected by it, and expressing their anger in different ways. Many people who identify with the Body Center Points (Eight-Nine-One) have a distinct experience with the emotion of anger or rage. All humans experience anger; this is an undeniable fact. However, for Eight-Nine-Ones, anger is the catalyst for many of their patterns of behavior.

During times of pain and suffering, either internally or externally, Eight-Nine-Ones experience a visceral response that often transforms into bodily action and instinctual external rage. This pattern consequently connects Eight-Nine-Ones to action and results more so than the other centers. The Body Center is concerned with creating boundaries for themselves in order to resist being affected by external factors. The boundaries created are dependent on how the Point in question is attempting to protect themselves, fulfill the core motivation, and avoid the basic fear.

We call the Body Center the *Defenders,* because that is exactly what they do—defend against threats to themselves as well as to others. Each Point *defends* in its own way, which we dive into in each section, but they all take action based on what they feel in their bodies. The instinctual motivation to protect or to defend human survival resides within the Body Center. When operating from a healthy space, Eight-Nine-Ones are fierce defenders of justice, equity, and fairness and will lead with kindness, courage, and honor. They are the center that gets things done, because they are wired to take action more readily than most.

On the other side, the action and anger residing in the Body Center can leave a considerable amount of destruction in its wake. When operating from an unhealthy space, Eight-Nine-Ones can be explosive and vengeful, judgmental and overreactive, and fall into a toxic pattern of *defending* for the wrong reasons. Many people within the Body Center experience a wall of anger and rage surrounding a particular unhealed or unexplored internal wound. This wall can be brought down by diving into the inner work necessary to move through the passion, fixation, and virtue and activate as an Ally, Advocate, or Love Warrior.

We all have access to the Body Center energy, and sometimes the anger we pick up from these Points can serve as a wake-up call or a catalyst for helping us land in our virtue. Not all anger needs to be destructive.

BODY CENTER STRENGTHS

Steadfastness, instinctual awareness, leadership, inspirational, supportive action, trustworthiness, loyalty, morality in virtue, social justice awareness, communication, mercy, courage, pragmatism, visionaries, balance, honor, fairness, philanthropy, ready to take action

BODY CENTER CHALLENGES

Anger, boundaries, separation, control, passivity, reactivity, excessive action, judgment, aggression, morality vs. action, compassion, vulnerability, conflict, repression, independence, intention vs. impact, internal unhealed wounds, explosive rage, internal reflection

ENNEAGRAM
POINT 8

Darkness cannot drive out darkness; only light can do that.
Hate cannot drive out hate; only love can do that.

—MARTIN LUTHER KING, JR.

If you're going to hold someone down you're going to have to hold on by
the other end of the chain. You are confined by your own repression.

—TONI MORRISON

Courage is what it takes to stand up and speak;
courage is also what it takes to sit down and listen.

—WINSTON CHURCHILL

The strongest love is the love that can demonstrate its fragility.

—PAULO COELHO

OVERVIEW

If Point Eight is where you stand on the Enneagram map, there is an unmistakable energy that resides within you. Instinctual protection, strength, control, and power are just a few of the assets you were born with—and as we like to say, "You will move mountains." The Eight is recognizable in Enneagram teachings as the *Challenger*. In the IDEA space we experience this powerful energy in distinctly different ways. Eights can show up with the energy of the *Guardian*, the *Aggressor*, and the *Oppressor*. IDEA work is the place to demonstrate your capacity for strength and compassion and show up as a force to be reckoned with.

If the dominant energy you experience is at Point Eight, you may feel compelled to exert tremendous energy in the direction of everything you do. You often experience a need for control to keep yourself protected from whatever might render you vulnerable. This need for control is constantly driving your actions and can be quite exhausting. Power *with* rather than power *over* others is sometimes a difficult space for you to occupy. It can feel uncomfortable to let go of control of your environment, including control over anything external that might influence your environment. I coach and mentor many people from all walks of life and have witnessed this protective stance from Eights with respect to the vulnerability of their hearts. Most Eights are bighearted, action-oriented, and ever ready to get things moving. The amount of energy, strength, assertiveness, and ability to take charge and move forward as a normal way of being for Eights is a true wonder to behold. Most of us would love to be able to tap into that energy bank. The challenge, if you are an Eight, is that every perceived mountain may only be a molehill. When you exert too much energy, be it in a conversation for you versus a confrontation for the person you are speaking with, you are likely to lose rather than gain Allies and connections. That is not the mission. Maintaining control creates a comfort zone for you; however, this work requires learning how to meet people where they are and accept how they show up across differences. You will have just as much *un*learning as learning to do.

At your best, you are often an evolving Ally, Advocate, and guardian of the downtrodden and the Love Warriors. You seem to find a way to stand up to anything or anyone that causes the unjust or unfair treatment of others, at least through your Eight lens. The deep fear of being controlled or harmed by external influences may cause you to construct walls around your big heart to protect yourself from heartbreak and your own innocence. While radiating an energy that manifests the appearance of an invulnerable human being who can take on anything, your heartbreak at Point Eight is equally as powerful as your strength. When you let your guard down, there is a lovable, kind, and tenderhearted human, sometimes hidden under a prickly exterior. If this is resonating with you, remember this: there is no need to *always* appear strong and assertive. It is a counterproductive way of moving through the world and can be intimidating and unnecessarily confrontational to some, which can amplify disconnects across differences. Remember, your evolutionary path is toward Allyship and Advocacy.

The experience of being feared or of being seen as dominating and overbearing may not be an uncommon experience for you at Point Eight. Even if your actions are well-intentioned, you may be unaware of the true impact of your words and behaviors. The aggressive stance and powerful energy you embody may be from a protective or well-intentioned place, but the message you may be unintentionally projecting can have a profoundly different effect on people. Aligning your intent with your impact is just another step to becoming a whole human being who strives to do better.

If this sounds like you, welcome to the IDEA community. You can be an essential Ally for any cause, and I hope you will join us on our path to heal humanity.

As an Eight, you have great strength, power, and valuable vulnerability. If Eight energy is where you have determined your place resides on the Enneagram map, discover the journey of how you can harness the gifts from all the different components of the Enneagram: explore your basic desire, basic fear, core motivation, passion/blind spot, fixation/trap, virtue/your true self, and the Eight's connections to Points Two, Five, Seven, and Nine.

Let's go over a few things to prepare you for your journey.

- The Eight blind spot, or passion of lust as it is called in the Enneagram, is a deep desire to take on life with all of the energy you can produce.

- Your Eight energy seeks more challenges, more control, more action, more intensity, more of everything.

- The intensity that your Eight energy brings into everything matters and drives you to push the limits in your life landing you in no-win oppositional situations. This conscripted stance is the default to enforce power over whomever you perceive to be the adversary.

- Your unique way of navigating challenges can lead you to a thirst for revenge, a concept that is taught as the fixation of vengeance. This is where you get trapped and your rage becomes the guidance for your automatic pilot.

- The dominant stance and reacting with a vengeful force are your ways of masking your Achilles' heel: *vulnerability.*

- The invitation to move into activation is attainable when you access the gift of reason at Point Five, moving away from rage, lust, and vengeance as they are specious emotions that are blocking your true heart.

- Enter the transformative space of the heart at Point Two, where you can rediscover your innocence, taught in the Enneagram as the Eight's virtue. This is where you will reclaim your balance and peace as a Love Warrior, Ally, or Advocate.

SUMMARY OF 8s IN THE IDEA SPACE

The images of powerful historical icons in IDEA work, both positive and negative, can easily serve as a visualization for the people who stand at Point Eight: Martin Luther King, Jr., Kamala Harris, Toni Morrison, Alexandria

Ocasio-Cortez, Winston Churchill, Indira Gandhi, Saddam Hussein, Donald Trump, and Fidel Castro.

Eights in the IDEA space are influential, outspoken, strong-willed leaders, sometimes advocating for humanity and sometimes contributing to the marginalization of humanity. There is a very distinct energy of confidence and control that is inherent for all Eights. The energy that we all have the opportunity to access from Point Eight is the strong internal sense of justice and the inner drive to protect the disadvantaged, disenfranchised, vulnerable, downtrodden, and underrepresented. The polarity here that must be managed is creating the space for the honoring of connection and advocacy through authentic vulnerability and a compassionate approach to conflict. For the most part, people at Point Eight are directly opposed to vulnerability—or what they consider to be weakness—however, vulnerability is the key to accessing the heart space and developing a compassionate objectivity instead of gut reactivity that many find overly aggressive, intimidating, or overpowering.

People who possess the dominant energy at Point Eight can be the true guardians of the IDEA world. The instinctual protection, strength, control, and power at Point Eight is unmistakable, and it has the ability to affect everything and everyone who comes in contact with this particular energy. You will find Eights in every walk of life. Often, they are in top positions of power or are capable of enacting real changes in systems and societal structures, for better or for worse. Eights are the leaders we follow, the speakers we listen to, and the people we look to for strength in times of pain and suffering. Eights make people feel confident that anything is possible as long as we fight hard for what we believe in.

———

Activation is possible when you engage in doing intentional inner work, continue to educate yourself, and create new and more compassionate connections across differences. You can avail yourself of opportunities to choose love and compassion, allowing your actions to manifest as a power with rather than power over other humans. In the next few sections, observe the evolution of a true Eight Advocate as we move you from the unhealthy, average, and healthy levels of development. You may notice yourself in each of the levels; we are all learning and growing, and it is vital to remain present, grounded, and honest as you allow your inner observer to guide you through this process. As you work your way through the descriptors and examples, pay attention to how you react and respond while you process the information about your attitudes, behaviors, and beliefs. This is a fluid process, and as human beings we are capable of accessing the high road and falling into destructive behaviors and old beliefs, all in the same day. The journey here is being open to a new way of navigating your Enneagram energy to resolve the challenges you face across differences and uncover your hidden implicit biases.

PATH OF ACTIVATION

As we illustrate the path of activation from active othering to passive othering and ultimately to Advocacy, the levels of development (unhealthy, average, healthy) demonstrate how the Eight energy manifests in the IDEA space. In our exploration of the various stages of activation, we can uncover the complexities of Eight energy by observing the nuances of the evolution of the journey.

THE OPPRESSOR—ACTIVE OTHERING

In the unhealthy levels of development, we experience active othering, a space occupied by the *Oppressor*—a person who consciously acknowledges and reacts based on a distorted reality that is filtered through the Eight's blind spot/passion of lust. The blind spot for the Eight manifests as a relentless search for a challenge, cause, or recipient of/for the intensity of an overabundance of energy. In this space we find the ruthless, unrelentingly cruel, vengeful, omnipotent, and extremely destructive individuals who justify their actions and beliefs from the unhealthy energy of Point Eight. Fear, anger, and control are the primary motivators that distort reality, resulting in disdain for humans who may be perceived as a threat to their way of life.

For people who reside within the automatic advantage, disengaging from reactionary bias and bigotry in order to move toward activation as an Ally or Advocate can seem like a sign of weakness or vulnerability. This can trigger the defense mechanism of denial, which will further fuel feelings and expressions of deep rage. At this level, people who are born into automatic advantage can become deeply oppressive, vengeful, cruel, and tyrannical. These are the people capable of dehumanizing large groups of people and amassing a huge following of like-minded individuals. They are demonstrative in their cruelty and aggressively defend their beliefs in order to appear strong and in control when deep down what is really being defended is their vulnerability and personal trauma. For some unhealthy Eights with automatic advantage, this space can be the result of a power dynamic shift in which there are feelings of fear around losing position or control to another person or group. The fear of being in a weaker position can trigger a deep rage aimed at whomever or whatever is challenging the position of power.

People who have developed positional power and fall into the unhealthy levels of development can become vengeful and oppressive, consciously rejecting the people, the circumstances, and the details of their journey. An intentional distortion of reality creates an "I did it all myself" attitude which serves as the justification for the dehumanization of anyone who challenges their position or serves as a reminder of their origin. We can experience the concept of horizontal bias at this level, where people who share similar dimensions of diversity can dehumanize other people within the same category in order to gain more power and control.

The *Oppressor,* in regard to the Love Warriors who have found themselves pushed to the margins, can be those who seek to turn the tables in a vengeful and deeply destructive manner. They often find it difficult to address their own internal wounds and trauma; fearing vulnerability, they will strike out and perpetually exert their energy with rage and a thirst for revenge. For the Love Warriors, the unhealthy Eight energy manifests as intense rage masking deep pain that traps people into a pattern of behavior of vengeance, also known as the fixation: lashing out with intimidating bouts of anger and a hunger for reciprocal action. This space is heartbreaking to witness as anger, vengeance, and outrage take over a person's ability to heal, engage in productive conflict resolution, or find compassion for themselves and others.

My Son, Will This Be Your Life?

When my firstborn was a toddler, I found that running around in circles in the open space of a shopping mall brought him great joy. For me it was just enough time to read a chapter in a book and let him wear himself out. Sadly, I can never forget the day that I no longer felt comfortable allowing him his freedom of movement in that space.

I was sitting on a bench watching him play when another little toddler who happened to be White-bodied came over and began running in circles with him. The children were having a wonderful time just enjoying one another. The little sounds of laughter made me smile and warmed my heart. I looked back down at my book and thought all was well with the world.

*Moments later I heard a loud, harsh male voice bellowing from where the children had been playing. I was startled when I looked up to see a man snatch this child by his waist in one swift movement. He violently shook the little one and, staring piercingly into this little boy's eyes, he screamed, "Don't ever let me catch you playing with a n***** again!" The little boy started to cry. The man held up the boy out of my son's reach, as if my two-year-old posed a threat to him. I ran over and I picked up my son, and I held him to my chest. My heart was beating so fast, and I was holding him so tight that I feared I was hurting him. I wanted to protect him and tell him everything was okay and he had done nothing wrong. But I could not speak; I could not even catch my breath. So I held him close to my heart and prayed that he understood he was safe now in my arms. I looked into his innocent eyes as we both burst into tears.*

I will never forget that day. I know the memory of it lives somewhere in my son's body, though he has no recollection of the incident and I've never spoken a word of it since. As parents, we all try to protect our children from pain and suffering, and I could not let this be my son's first memory of how the world treats young Black boys. This was a moment of unbridled rage, and my son had been caught in the middle of this grown man's hatred and racism. This was the energy of anger, bigotry, hatred, and fear. While the memory of this traumatic experience undoubtedly resides within my son's body, I know it is also present in that little White-bodied child who only saw my son as a playmate and probably had no biases against anyone until that very moment.

I will never know this man's Enneagram type. He could have been any type on the Enneagram map, but the energy that I experienced on that day was the powerful energy of rage that I have experienced on the low side of Point Eight. His actions, as experienced by me, were unjustifiable, despicable, and mean-spirited. His rage and the articulated reason for the outburst literally took my breath away. From his lens he was protecting his child from what? My child's skin color?

As I have lived and learned, bigotry and grace can be accessed at all nine Points of the Enneagram. I have one specific regret about that moment: I wish that any of the powerful Eight Allies that are in my life now had been present with me on that day to meet his energy.

THE AGGRESSOR—PASSIVE OTHERING

The *Aggressor* resides in the murky waters of passive othering, where we experience varying average levels of development. On the unhealthy side of average, we find Eights who consciously choose to remain in the pattern of behavior, or fixation, of vengeance; they seek outlets for their angry energy and avoid dealing with the true causes of their rage. In this space Eights are unpredictable, overly confrontational, egocentric, belligerent, vindictive, angry, and callous. When we move to the average levels, we have a space that most people find themselves reverting to as a comfort zone during times of stress: Eights become boastful, willful, insecure, emotionally demonstrative, vindictive, and intimidating—inhumanity caused by resistance to vulnerability. These areas of passive othering can feel uncomfortable and challenging for some Eights, as they are generally driven by a desire to authentically support and protect wherever they perceive a threat to those with less power. Most Eights who have been stuck in the role of the *Aggressor* for a long time find it difficult to move past the basic fear of being vulnerable, controlled, or harmed, which ultimately lands them firmly in a pattern of vengeance, the fixation of an Enneagram Eight.

For Eights born into automatic advantage, the *Aggressor* takes the form of an outwardly angry human being who is trying to mask and deflect their own pain and vulnerability. Similar to the behaviors of the Eight at the *Oppressor* level, this is a person who is likely struggling with a shift in power dynamics and feels like they are losing control of their environment to someone or something. Many people at this level feel insecure with their surroundings. Believing that they must provide for and/or protect themselves, they build up walls to keep everyone and everything out. The fear of betrayal and being let down by others leads the *Aggressor* to unleash a toxic energy of vengeance that alienates people and creates divides in many relationships. The opportunity to pause and engage in honest emotional reflection and objectivity becomes a struggle for Eights at this level. They often react with forged strength and a gut reactivity in the hopes of concealing their vulnerability and capacity for gentleness. The fear of opening up and communicating with a person who may challenge their strength quickly buries their ability to find the compassion that is hidden deep in their big hearts.

Eights who develop positional power and fall into the role of the *Aggressor* can be highly defensive individuals who react and behave in vengeful and destructive ways out of fear of losing their power or control over their situation. They have undoubtedly fought hard to get to where they are, oftentimes leaving a path of deep divides caused by their outward anger and rage-induced actions, and they are not likely to let go of their power for any reason. These individuals become cruel and emotionally demonstrative when faced with challenges across differences; they may experience a moment of empathy toward people in similar situations, but the fear of giving up their control or power quickly shifts them into a defensive stance.

For the Love Warriors pushed to the margins, this space of unhealthy anger and the fear of their own vulnerability leads to complications when addressing and healing the internal trauma and wounds caused by deep suffering and pain. They can fall into destructive patterns of self-betrayal and vindictive actions, and hold on to a seething anger aimed at external factors as a way of hiding the deep pain they have experienced. They are oftentimes wounded individuals attempting to conceal their vulnerability by lashing out with vengeance and hollow acts of aggression aimed at anyone who threatens their perception of strength and control. They may experience moments in which compassion seems like a viable option, but their unresolved anger quickly shifts them into a dehumanizing state.

The Coup

My work as an IDEA consultant is best accomplished when I work with the leadership team at the top level and with people who occupy the lowest-paying positions in the organization simultaneously. It is not uncommon to find pockets of resistance at any level.

In one organization the resistance was palpable at the lower level and the employees began talking about not wanting to "drink the IDEA Kool-Aid." I dispatched a team of trainers to work with this group, and when I tell you they ate my trainers for lunch, well, let's just say that's only a mild exaggeration. I decided to take the matter into my own hands and scheduled myself to do the group's next round of training.

As usual there was a leader of the pack. "Hey, doc, you coming out here with some more of that Kool-Aid? I told your folks we're not drinkin' it!" The training room erupted with laughter, and I laughed right along with them. I walked over to where my chief rabble-rouser was seated.

"What's your name?" I asked.

He responded, "Charlie, and I don't know why you are out here wasting our time."

"Well, Charlie," I said, "I'm sorry you feel that way. I stayed up most of last night mixing up a special flavor of Kool-Aid for you." We locked eyes. I stood my ground as he gazed up at me. I

continued, "I'll make a deal with you. If you sit through this class and try to listen without being disruptive, we can talk to your supervisor and see if we can get you assigned to be somewhere else for the rest of these classes." I could tell he was struggling to come up with a sarcastic comeback. "Deal?" I asked.

He paused for a brief moment and replied, "Deal."

The training began, and with Charlie somewhat silenced, the group came around and began to engage. Little by little I was able to draw them in. Charlie sat in the back of the room fuming at how things had unfolded. He was stuck between the proverbial rock and a hard place. He began pounding his fist on his desk. The rest of the group ignored him, and I continued.

We had reached the part of the training where I began teaching the Enneagram Points. Eight is always the first energy I teach, and I felt this was divine intervention at this moment. I began reviewing the Eight energy: outspoken, domineering, angry, powerful, willful ... There were several outbursts of laughter, some serious reflection, and a lot of questions. One brave soul spoke up. "Hey, Charlie! That sounds a lot like you, man!" Charlie quickly gave him the death stare.

When the class was over, Charlie was the first one out the door, moving swiftly and purposefully to escape the obvious discomfort he was experiencing. Many of the determined non-Kool-Aid-drinkers lingered to ask more questions. I sensed they were interested in learning how to deal with the energies that had dominated the workplace culture for so many years.

Charlie never requested that I make good on our deal, nor did he return to any of the future training sessions. It had been brought to my attention that he tried to intimidate a few of his co-workers to stage a coup to prevent the group from coming to the training and conversation circles. It did not work. I returned week after week and continued training in that organization for many years. Charlie never challenged me again, and the workplace flourished with a new culture of respect and compassion.

THE GUARDIAN—ADVOCACY

The healthy levels of development, where we experience the true Advocacy of Point Eight, are home to the *Guardian*—a strong and merciful defender of humanity. These are the people who embrace their authentic selves and understand that they do not need to show force and strength in order to protect themselves and others. The *Guardian* finds strength through vulnerability and a return to the purity of an innocent heart. They are able to take action through compassion and empathy, leading others into a space of healing and the honoring of our collective humanity. The emergence of their true spirit allows them to overcome their basic fear of being controlled or harmed by outside influences; they surrender to the reality that they cannot control everything and they harness their real strength as a selfless guardian and protector for all of us. These are the leaders who genuinely access their heart space and begin to operate from love and true awareness in the face of divisiveness, confrontation, and conflict instead of attempting to confront the challenges with forged aggression. The surprising capacity for gentleness and love residing in the Eight energy is more powerful than anyone expects.

An Eight born into automatic advantage who has done the inner work necessary to move into the space of the *Guardian* has found innocence, the gift or virtue of the Eight, in the process of defending and showing compassion for themselves and others without the need to maintain a false sense of control over everything and everyone around them. These are the people creating and honoring the space for others to be brought back in from the margins and authentically standing as *Guardians* who protect and defend humanity. For people born into automatic advantage, activation and Advocacy takes the form of formidable power and strength to enter the fight for humanity to achieve equity, equality, and justice. At this level, Allies and Advocates have the capacity to enter spaces unobstructed where Love Warriors are underrepresented and unwelcomed. Allies can stand with others and Advocates can open doors for others by using their energy, position, power, and automatic advantage to defend the rights and dignity of all involved.

People who gain positional power at this level of development are capable of being instrumental in creating sustainable change. The unique perspective of being present within multiple hierarchies of society allows these *Guardians* to not only open doors but to also know which doors to open. They have faced the margins of society, found their way back, and recognize the path to bring others along to reconnect the divides our community faces. Many *Guardians* who are in positions of power become the historical humanitarians we honor and celebrate.

Love Warriors who stand at Point Eight and have moved into Advocacy may use their abundance of energy to fight back and reclaim their own power. When a person is willing to engage in the inner work necessary to heal their inner wounds and choose self-love, compassion, and personal power over vengeance and retribution, they can lead the way for their communities and serve as defenders of "others." The Love Warriors who step into Advocacy can become forces of nature, guarding the path and leading causes with a heroic and courageous amount of compassion. Oftentimes these Love Warriors are able to gain positional power and become prominent figures in true historical change, leaving legacies that can be felt for generations to come.

Got My Back

The loyal and protective nature of those who have their dominant energy at Point Eight, when healthy, brings strength, fearlessness, and action to the Advocacy. I have noticed time and again that my social justice journey has been sprinkled with Eights who check in, lend a hand, and then move on. In organizations, I have marveled at the Eight leaders who sit at the helm of a culture change or an IDEA initiative. This is when the energy of Eights makes for a fearless, no-nonsense, kick-ass Advocate who is not taking no for an answer. I have learned to embody this powerful energy for myself when needed.

It does not come as a surprise that some of my strongest Allies stand at Point Eight. A few years ago, I was presenting at an Enneagram conference and having difficulty getting my presentation materials delivered to the conference center. My creative design consultant and I were beside ourselves. The resolution to our problem surfaced at Point Eight. Sensing our frustration, a lovely human approached us saying, "Have everything shipped overnight to my place. We can coordinate to get it to the conference center and there won't be any confusion about getting it to you." We smiled with relief and quickly accepted the gracious offer.

Later in the week when my session on the Enneagram and IDEA was about to begin, I noticed the room had more participants than usual. A lot more than usual. I scanned the room and was extremely heartened by what I discovered. This same lovely human was sitting in the front row of my session and had obviously recruited others to come along. Historically, the Enneagram community hadn't fully embraced my sessions and often avoided the tough conversations that developed from them. The attendance would always pale in comparison to other sessions, but I would always find a few Love Warriors to bring into the journey. In this session, my Ally had exponentially increased the amount of Allies and Love Warriors who were present and created space for my message to be heard.

This Ally has always treated me with love, warmth, kindness, and respect. With just the right touch of checking in, this Ally showed genuine concern over whether I was being included or treated differently, considering the topic of my presentations.

Over the years my Ally's support for my work has been unwavering. We have talked about what we might cook up together as an offering to make the Enneagram more accessible to communities of color and Love Warriors, wherever they may reside. When George Floyd was murdered, many people reached out to me from around the globe. This individual who stands at Point Eight was one of the first to reach out. I appreciate the support and the willingness to offer whatever assistance is needed. While my Ally is not intrusive, I have only to ask, and I know that I can rely on time-tested loyalty and authenticity of intention to have my back. Recently I have experienced more Point Eight Allies coming forward. A heartfelt offer to work together to bring more understanding and healing through somatic awareness is in progress for 2022, a collaboration with an Eight Advocate who is working with me on my own healing. A close relationship with another Eight colleague who has looked me right in the eye and stated, "I want to do more." And she will do more as she has the platform to do so. Hearts bigger than anyone can imagine, and rarely more talk than action, the Guardians who stand at Point Eight are priceless.

While George Floyd was a wake-up call for many, Allies who embody Eight as their dominant energy have transformed into Advocates. Eights from all over the globe have made their presence known and their support is unwavering. From Canada to Copenhagen and back to California, they are engaged, activated, and always elevating the Love Warriors with the force of their full presence.

The authentic strength that radiates from the heart of Point Eight brings true power to any challenge.

At Point Eight your greatest strength is your sense of justice and inner drive to protect the disadvantaged, vulnerable, downtrodden, and underrepresented. Use your innate power and strength for good, and channel your forceful energy through a lens of love and light to become a social justice Advocate and protector of equity and fairness.

Consider this prework to practice and explore as you prepare yourself for the path of activation as an Ally, Advocate, or Love Warrior:

- The objective time-out and intentional pause at Point Five in your Head Center can accelerate your movement with the arrow toward Point Two.

- Take a moment to pause and cool down. Going against the arrow to Point Five first gives you the opportunity to access and quiet your Head Center to create additional space for reflection and processing.

- Breathe in and embody peace through internal reflection, and explore the positive qualities at Point Five. Learn to still the rumination about anger and vengeful action, and find perspective with objectivity and a curious spirit.

- In the Heart Center at Point Two, begin to address the value in your vulnerability. The connection to your heart allows people to see the real you in all of your power and strength. You can connect with others across the differences with compassion and kindness. Step into your vulnerability and allow yourself space to heal and address your inner wounds.

- Allow yourself to reflect on the intentions behind your actions. What is at the core of your intentions? Reflect on the true impact of your actions and behaviors, and find multiperspective balance in how you navigate through the world.

ENNEAGRAM
POINT 9

Change will not come if we wait for some other person or some other time. We are the ones we've been waiting for. We are the change that we seek.

—BARACK OBAMA

Burnout is a way of telling you that your form of activism was perhaps not very full circle.

—GLORIA STEINEM

Great leaders are almost always great simplifiers who can cut through argument, debate and doubt to offer a solution everybody can understand.

—COLIN POWELL

You cannot escape the responsibility of tomorrow by evading it today.

—ABRAHAM LINCOLN

OVERVIEW

If Point Nine is where you stand on the Enneagram map, the need to keep peace and find harmony is the driving force behind your actions and behaviors. In a world full of challenges and struggles, most humans try to find ways of resolving conflict in their own way, but for you at Point Nine, this is a way of life. In the Enneagram world, the Nine is appropriately known as the *Peacemaker* or the *Mediator*. In the IDEA space, we experience this energy in distinctly different ways. Nines can show up with the energy of the *Knight*, the *Sleepwalker*, and the *Shadow*. IDEA work is the place to expand your capacity for presence, harmony, and extraordinary strength to show up as a crusader for equity, justice, and connection for all humans.

As a Nine, you are the type most devoted to finding internal and external peace and creating harmony in the world. Stability, avoiding conflict, compromise, and mediation create your comfort zone. You are the quiet waters that run deep beneath our collective human experience. Many Nines share the experience of being complacent during times of conflict, which can cause you to fall asleep to yourself and to the true depth of your powerful presence in the world. You have a strong drive to maintain balance and harmony, both internally and externally, in order to not feel loss or separation from whatever resides within your comfort zone.

At Point Nine, the gaze is automatically drawn to finding ways to either avoid or resolve conflict; if you are a *Peacemaker* or a *Mediator*, you have the ability to see the big picture and the many ways of addressing (or not addressing) situations. The lens through which you view the world is one of quiet internalization, and sometimes a repression of true feelings in order to not wake up to reality. The repression of your true self can cause a deep, tortuous anger to build within you. This anger is perfectly demonstrated through the metaphor of a volcano. The volcano runs deep with searing magma; warning signs of an eruption may appear but are quickly replaced with a quiet stillness, then unexpectedly the volcano erupts. Lava flows and torches the world around it but also scorches the volcano itself. Nines will erupt in anger, but it is clear the anger is just as painful for them as it is for the person it may be aimed toward. You avoid dealing with your anger and instead numb out and deflect your true emotions. This will only lead to more disconnects and deprive you of true peace. Presence is the main obstacle for most Nines, whether in the IDEA space or in their everyday lives. At Point Nine you are capable of tremendous contributions as long as you stay present.

At your best you are often an evolving Ally, Advocate, and defender of humanity's capacity for peace and harmony. You seem to find a way to communicate and find common ground across differences, even when others are unable to get there. However, the deep fear of having your equilibrium disturbed in one way or another may cause you to repress your true emotions and feelings, believing that they won't matter anyway. While radiating an energy that manifests the appearance of a calm serene human who has it all figured out, your indifference at Point Nine is equally as powerful as your presence. Your passive stance and seemingly lackadaisical apathy say more than you think, especially during conflicts that may arise. When you let yourself become present to your true strength, there is a fierce, passionate, and engaged human sometimes hidden under a calculated stoicism. If this is resonating with you, remember this: you know you have the capacity to do great things, but you are afraid to engage and become present to your power. This is a counterproductive way of moving through the world and can be disheartening and unintentionally destructive, which will amplify the disconnects you face across differences. Remember, your evolutionary path is toward Allyship and Advocacy, but you must remain present to stay on this path.

The experience of being complacent or of being seen as hopeless and indifferent may not be an uncommon experience for you at Point Nine. One of the biggest obstacles for Nines to gain access to the gift, or virtue, is the daily repression of your authentic selves in order to not feel anything that may affect your environment—passive-aggressive behaviors, saying yes when you really mean no, avoiding conflict to maintain false connection with others, choosing to remain asleep to addressing your own pain and suffering, thus denying the existence of the pain and suffering of others. Becoming present is just another step to becoming a whole human being who strives to do better.

If this sounds like you, welcome to the IDEA community. You can be an essential Ally for any cause, and I hope you will join us on our path to heal humanity.

You have great strength and power, and the capacity for a valuable perspective. If Nine energy is where you have determined your place resides on the Enneagram map, discover the journey of how you can harness the gifts from all the different components of the Enneagram: explore your basic desire, basic fear, core motivation, passion/blind spot, fixation/where you get stuck, virtue/your true self, and the Nine's connections to Points Six, Three, Eight, and One.

Let's go over a few things to prepare you for your journey.

- Your Nine blind spot, or passion of sloth as it is called in the Enneagram, supports your deep desire to remain unaffected by reality and the challenges you may face in the hopes of maintaining a false sense of inner peace.

- Your energy seeks to avoid anything that may challenge your ability to numb out or to cope with the demands of your own feelings and the feelings of others.

- The inactivity that your energy can foster is a destructive pattern of behavior that is intentionally designed to deny you the ability to engage in life and live up to your full potential.

- This leads to your acceptance of a delusional approach to life, a concept that is taught as your fixation of indolence. This is where you get trapped, and your anger and apathy become the guidance for your automatic pilot.

- You protect yourself from being disrupted or forced to wake up by running away from challenges, oftentimes seeking out painless solutions to detach from being held accountable for your actions. There may be a sense of fatigue when you become overwhelmed or disheartened by the current state of things.

- The invitation to move into activation is attainable when you access the gift of objective reasoning and a clear focus to address your true feelings at Point Six; move away from anger, sloth, and indolence as they are duplicitous emotions that are blocking your true heart.

- Enter the transformative space of the Heart Center at Point Three, where you can harness your ability to take action, taught in the Enneagram as the virute of the Nine. This is where you will reclaim your balance, strength, and presence as a Love Warrior, Ally, or Advocate.

SUMMARY OF 9s IN THE IDEA SPACE

The images of leaders in IDEA work, both positive and negative, can easily serve as a visualization for the people who stand at Point Nine: Barack Obama, Alicia Keys, Ronald Reagan, Colin Powell, Carl Jung, Abraham Lincoln, Gloria Steinem, Queen Elizabeth II, Whoopi Goldberg, Joseph Campbell, Morgan Freeman, Dwight D. Eisenhower, and Audrey Hepburn.

We all know someone considered the mediator, the referee, the peacekeeper, or the negotiator, and chances are if you stand at Point Nine, people have referred to you by one of these monikers. Nines are able to step back and see the big picture through multiple perspectives and are predisposed to finding a reasonable solution for everyone. A lot of historical social justice leaders, Advocates, and humanitarians who stand at Point Nine are the unsung heroes of true change and growth. Contrastingly, there have been an alarming number of U.S. presidents throughout history whose unhealthy Nine energy fostered apathy and the furthering of marginalization of American society.

The energy that we all have the opportunity to access from Point Nine is the calm level-headed approach to conflict resolution when communicating across differences. There is a distinct energy within most Nines that exemplifies the human capacity for serenity, but sometimes this energy is polluted with the underlying repression of anger. The polarity here that must be managed is creating the space for connectivity and engagement while maintaining presence and emotional honesty. While most people who stand at Point Nine seem calm, cool, and collected in the face of conflict, the inner dialogue of a Nine is tiptoeing around the line of indolence and action. Presence is the key to remaining active as an Advocate and vocal defender of social justice.

People who possess the dominant energy at Point Nine can be the still waters that run deep beneath the problems at hand. The inner drive to avoid conflict actually serves as a motivating factor when navigating the work of social justice. Nines, when awake, will ride into battle as the *Knights* (nonbinary) in shining armor and fight for resolution at any cost. You will find Nines in all walks of life; often they are the quiet but fierce defenders of justice and peace for the Love Warriors and disenfranchised. Nines have an effect on people that makes everyone feel a little more at ease and comfortable, even in difficult moments.

———

Activation is possible when you engage in doing intentional inner work, continue to educate yourself, and create new connections across differences with a powerful presence. You can avail yourself of opportunities to choose love and presence, allowing your actions to manifest as a true awareness for the power of connections to other humans rather than an apathetic approach to disconnection. In the next few sections, observe the evolution of a true Nine Advocate as we move through the unhealthy, average, and healthy levels of development. You may notice yourself in each of the levels; we are all learning and growing, and it is vital to remain present, grounded, and honest as you allow your inner observer to guide you through this process. As you work your way through the descriptors and examples, pay attention to how you react and respond while you process this information about your attitudes, behaviors, and beliefs. This is a fluid process, and as human beings we are capable of accessing the high road and falling into destructive behaviors and old beliefs, all in the same day. The journey here is being open to a new way of navigating your Enneagram energy to resolve the challenges you face across differences and uncover your hidden implicit biases.

PATH OF ACTIVATION

As we illustrate the path of activation from active othering to passive othering and ultimately to Advocacy, the levels of development (unhealthy, average, healthy) demonstrate how the Nine energy manifests in the IDEA space. In our exploration of the various stages of activation, we can uncover the complexities of Nine energy by observing the nuances of the evolution of the journey.

THE SHADOW—ACTIVE OTHERING

In the unhealthy levels of development, we experience active othering where the *Shadow* lingers—a person who consciously acknowledges and reacts based on a distorted reality, which is filtered through the Nine's blind spot/passion of sloth. The blind spot for the Nine manifests as a deep state of denial and avoidance of all things: feelings, reality, hope, presence, humanity. In this space we find the deeply repressed, ineffectual, blindly loyal, and painfully angry individuals who justify actions and beliefs from the unhealthy energy of Point Nine. These Nines are capable of embodying true apathy: destructively cavalier, distant, unfeeling or indifferent, a repressed anger lurking within a cold and detached individual. Anger and denial are the primary motivators that distort their reality, resulting in a disdain for humans who may disrupt their inner peace or force them to wake up to or acknowledge their anger.

For Nines who were born into automatic advantage, disengaging from reactionary bias and bigotry in order to activate as an Ally or Advocate can force a state of presence that may trigger deep internal anger. These asleep Nines feel hopeless in the face of challenges and change and often revert to a level of numbness that allows their inner peace to remain falsely still. They can often be found among the masses of the unquestioning and complacent, blindly attaching themselves to anything that lets them release their anger, even if it is misdirected or unrelated. These are the individuals so detached from humanity that they develop a complete disregard for basic human decency. Presence is a true challenge for Nines who stand in the *Shadow* role; when they neglect the importance of their inner voice and bury their true emotions, they remain too stubborn to wake up and deal with reality.

People who develop positional power at this level of development can become deeply repressed and cruel to other humans. They forget their own struggle and often dehumanize others on the same path. Their tendency toward indifference and apathy increases as they drop deeper into the unhealthy levels. The callousness and detachment create a hotbed for hatred, bigotry, and bias to flourish unchecked. The "not my problem" mentality sets in and becomes the justification for the repressed anger and laziness. At this level people with positional power oftentimes feel a deep anger at the injustice they had to overcome in order to get to wherever they may be, and they can misdirect this anger onto others who mirror their own struggle. Dehumanizing behaviors become second nature and pollute the Nine's ability to find compassion for themselves and others.

The *Shadow*, in regard to Love Warriors who find themselves pushed to the margins, can appear to be truly hopeless and will accept false reality. They live in a state of denial and avoidance of the real pain, suffering, and anger that has been experienced. At Point Nine, they find it difficult to acknowledge and address their own internal wounds and trauma. The fear of waking up to the true cause of the deep pain creates a sleep state of indolence, denying any opportunity to deal with life. This space is heartbreaking to witness as anger, apathy, and fear take over a person's ability to heal or find compassion for themselves and others.

Hiding in Plain Sight

There are many people who log on to my website asking for advice or help for themselves. Among them are the worried souls who want guidance for loved ones as we face the challenge of trying to love and understand one another in an increasingly diverse world. A fairly recent phenomenon has been the influx of requests from people asking for help as they have watched spouses, children, siblings, relatives, and close friends cross over into the space of activism and anarchy. As membership increases among groups that are segregated and violent by nature, it is difficult for many to understand how people that are known to be mild mannered and peaceful by nature are connecting with groups that are steeped in violence, rage, and destruction. This is the Shadow *Nine. If this is your personal experience or the experience of someone beloved to you, remember that only love will bring you/them back. The need to belong is an integral part of our hierarchy of needs. If you are finding a space of belonging that is aligned with violence and othering, take the time to practice presence and honor the connection to goodness and love that is always present within you. Explore your values and bring them back to life. You do not have to find your place in darkness. Look for it in the light. Honor our universal connection and allow this to help you become healthy and whole. I have held the hands and hearts of so many people who love one another but are on opposite sides of the "ism" issues. I don't think of these cases as stories that I am willing to share. I can say that the peaceful and mild mannered among us, when falling to unhealthy levels, can release an incredible amount of pent-up rage directed toward those whom we believe will replace us. This rage is also internalized, and the passion/blind spot of anger consumes its victim (the unhealthy Nine). If your life experiences seem to be of such that you feel that nothing that you say or do matters to anyone in your inner circle, you may allow yourself to be chosen to be a part of a group that taps into the internal rage that lives in you that you have denied.*

If you're an unhealthy Nine who has lost yourself in the numbness of life, unhappy with work, home life, or otherwise, you will inadvertently seek out places to feel connected and part of a community, regardless of how it aligns with your ideals. You may have grown up knowing love, compassion, and kindness, but when you find yourself unhappy, alone, or without a comfortable atmosphere, you will forget your heart and become cold, distant, and cruel. Finding refuge in a group of people who make things feel comfortable or at ease, you turn a blind eye to any toxic or destructive beliefs, behaviors, or actions the group may harbor. As if by osmosis, you begin to unconsciously absorb these messages, and then all of a sudden your beliefs, behaviors, and actions begin to mimic the environment you find yourself in. Finding solace in your time of need, you defend your newly acquired actions and beliefs when challenged, disregarding your true nature for kindness and compassion.

THE SLEEPWALKER—PASSIVE OTHERING

The *Sleepwalker* resides in the destructive limbo of passive othering, where we experience the varying average levels of development. At the unhealthy level of average, we find Nines who consciously choose to remain in the pattern of behavior, or fixation, of indolence; they avoid external influences that may force them to wake up to the pain, suffering, or anything that may be disturbing. In this space, Nines are projecting a false sense of calm, unwilling to engage authentically, hopelessly indifferent, blindly neglectful, stubborn, angry, cruel, and apathetic. In the average levels of development, we have a space that most people find themselves reverting to as a comfort zone during times of stress—Nines become emotionally numb and self-effacing, deflecting authentic reflection, and embracing a "going with the flow" mentality. They fall into apathy caused by the inability to maintain presence. This area of passive othering is unfortunately a natural state for people who stand at Point Nine. The basic desire to have harmony, peace, and inner stability causes many Nines to remain asleep and impedes access to Nine's gift, or the virtue, of action. Nines who have been stuck in the role of the *Sleepwalker* for a long time find it extremely difficult to move past their basic fear of experiencing loss and separation. This keeps them from accessing their authentic selves, and ultimately lands them firmly in a pattern of indolence, the fixation of Nines.

For people born into automatic advantage, this space of passive othering is truly heartbreaking to witness as the dehumanization and disregard for common decency flourishes from within the Nine. Their disregard for other people in the hopes of preserving their inner peace leads them to turn a blind eye to blatant atrocities that may be happening right under their noses. Sometimes they experience a false realization that they cannot make a difference and their voice, actions, or influence won't matter. The "not my problem" outlook becomes a fallback, leading Nines down a dark path of denying or justifying their complicity in the widespread dehumanization of people. Some Nines at this level have outbursts of misplaced anger and hateful or bigoted reactions that can shock others, even the people closest to them. The volcano metaphor of the Nine anger is an ever-present factor for these individuals. On the other hand, they may experience a flicker of hope when they begin to find presence, but it is short-lived as they find the presence too disruptive to their routine of passivity.

Nines in positions of power at this level can become apathetic and indifferent to the circumstances that challenge our collective harmony as a global society. The overwhelm and chaos create a fatigue that can settle into the body of the Nine. They often focus on work or other areas in order to create a false sense of calm and deflect their anger and apathy. Many asleep Nines at this level will turn a blind eye to obvious inequities or daily indignities forced upon others; they adopt a subtle ignorance in the face of challenges. The outbursts of misplaced anger and bigotry can unexpectedly rattle the Nine and the people on the receiving end of whatever just spewed from their mouths. Instead of using their positional power to address the problems at hand and offer support or Allyship, they revert to a detached and aloof state believing their presence won't make a difference. Some Nines at this level will experience moments of compassion and connection during conflict, but the ability to remain present or acknowledge the impact of their presence can seem overwhelming and cause them to detach further.

For the Love Warrior who stands at Point Nine, this space of inaction and passivity leads to complications when addressing and healing the internal trauma and wounds caused by denial and indolence. They can fall into patterns of self-betrayal and painful indifference when the anger and numbness take over their hearts. At this level, people often feel a deep anger at the injustice they had to overcome or currently face in order to get to wherever they may be, and they misdirect this anger onto others who mirror their own struggle. Dehumanizing behaviors become second nature and pollute the ability of the Nines to find compassion for themselves and others. They become enablers in their own dehumanization by ignoring their problems and reverting to a state of helplessness in the face of challenges. The fleeting moments of presence they may experience are quickly replaced with the pessimistic approach of numbing out.

Live and Let Live

When working in an organization to help bring about a culture change, a strong level of engagement is a must-have with the leadership team. When the Nines on the team fall into the Sleepwalker *level of transformation, their energy of being checked out can drain the enthusiasm from the entire team.*

I was working with a leadership team to help to course correct some deeply entrenched racist, homophobic, and misogynistic attitudes and behaviors. This was not an easy assignment. The employee workplace culture assessment was frightening. It was hard to believe that anyone in a supervisory position had allowed even one of these incidents to go unchecked, much less to thrive, fester, and flourish. As I began to work with this team, it became clear that they were not engaged with the employees and took no responsibility for the horrible incidents that occurred on their watch. This was a leadership team of five. Three of them were Enneagram Nines. I interviewed each leader. "I understand the racial slurs are ubiquitous among your employees. What are you doing to curtail it?"

"I'm sorry, ma'am. I'm not sure what you are talking about."

Needless to say, that response irked the hell out of me! "Your employees have shared in the survey that Blacks are subjected to a constant barrage of racial slurs on a daily basis. Women are referred to and expected to respond to derogatory names, just to identify a few of these extremely disturbing allegations."

This human being sitting in front of me looked confused. "I know some cussing goes on every once in a while, but it's not like it's a big deal. No different than any other workplace." I was shocked. Not because of what he said, but because I could see that he believed it!

I went on to interview the rest of the team. All of the Nines on the team downplayed the results of the report. While no one was pleased with the survey results, the two remaining senior executives were well aware of the accuracy of the report. As I continued to work with this team over time, they came around and began to own their part in the toxic culture.

Only one of the Nines (let's call him Jim) totally lost it. During a roundtable strategy session, he blew up. "I'm sick of this bullshit! These sons of bitches run around here doing and saying whatever they want, and I leave them alone. Live and let live, and now I'm the bad guy? I'm not taking the hit for a bunch of ni ... " He caught himself before the word was fully formed. His eyes met mine, and he seemed to be trying to gain control of his emotions. His eyes teared up as he grabbed his things from the conference table and stormed out of the room.

The CEO looked at me and asked, "What just happened?"

"The volcano erupted, and it appears there is a lot more underneath wherever that came from," I answered.

"Do I need to go after him?" the CEO asked.

"No, give him some space to cool down," I replied.

"I've never seen Jim angry. I didn't even know that he had the capacity for that kind of anger! I wish he would put some of that fire into his job. Maybe things wouldn't have gone off the rails around here."

Jim put in his letter of resignation the next day. He came to see me after dropping it off at HR. "I'm sorry, Dr. E. I don't want you to take this personally. If more of the women and your people were like you, this job wouldn't have been so hard." He had no idea that his words were insulting and definitely triggering for me.

"Is that so, Jim? What exactly do you mean by that?" I asked.

"These people are just different from me, and not in a good way. I've learned to just ignore them and let them work things out for themselves. It's not my battle to fight. Sometimes I feel like I'm a ghost around here. They don't appreciate or recognize anything that I do for them, and I've done a lot," he said.

"Can you share with me a few things that you've done that have not been appreciated?"

He was silent for a moment, and when he spoke, it was the voice of someone who was totally defeated. "I left them the fuck alone. Nothing that I did would have made any difference anyway."

If you recognize this energy on the downside of Nine, take back your power and step into the reality that you and your actions matter. You can resolve to restore the Peacemaker's peace or contribute to the disintegration into chaos.

THE KNIGHT (NONBINARY)—ADVOCACY

The healthy levels of development of Point Nine are where we experience the powerful presence of the *Knight* (*nonbinary*)—an engaged and forceful defender against all threats to our collective humanity. These are the people willing to face conflict with an unexpectedly powerful impact and a calm but present serenity. The *Knight* is a fierce defender of humanity, a quiet but surprisingly assertive leader on the front lines of the battle for love, compassion, and reconnection. They navigate life through an inner strength and the courage of honoring their authentic selves in the face of divisiveness, confrontation, and conflict. The need for maintaining inner peace and stability at any cost evolves into an externalization of finding peace and harmony for everyone through honest, reasoned, and harmonious approaches. The unexpected strength and influence residing in the Nine energy is more powerful and meaningful than anyone expects.

People who are born into automatic advantage, when operating within healthy levels of development and Advocacy, can lead the world into reconnection and harmony through a deep awareness and a sense of responsibility and accountability. A Nine who has done the inner work necessary to move into the space of the *Knight* has found the ability to take the right action and remain present without the fear of being affected by disruptive influences. They recognize the power of their presence in facing challenges across differences and serve as defenders of the reconnections to humanity. Using their position as an Ally, they stand firmly in spaces with Love Warriors and other Allies, rarely backing down from a challenge to justice. The surprising capacity for presence and strength residing in the Nine energy can catch people off guard and encourage them to take action alongside the Nine in whatever battle they may be fighting.

The *Knights* who gain positional power at this level of development are inspiring leaders on the front lines of true historical change in the social justice arena. The unique perspective of facing the margins of society and using their impactful presence to regain their power allows these defenders of humanity to become motivators for people who find themselves feeling hopeless and abandoned. They have acknowledged the true impact of their full presence and hold steady in the face of conflicts while bridging the divides. People are often caught off guard by the surprisingly powerful voice of these Nines and will find inspiration in the forcefulness of the Nine's ability to stand on the frontline of conflict.

The Love Warrior who has done the inner work necessary to move into true Advocacy has woken up to reality, addressed their trauma, begun to heal their inner wounds, and found strength in their ability to remain present as a defender of humanity. These Love Warriors can appear quiet or even unconcerned, but internally they are experiencing a deep healthy anger targeted at addressing the inequities and disparities. They can internalize the challenges in order to find right action, which allows them to remove themselves from the anger and find objectivity. When they hit the moment of "enough is enough," they may uncharacteristically give voice to these emotions and catch people off guard with the forcefulness of their response. Oftentimes, these Love Warriors can become the fierce and noteworthy leaders who create sustainable change within systems by presenting a steady strength during difficult challenges.

Two Knights in Shining Armor

2016 was the year that seemed to push every button of my internal operating system to see exactly how deeply dysfunctional I could become. After an internal reset that landed me squarely in the center of Enneagram activism, I leaned heavily into my spiritual practices: prayer, meditation, and acts of service. I had forgotten the phrase "new level, new devil" until it arrived on my doorstep.

It was a Friday morning not unlike any other Friday morning. Most people in the neighborhood could set their clocks by the sight and sound of my husband going out for his morning run. On this particular morning, dressed in his usual Under Armour running gear, which included a reflective vest and reflectors on his shoes, he was suddenly brought to a halt by lights coming toward him from all directions. The lights were coming from police and county sheriff cars. They called out, "Stop! You there, stop now!" My husband stopped and slowly extended his arms as the officers got out of the car. They handcuffed him and forced him to the ground, his face in the dirt. The dogs were brought out to check for drugs. Apparently there had been an early morning robbery nearby and the police officers said he "fit the description." They asked him his name and information—where was he going, what was he doing out, and all the questions that had obvious answers. He responded to the best of his ability while handcuffed, facedown on the ground.

The early-morning workout crowd from our neighborhood was turning in to the fitness center where my husband was being detained. For 16 years, he had been a member of the fitness center, where he worked out in the mornings after his run. The cars all turned in. No one stopped. My husband, who is annoyingly humble about using titles, actually used his titles that day. He told the officers that he was Colonel Dr. Walter Eugene Egerton III and that our home was just a few yards away. He pointed out that his car was parked in the parking lot of the fitness center. He tried to speak again, adding that he was a physician, hoping that they would recognize that they had made an error in judgment. He was composed, methodical, thinking logically and carefully. He did and said all the right things. All the things that we had taught our sons to do. Nevertheless, he was still on the ground with his hands cuffed behind his back. One of the sheriff's department officers began to speak to him. "You can sit up if you'd like."

My husband shared with me that he attempted to look at the officer and say, "Now exactly how is that even possible?"

Eventually he was pulled upright. After running the check on him, they of course discovered that he was in fact Colonel Dr. Walter Eugene Egerton III: a retired United States military full colonel; a physician; a husband, father, grandfather, church leader; and a Black man living in the USA—I have to pause for a moment. This story is still so difficult to tell.

When my husband went into the fitness center, he was greeted by a group of people standing in the front lobby, all very happy to see that he was fine and curious about what happened—the same group of people who had never stopped to check or offer a helping hand while this was unfolding. When he finished his workout, he came home. I got up that morning and found him in his office. I went in, and he was in his lounge chair, his eyes closed. I kissed him on his forehead. He opened his eyes and looked at me as I asked, "How was your run?"

He answered, "Well, it was eventful," and recounted the events of the morning. He spoke calmly, as if he were telling me that he stopped at Starbucks just to get a cup of coffee.

I was outraged. I looked at him and said, "This is not acceptable. We need to deal with this, and we need to deal with it now."

He looked at me and placed his hand on my forearm, responding gently, "Honey, I'm a Black man living in the United States of America. You know this is just how it is."

My heart shattered. I looked at him, and the words would not come, but the tears flowed freely. I felt the depth of his pain that he was not giving a voice. I felt every bit of the pain that he was not allowing himself to feel. I recognized that he was numb to the daily indignities that he had endured over his lifetime. The death by a thousand cuts. I thought at that moment that he did not have the capacity to recognize how much he mattered, not just to me and his family, but to the entire world, and that he had a voice that he could use. I viewed this as a low point for my loving Nine spouse, but I was wrong. He had a plan.

He asked me to call the Monseigneur at our local parish. He was a very dear friend and also an Enneagram Nine. My husband, my priest, and I paid a visit to the sheriff's office a few days later. I watched as these two men—one White, one Black—weaved a web of accountability around the people seated in that room. My voice provided some context, as I had worked with law enforcement in police academies, police officers working in low-income neighborhoods, emergency response teams, and firefighters to provide IDEA training and consultation. I was well versed in their attachment to profiling, and I knew that implicit bias training was not yet integrated into their curriculum. I expressed my concerns about this and received a guarded response.

My priest spoke up. "I have a question for you. If the robber had been a young White guy and you encountered me out running, gray hair and obviously an older person, would you have subjected me to the same disrespectful treatment?" There was complete silence in the room. When no one responded, our priest spoke again. "I'm going to answer that for you. The answer is no. You would have pulled up beside me, rolled down your window, and asked if I had seen anything while I was out running. When I told you that I had not, you would have told me to be careful and stay safe and then driven off."

My spouse looked around the room, and I noticed a hint of a grateful smile crossing his face as he began to speak. "Now that we have your attention, let's talk about how we are going to prevent this from happening to anyone else in the future." I sat back and listened as the real work of this meeting began. There were additional meetings that took place to try to bring about a peaceful resolution that would represent tangible change. My husband was an eloquent and fearless Advocate for the prevention of unnecessary violence and degradation of the BIPOC community. Our priest was his Ally and Advocate every step of the way. Both men took on the role of the Knight as they used their positional power for the good of the community.

The memory of this incident still lives in my body. I allow the tears to fall as a vector for the release of some of the pain. I am all too aware that I could have lost him that day, and this experience would have been expressed very differently. I still marvel at his handling of the situation, his calm and reasonable approach to what a tangible outcome that led to restitution and justice looked like for him. He wanted a public apology but received a private apology. More importantly he wanted change in policy and practice. We no longer live in that neighborhood, but I believe that my husband and my pastor made it a safer place for the BIPOC community before we left. They remain my Knights in shining armor.

At Point Nine, your greatest strength is your natural tendency for mediation and balance in the midst of deep divisions, as long as you stay present. You use your innate ability for seeing the big picture, finding solutions, and reconnecting across divisions to serve as defenders and Advocates for inclusion, diversity, equity, and anti-racism in the social justice arena. You become invested in all humans gaining the capacity to know justice and peace, and you are vital to the healing process we must all undergo if we are to reconnect as one human race.

Consider this prework to practice and explore as you prepare yourself for the path of activation as an Ally, Advocate, or Love Warrior:

- The objective time-out and intentional pause at Point Six in your Head Center can accelerate your movement with the arrow toward Point Three.

- Take a moment to pause and engage in honest reflection. Going against the arrow to Point Six first gives you the opportunity to access and quiet your Head Center to create additional space for reflection and processing of your anger.

- Breathe in and embody peace through internal reflection and explore the positive qualities at Point Six. Learn to find focus and presence while processing the world around you constructively and intentionally.

- In the Heart Center at Point Three, begin to address the value in your presence. The connection to your heart allows people to see the real you in all of your power and strength. You can connect with others across the differences with a forcefulness that will inspire others to engage in a meaningful and heartfelt way.

- Allow yourself to reflect on presence. What is preventing you from finding and maintaining presence during difficult situations? Why do you feel the need to repress or deflect your true emotions or beliefs when you experience something that disturbs your inner peace? Try to find a clear focus on how to process information in order to take action.

ENNEAGRAM POINT 1

*Our human compassion binds us one to the other —
not in pity or patronizingly, but as human beings who have learnt
how to turn our common suffering into hope for the future.*

—NELSON MANDELA

*A small body of determined spirits fired by an
unquenchable faith in their mission can alter the course of history.*

—MAHATMA GANDHI

*You may not always have a comfortable life, and you will not always
be able to solve all of the world's problems at once. But don't ever un-
derestimate the importance you can have, because history has shown us
that courage can be contagious, and hope can take on a life of its own.*

—MICHELLE OBAMA

OVERVIEW

If Point One is where you stand on the Enneagram map, you may have a strong calling or mission that guides you in everything that you do. In a world that embraces and functions from a state of binary thinking—good and evil, right and wrong, light and dark—Enneagram Ones find this not to be merely a concept but a way of being. The One is known in the Enneagram community as the *Perfectionist*, the *Reformer*, the *Idealist*. In the IDEA space we experience this powerful energy in distinctly different ways. Ones can show up with the energy of the *Luminary*, the *Critic*, and the *Vilifier*. IDEA work is the place to find your purpose as a beacon of light for justice and peace by instilling hope in humanity.

If the dominant energy you experience is at Point One, you may be compelled by your moral compass. Integrity, a strong sense of purpose, and a need for order and justice create the comfort zone for the One. Dualistic concepts are more appealing for you, as they lend themselves to removing complexities and shades of gray. When things are black or white, good or bad, the choices lend themselves to being contained to decisions that are more likely to be right. At Point One you have a deep investment in being right and truth-telling. You are imbued with a personal sense of obligation to do no harm, and more than likely you have an aversion to making mistakes or being wrong based on your experience of the inner critic. The inner critic at Point One is relentless; this taskmaster is constantly intruding and evaluating the choices you make and actions you take. If the decisions, choices, and actions qualify as good, you may receive a passing grade, though the internal narrative that reminds you of how you or the person you are judging could have done it better is ever present. When you "get it wrong," the condemnation of the inner critic provides more than enough motivation to prevent you from ever making another mistake.

At Point One the gaze is automatically drawn to what is wrong; if you are a *Fixer*, *Perfectionist*, or an *Idealist*, you can automatically see what needs fixing or improvement. The lens through which your world is viewed is one of constant need for improvement, self included. The improvement and correcting of others are done in the spirit of "getting it right," though others may not view it as such. Often, the constant need for improvement, sometimes seen as a quest for perfection, is imposed upon others without regard for whether or not they desire or even need fixing.

At your best you are often an evolving Ally, Advocate, and Defender who guides humanity to do better in every way. You are a trustworthy teller of truth who seeks out ways to make the world more equitable, fair, just, and good. However, the deep fear of being wrong or causing harm may amplify your constant search for perfection or for seeking out what is wrong in order to correct it. This imbalance may cause you to impart your own values, beliefs, and ideals onto other humans with little regard for the true impact of your good intentions, which leaves you frustrated and resentful. Your composed exterior is masking a seething anger aimed at everything that you see as a challenge to what you deem right/correct/good. If this is resonating with you, remember this: there are no absolutes in life. The world is full of possibilities, and your idea of what is right may not be the case for someone else, and that is okay. The counterproductive practice of holding on to rigid polarities and becoming resentful and judgmental when things don't follow your specific guidelines of good and right is only causing harm to you and those around you. Remember, your evolutionary path is toward Allyship and Advocacy.

The experience of being cold, controlling, and judgmental may not be an uncommon experience for you at Point One. Even if your actions are well-intentioned, you may be unaware of the harmful impact of your words and behaviors. The constant need to critique, fix, or point out flaws may come from a well-intentioned place, but for people on the receiving end it may be unwelcomed, intrusive, judgmental, and harsh. Aligning your intent with your impact is just another step to becoming a whole human being who strives to do better.

If this sounds like you, welcome to the IDEA community. You can be a true Ally for any cause, and I hope you will join us on our path to heal humanity.

You have great integrity and purpose at Point One. If this is where you have determined your place resides on the Enneagram map, discover the journey of how you can harness the gifts from all the different components of the Enneagram: explore your basic desire, basic fear, core motivation, passion/blind spot, fixation/where you get stuck, virtue/your true self, and the One's connections to Points Four, Seven, Two, and Nine.

Let's go over a few things to prepare you for your journey.

- For the One, your blind spot, or passion of anger as it is called in the Enneagram, is a compelling desire and futile attempt to right all of the wrongs in an imperfect world.

- Your One energy seeks out mistakes, opportunities for improvement, and corruption. The constant drive to fix things, from your point of view, can create disconnects when communicating and interacting across differences.

- Your unique way of navigating challenges can lead you to a perpetually critical stance, sitting as judge, jury, and executioner; a concept that is taught as the fixation of resentment. This is where you get trapped and your anger and judgment become the guidance for your inner critic and automatic pilot.

- This hypercritical position and the subsequent judgments and assessments you place on other people is your way of deflecting the gaze from your own imperfections.

- The invitation to move into activation is attainable when you access the gifts of emotional honesty and internal reflection at Point Four, moving away from anger, resentment, and judgment, as they are toxic emotions that pollute your true heart.

- Enter a transformative space by accessing the energy at Point Seven, where you reclaim your serenity, taught in the Enneagram as the One's virtue. This is where you will find true emotional balance, flexibility, and joy in the possibilities of life.

SUMMARY OF 1s IN THE IDEA SPACE

The images of historical icons in IDEA work, both positive and negative, can easily serve as a visualization for the people who stand at Point One: Mahatma Gandhi, Nelson Mandela, Ruth Bader Ginsburg, W.E.B. DuBois, Rudy Giuliani, Osama bin Laden, Thurgood Marshall, Joan of Arc, Sandra Day O'Connor, Eleanor Roosevelt, Margaret Thatcher, Michelle Obama, Angela Merkel, Al Gore, Hillary Clinton, Pope John Paul II, and Phyllis Schlafly.

Social justice work is intrinsic to people who stand at Point One on the Enneagram map. Point One represents the position of our north star or moral compass, when operating within the healthy levels of development. The energy that we all have the opportunity to access from Point One is the strong internal push to do the right thing. The challenge here is that if you are a One, you view life through the lens of "problems to solve" and have difficulty recognizing that some challenges are, by nature, polarities to manage. Racism and othering are problems to solve and the journey at Point One is to learn to recognize and manage the polarities along the way. Intersectionality and the complexities of challenges faced depending on how a person identifies is a distinctly difficult polarity for Ones to manage, as it contains many confounding factors that must be acknowledged and measured. The duality of Black and White or male and female, for instance, can become a disorienting concept when any aspect of multidimensional diversity is added to the equation. The possibility of more than one "right" perspective is a balancing act that many Ones may find particularly challenging. At Point One, the injustice and inequities found at the core of racism, sexism, homophobia, bias, bigotry, and all othering require space for the embodiment of wisdom and grace. Doing the right thing can feel intuitive to a One, depending on where they are on the path to heal humanity. The challenge is to expand the vision beyond what they allow themselves to see from this particular perspective. It may be the right thing for the One, however, it may be totally counterintuitive from a different Point on the Enneagram.

People who possess the dominant energy at Point One can be the metaphorical lighthouse in the storm of the IDEA ocean. The desire to make a difference in the world rings true when their actions are aligned with their words. You will find Ones in every walk of life; they are changemakers, luminaries, and seekers of justice. Ones have an effect on people that makes us square our shoulders and stand a little straighter when they are around. From a nurturing point of view, it is the feeling of being held accountable for your actions, helping you to understand that your actions have benefits and consequences. From a protective stance, it resonates as more of a demand for you to "come correct" and to show up in your power for justice and equality in the "right" way.

Activation is possible when you engage in doing intentional inner work, continue to educate yourselves, and create new connections across differences. You can avail yourselves of opportunities to choose love and empathy, allowing your actions to manifest as a balanced approach to reason and perspective rather than a judgmental and angry reaction to challenges. In the next few sections, observe the evolution of a true One Advocate as we move through the unhealthy, average, and healthy levels of development. You may notice yourself in each of the levels; we are all learning and growing, and it is vital to remain present, grounded, and honest as you allow your inner observer to guide you through this process. As you work your way through the descriptors and examples, pay attention to how you react and respond while you process this information about your attitudes, behaviors, and beliefs. This is a fluid process, and as human beings we are capable of accessing the high road and falling into destructive behaviors and old beliefs, all in the same day. The journey here is being open to a new way of navigating your Enneagram energy to resolve the challenges you face across differences and uncover your hidden implicit biases.

PATH OF ACTIVATION

As we illustrate the path of activation from active othering to passive othering and ultimately to Advocacy, the levels of development (unhealthy, average, healthy) demonstrate how the One energy manifests in the IDEA space. In our exploration of the various stages of activation, we can uncover the complexities of One energy by observing the nuances of the evolution of the journey.

THE VILIFIER—ACTIVE OTHERING

In the unhealthy levels of development, we find active othering where the *Vilifier* resides—a person who consciously acknowledges and reacts based on a distorted reality that is filtered through the One's blind spot/passion of anger. The blind spot for the One manifests as an internalized fury aimed at anything that challenges their idea of right or good in their pursuit to fix the world's mistakes, or anything that points out the One's own flaws. In this space we find the self-righteous, deeply judgmental, inflexible, and cruel individuals who justify their actions and beliefs from the unhealthy energy of Point One. They become vessels for hatred and resentment, harshly judging anyone and anything who challenges their moral compass. Anger, fear, and control are the primary motivators that distort reality, resulting in a resentment for humans that do not fall in line with the One's ideals.

For people who are born into automatic advantage, disengaging from reactionary bias and bigotry in order to activate as an Advocate can seem counterintuitive or a direct threat to the One's moral compass. This can trigger the defense mechanism of reactive formation, in which the One develops contradictory actions and behaviors in order to hide their true emotions and beliefs. This paradox leads to a deep internal anger that corrupts the One's ability to see people as people, and instead they view them as objects. At this level, people born into automatic advantage can use their "higher calling" as a way to dehumanize, objectify, and oppress people that challenge their idea of right and wrong, good and bad. Their actions can be highly judgmental, cruel, heartless, and openly critical of other people as a way of justifying to themselves that they are right and others are wrong.

People who have developed positional power and fall into the unhealthy levels of development can become deeply resentful and inflexible, consciously rejecting the people, the circumstances, and the details of their journey. An internal distortion of reality creates an "I am right and good and I have the moral high ground" attitude, which serves as the justification for the dehumanization of anyone who challenges their beliefs and values or resides outside of their ideals. We can experience the concept of horizontal bias at this level, where people who share similar dimensions of diversity can dehumanize other people within the same "category" in order to deflect the resentment they hold on to around polarities.

Love Warriors who have been pushed to the margins and who fall into unhealthy levels of development can become deeply resentful of the position of the oppressors, often becoming unwavering in their judgment and seeing the oppressor everywhere and in everyone. No member of the group who represents the oppressor is given the benefit of the doubt or embraced as an Ally or Advocate. At this level of development, Ones can be especially cold, inconsiderate, and rigid when it comes to acknowledging, accepting, and communicating across differences. The polarity of one way versus another way, right versus wrong, is a mountain to climb when operating from an unhealthy level, and many are unwilling to make the climb. They may consider the idea of a multiperspective approach a direct challenge to their core values, and in turn lash out and hold on even tighter to their way of thinking.

The Intervention

There are few things more terrifying if you have studied the Enneagram than seeing the unhealthy level of your own dominant Point up close and personal. I have had this experience on several occasions; however, one moment very clearly stands out in my mind.

I answered a call from a friend who reached out to me because she was beyond frustrated with her boss. Let's call them Fred and Miriam. I knew this was going to be problematic, as she was asking for advice about how she and all the employees could stage an intervention with him and wondered if I would be willing to lead it. I gave her all the reasons that this was a bad idea, but I did agree to have lunch with just her and her boss if he was amenable.

We met at a remote location to avoid being seen by anyone from their workplace. She introduced me and launched right into the reasons she had invited me to meet with the two of them. I stopped her before she went any further into what was going to be a very long, dirty laundry list of offenses. I asked Fred how he felt about meeting with me to discuss the tension in the workplace. He said he was fine with it and that Miriam should continue laying out the "laments of the ignorant." Miriam shot me a look. After that comment, I settled back in my seat and let her talk.

When she finished talking, I asked if he would like to add or refute anything that she had stated. He responded, "No. She's summed it up pretty well. I have been saddled with the responsibility of managing a bunch of mindless, incompetent, lazy people. They have no pride in what they do, no work ethic, and absolutely zero integrity. I am not there to be their friend. I am there to do the right thing, and that is to make sure the job gets done." Miriam was in tears. I knew she was thinking about the retribution that he would exact from her. I asked him if he was interested in having a coach, and he responded as expected. "Not really," he said. "Their problems are not my problem. My problem is making sure they do their jobs."

I asked Miriam if she would mind leaving so that he and I could talk. It was a 3-hour-and-45-minute discussion. I listened to him vilify, disrespect, and defame the character and conduct of every single one of his employees. This man was not only toxic, he was dangerous. Underneath his disdain for all of his employees were racism and sexism, and he was blatantly and unashamedly homophobic. He was actively trying to purge the workplace of people that he felt were less than human. When he started justifying his actions with Bible verses, I was done. I can give myself an A for effort, but in all fairness my reaction formation defense mechanism kicked right in. The more he talked, the more I judged him with my calm and appropriate demeanor. I wanted to throttle him! I began to breathe my way through his diatribe of hatred. He paused just long enough for me to insert a few questions. I got him to turn his focus inward, and he began to talk about himself. He knew the Enneagram and was aware that his dominant Point/type is One. He was a tortured soul. It was not easy to sit in the space of empathy with someone who felt so much disdain for my own being but was unburdening himself in my presence. This was literally a One-to-One crucial exchange that there was not going to be any coming back from. He began to ask me some questions and was shocked to learn that I was Black. He didn't see me "that way." He didn't want to see me that way, so his brain tracked for what he needed to be true in that moment.

I went on to become his coach. His stuff was deep, but he worked at it. He's retired now and calls me from time to time for recommended reading. His journey continues, and I pray he is in a better place.

THE CRITIC—PASSIVE OTHERING

The *Critic* lives in the murky waters of passive othering, where we experience varying average levels of development. In the unhealthy level of average, we find Ones who consciously choose to remain in the pattern of behavior, or fixation, of resentment; they actively engage in directing their anger and judgment toward others and avoid acknowledging the true reason for their anger. In this space, Ones are unwilling to listen, stubborn, highly judgmental, abrasive, scolding, cruel, angry, and uncompassionate. In the average levels, we have a space that most people find themselves reverting to as a comfort zone during times of stress—Ones become emotionally constricted, internally motivated without external motion, overly opinionated, moody, irrational, rigid, unfeeling, and intrusive. This area of passive othering is uncomfortable and counterintuitive for Ones, as they are generally driven by improvement and idealistic tendencies. However, as we all know, passive othering is the hardest place to move out of in the IDEA space. Most Ones who have been stuck in the role of the *Critic* for a long time will find it difficult to move past the basic fear of being wrong or making a mistake, which ultimately lands them firmly in a pattern of resentment, the fixation of an Enneagram One.

Ones born into automatic advantage who fall into the space of passive othering are oftentimes deeply judgmental humans who conceal a great deal of anger for self. No one escapes the judgment. The anger morphs into a resentment of all things that point out their mistakes or corruption to their morality. Ones in this position will lash out in a hypercritical but polite way to redirect the blame onto other people as a way of maintaining a false sense of integrity. The fleeting moments of compassion and understanding are quickly replaced by an overwhelming fear of "getting it wrong" or having their integrity questioned.

Ones who develop positional power and fall into the role of the *Critic* can be emotionally repressed individuals who react and behave in resentful and judgmental ways out of fear of being wrong or having their flaws and mistakes pointed out by other people. They have undoubtedly fought hard to get to where they are, oftentimes leaving a path of disconnection caused by their deeply critical remarks and thinly veiled anger around maintaining their self-image of being good or right. These individuals become cruel and self-righteous when faced with challenges across differences; they may experience a moment of empathy and understanding toward people in similar situations, but the fear of having their integrity or ideals questioned quickly shifts them into a reactive state where they can justify their behaviors and actions.

For the Love Warriors residing on the margins of society, this state of passivity causes an incessant inner critic to manifest and run the show, leading to complications when addressing and healing the internal trauma and wounds caused by deep suffering and pain. Emotional honesty becomes a hurdle many are afraid of or unwilling to jump, leading them to live in a constant state of resentment and suppressed anger aimed at the world's faults. The constant pursuit to improve anything they may encounter and their inability to fix everything can foster a deep resentment around the causes of these imperfections. They may experience a flicker of hope and balanced perspective during challenging situations, but the anger and resentment they hold on to quickly pollutes their ability to remain compassionate.

Across the Border

Very early in my career I gravitated toward work that created opportunities for marginalized communities. While living in El Paso, Texas, the path for the youth held limited access to opportunity. I took a job working for a government-funded program and began mentoring and tutoring Mexican American students to help them find employment after they graduated from high school. The job included driving an old school bus to pick them up and drop them off in the evening. I was pretty proud of my ability to get that bus down those tiny, narrow streets.

When students disappeared from the program, I'd worry. I was aware of their comings and goings across the border, but I had no clue as to who was at risk for being detained at the border crossing. I learned a lot about their personal lives and the circumstances that they had to navigate. I worried about their safety and well-being. I wondered where they went or who they turned to when things got rough at home. This worry led me to look for a runaway shelter so that I could add its location to my list of resources. I discovered that there was no runaway shelter anywhere in El Paso. I had some strong thoughts and feelings about it, and I was determined to fix it. I took the anger in my belly, the love in my heart, and the God-given intelligence of my brain and went to work. I became a consultant for the City of El Paso and began reviewing social service programs that operated with city and federal funds. I was able to broker a deal between the Lee and Beulah Moor Children's Home and the City of El Paso for funding for a new runaway shelter. The private funding that came from the Lee and Beulah Moor Children's Home would enable a runaway shelter to sustain itself when there were gaps in the government funding.

When I say I was determined to "fix it," I wasn't playing around. I lectured everyone and anyone that I held responsible for this oversight. I was edgy, critical, and demanding. When the city gave me the green light and the children's home consented to the partnership, I sprang into action. I secured a location, interviewed, hired, and trained the staff, and ultimately resigned from my job as consultant for the city and became the director of a runaway shelter in El Paso.

My One energy was tested so many times as I watched young people come in and out of the shelter. The daily flow of underage youth who had been abused by people who should have been better humans was heart-wrenching. As a human who stands at Point One, the anger that I felt coursing through my veins was unbearable. I felt the need to do something that would provide protection for these young people, and I was hell-bent on changing the system. Fortunately for those young people, I was not a bridge burner, so I was able to find Allies. I was a force to be reckoned with. I recognized that the anger that I was experiencing served me well as a call to action, but I was unable to push past the resentment and the frustration that I felt toward the hierarchy and systemic injustice and my perceived indifference for young Love Warriors. My inner critic was on fire, and it wasn't directed just at me. I had so much anger and disdain for a system that was not protecting these children. Time after time, these young people would be sent back to the homes where the abuse had taken place. I wanted to do more. The fact that I could not find a solution all but wore me down completely. My anger threatened to consume me, and it took something from me that was more important than my own life.

I was pregnant and miscarried our child.

I returned to work as soon as possible, not wanting to deal with my own feelings. I came home from the shelter one evening and could not raise my eyes to meet my husband's curious gaze. "I don't think I can continue to do this any longer."

He knew immediately what I meant and responded with exactly what I needed to hear at that moment. "You won't have to. I got orders today. We are moving to Germany."

When I did not know how to access the grace to stop the pain, God stepped in and saved me. I didn't know the Enneagram back then. I was still judging everyone and holding myself to an impossible standard of perfection. I know now that I did my part and have great comfort and peace in understanding that what seems like imperfection is only a snapshot in time. My serenity comes now when I intentionally respond from a place of love and release the outcome. I recognize myself in the space of the Critic. *It's easy to get stuck there. Self-righteous, demanding, critical, and getting the job done. But at what cost?*

The shelter has gone through many highs and lows over the decades. The last time I checked, the runaway shelter in El Paso still exists. Hopefully this Critic *has moved on and has learned how to advocate for justice without resentment and can know peace by holding the space with love.*

THE LUMINARY—ADVOCACY

The healthy levels of development at Point One are home to the *Luminary*—an inspiring, compassionate, and benevolent defender of humanity. These are the people willing to be reasonable, kind, flexible, and hopeful in the face of divisiveness, confrontation, and conflict. The *Luminary* has found serenity in the imperfections of life by accepting what is instead of "what should be" while maintaining a pure definition of integrity and a genuine moral compass; they become flexible in their approach to finding solutions and communicating across differences. People are no longer objects; the One is able to move past polarities and treat other humans with dignity and respect instead of judgment and resentment. They are truly magnanimous and altruistic in their search for integrity, justice, and respect for all humans.

In the healthy levels of development and true Advocacy, people born into automatic advantage can move past the polarization of their ideals and use their innate moral compass to lead the fight against injustice wherever it may manifest. The polarity of right and wrong and good and bad evolves into a fair and objective perspective of finding wisdom in collaborative/moderate/flexible thinking. They seem to have the innate ability to intuit a response in their gut, filter it through their heart, and ultimately formulate a right response in the headspace. Many One Advocates become the leaders of social justice causes and create sustainable change that lives within the hearts of generations to come.

Ones who develop positional power at this level of development are capable of being instrumental in creating sustainable change. They have developed the self-awareness to address and heal their wounds and move into a space of hope, connection, and empathy. The unique perspective of being present within multiple hierarchies of society allows these *Luminaries* to not only open doors but to also know which doors to open; they do so with grace, kindness, and a balanced perspective of how the world operates. The polarities of right and wrong, black and white, good and evil are released, and a more flexible and objective approach can be cultivated. They have faced the margins of society, found their way back, and know the path to bring "others" along to reconnect the divides our community faces. Many *Luminaries* who are in positions of power become the historical and benevolent humanitarians we honor and celebrate.

In the healthy levels of development and Advocacy, Love Warrior Ones become beacons of hope and light and fight the systems within to dismantle inequities. They are the outspoken powerful leaders of true change and have a way of making everyone else see the path to joining causes to fight social injustice. The resentment and anger evolve into a wake-up call to find balance when faced with challenges. They become calm, purposeful, and hopeful in their mission to make the world a better place for all humans. These *Luminaries* are the heroes we celebrate, honor, and try to emulate when navigating through the social justice world.

Opening Doors
There have been many people in my life who have taken the time to mentor and inspire me on my journey. I believe that one of the

automatic advantages that I was afforded was being born and raised in New York City. Some of my earliest memories and influences came from Catholic nuns. As my life's journey began to go in a very different direction, one not necessarily aligned with being a Catholic school girl, I was "discovered" and became a child model. This was the end of childhood as I knew it. I found myself feeling rudderless without the affirming or condemning guidance from the nuns. I was on my own. Of course, there was always Mama, ever present and loving the world that I now had to navigate. I, on the other hand, did not love this new world I had been thrust into.

Fashion shows, magazine photo shoots, TV commercials, TV shows, and occasionally a movie where I just felt (and was) lost in a crowd. I remember the gasps when I walked the runway for the Simplicity Pattern Company. I was 10 years old and a rising star; therefore, I had an agent. My agent was truly a woman who had wisdom, vision, and insight. She knew I was young and clueless. She also knew what this opportunity meant not only for me but also for those who would come after me. I was fascinated seeing a woman sitting in a position of power with such grace. She was a stark contrast from the women I had looked up to in religious habits with folded hands and rosary beads. My agent was stylish and impeccably dressed from head to toe. Before every audition she would take me aside, tell me what was expected, and show me how to handle myself. After managing my expectations, she would smile and hug me and remind me that I was changing the world. During one of my photo shoots for a well-known bath soap, I called her because I was having a miserable experience. She came down to the set and looked at what was going on. The photographer was not prepared for the smack-down that was coming. Without raising her voice she said, "You can recast this photoshoot with someone who is stupid enough to put up with your demands. That girl is not Debby Threadgill.

Come on, sweetie, we are done here." I was smiling inside and out as we left together.

On the way home she told me that while I was among the first, many little Black girls would be able to realize their dreams because I had opened a door and held it open for them to follow. "I also want you to remember that if anyone ever does anything that you are uncomfortable with, you do exactly what you did today. You call me." I knew she would always protect me. And that's exactly what she did. She ran her empire with integrity and an energy that felt like she always knew how to do the right thing. She made sure I became a member of the Screen Actors Guild and the American Federation of Television and Radio Artists. She celebrated my successes right along with me and my mother while carefully planning the next steps of my journey. The civil rights movement was front and center during this period of my life. I had events to attend, causes to support, and eventually I would receive awards from the NAACP. My community was proud, grateful, and gracious. Next step, political presence. I was interviewed for and ultimately selected to be a Kennedy Girl. We wore signature NY black dresses and campaigned at events for Bobby Kennedy. Once again, she created opportunities where I was the first, only, or one of the very few people of color in that space. She had the energy of all of the attributes that I ascribe to the Luminary. She was feisty and fierce, kind and benevolent. Advancing the cause of "colored people," as we were sometimes referred to, was a goal that she kept at the center of her being. Gently nudging me forward with passion, purpose, and love.

At Point One, your greatest strength is your sense of integrity and the inner drive to answer to a higher calling or purpose. You use your innate moral compass and higher calling to enact right action in others and in yourself and become a beacon of light and hope for equity and justice.

Consider this prework to practice and explore as you prepare yourself for the path of activation as an Ally, Advocate, or Love Warrior:

- The objective time-out and intentional pause at Point Four in your Heart Center can accelerate your movement with the arrow toward Point Seven. Breathe in and embody compassion through internal emotional reflection and explore the positive qualities at Point Four.

- Going against the arrow to Point Four first gives you the opportunity to pause and drop into your heart space, where you create additional space to honor the humanity of other people through empathy and understanding instead of judgment and resentment.

- Take a moment to pause and find perspective. Get in touch with your true emotions and honor what you are feeling. Emotions are not a weakness; they are the key to finding compassion for yourself and thus extending this compassion to others.

- In the Head Center at Point Seven, learn to still the rumination about anger and resentment and find serenity in what *is* instead of what you think it *should* be. Allow yourself to be flexible and considerate when communicating across differences.

- Make space for yourself to reflect on the true impact of your intentions. What is at the core of your intentions? Reflect on the underlying factors that affect how you react and behave, try to find multiperspective balance, and let yourself breathe.

- Explore the value system you use to judge people. Uncover any hidden biases or messages that may be distorting your lens.

Chapter 6

THE HEALERS— HEART CENTER: 2-3-4

The Heart Center, or Feeling Triad, is home to Points Two, Three, and Four. These three energies have a connection to the emotional intelligence around accessing true compassion and empathy during moments of conflict or pain. This group is centered around emotions, self-image, and value. The shame around their own identities plays a key role in how these three Points show up in the world. Many people who identify with the Heart Center Points (Two-Three-Four) have a distinct experience with the emotion of shame or guilt, more so than the other centers. All humans experience shame and guilt; this is an undeniable fact. However, for the Two-Three-Four, shame is the catalyst for many of their patterns of behavior.

During times of pain and suffering, either internally or externally, Two-Three-Fours experience an emotional response that often transforms into internalized shame and redirected guilt. The Heart Center is concerned with their own self-identity and the hostility surrounding how they defend or project this image to others. The hostility and guilt around how they show up in the world is dependent on how the Point in question is attempting to find their true selves, fulfill the core motivation, and avoid the basic fear.

We call the Heart Center the *Healers*, because that is exactly what they do: heal the divides between who or what is being valued and devalued and connect to the emotional intelligence for themselves and for others. Each Point *heals* in its own way, which we dive into in each section, but they operate based on what they feel in their hearts and how they manage shame and guilt. The compassionate approach to connection and kindness resides in the Heart Center. When operating from a healthy space, Two-Three-Fours are genuine and authentic healers of the Love Warriors and the underrepresented; they connect to people with humility, benevolence, and empathy. They are the center that can access the heart space more readily because they are wired to tap into true emotion.

On the other side, the connection to emotions and shame residing in the Heart Center can create a distortion of authenticity and value. When operating from an unhealthy space, Two-Three-Fours can be manipulative of self and others, prideful and self-serving, and fall into a toxic pattern of validating emotional distortion from various angles. Many people within the Heart Center experience deep shame surrounding a particular unhealed or unexplored internal wound—often involving how their presence shows up in the world. This obstacle can be overcome by diving into the inner work necessary to move through the passion, fixation, and virtue.

We all have access to the Heart Center energy, and sometimes the shame and guilt we pick up from these Points can serve as a wake-up call or a catalyst for helping us land in our virtue. Not all shame and guilt need to be negative.

HEART CENTER STRENGTHS

Compassion, authenticity, connection to humanity, ability to see others as they are, humility, truthfulness, equanimity, internal reflection, generosity, altruism, charitable, benevolence, expression of emotion, authentic vulnerability, boundless empathy, charisma, infectious warm energy, kindness, ability to see the value and heart in people when others cannot

HEART CENTER CHALLENGES

Shame, guilt, self-image, identity, value, boundaries, vanity, self-serving action, emotional manipulation, over-sensitivity, humility, truthfulness, false image, fear of being true to self, courage, deceit, pride, envy, denial, repression of true emotion, suppression of authentic self, self-serving truth

ENNEAGRAM POINT 2

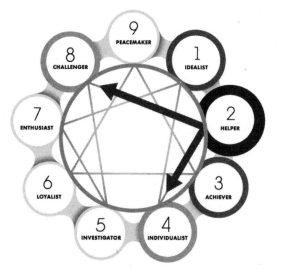

If you want peace, you don't talk to your friends.
You talk to your enemies.

— **DESMOND TUTU**

What humility does for one, is it reminds us that there are
people before me. I have already been paid for. And what I need
to do is prepare myself so that I can pay for someone
else who has yet to come, but who may be here and needs me.

— **MAYA ANGELOU**

The more we can be in a relationship with those who
might seem strange to us, the more we can feel like we're
neighbors and all members of the human family.

— **FRED ROGERS**

OVERVIEW

If Point Two is where you stand on the Enneagram map, the capacity for compassion, empathy, kindness, and the authentic desire to help all come naturally for you. The Two is known in the Enneagram community as the *Helper* or the *Giver*. In the IDEA space we experience this powerful energy in distinctly different ways. Twos can show up with the energy of the *Angel,* the *Appeaser,* and the *Manipulator.* IDEA work is the place to expand your innate ability to find compassion and connection and show up as a true healer for all humans.

If the dominant energy you experience is at Point Two, you may feel compelled by a desire to help and ensure that you are loved and needed by others, employing whatever strategies you can utilize to meet the mark. When we use the term *love* here, it is not only in the traditional sense of showing affection for someone, it is also in the deeper sense of wholeness and unity; love is a state of being, a sense of connectedness to one another.

You have a strong drive to help, and you seek out places where you can offer support and a caring approach to challenges. Kindness, compassion, and the need to develop connections create the comfort zone for you at Point Two. The energy at Point Two exemplifies the desire we all have to feel loved and to connect with others in a meaningful and heartfelt way, and the drive to be a source of benevolence and love in the world. This energy is relationship oriented—though not necessarily romantic—and can sometimes manifest in manipulative or people-pleasing ways. The need to create and maintain connections drives you to go out of your way to sustain the dependencies in other people that you have created.

At Point Two, your gaze is automatically drawn to how you can help. If you are a *Helper* or a *Giver*, you can see opportunities for connection through compassion. The lens through which the world is viewed is one of boundless love. If you identify with Point Two, you may resonate with the experience of not being able to say no easily—you reject your own feelings or needs in order to shift focus externally and feel valued and appreciated by others. When operating from an unhealthy space, the energy of the love you project can sometimes be tainted by a hidden agenda; creating dependencies allows you to feel valued and worthy but can lead to toxic and manipulative behaviors. The challenge, if you are a Two, is noticing when manipulation and shame are affecting your ability to access true compassion and stifling your inner strength to find value in your own beliefs.

At your best you are often an evolving Ally, Advocate, and healer of humanity. You seem to have a capacity for pure love and light beyond what most people experience. However, the deep guilt or shame you carry around your own self-worth can block your ability to access your authentic self and strip you of your humility. While radiating an energy that manifests the appearance of a selfless person, your distortion of self-worth challenges the very thing you live by: love and compassion. You may seek out causes and people "in need" but fail to follow through authentically when you realize there is no reciprocation of the energy you have invested. Your justification becomes a self-serving excuse of false martyrdom, which is entirely manipulative and hollow.

When you are able to move past people-pleasing and manipulative behaviors, your true worth shines through; you become genuinely selfless and deeply connected to other humans. You have the natural capacity to help others where you can intuit what may be missing and you can willingly support them. If this is resonating with you, remember this: your self-worth and value are not dependent on how much you offer but the authenticity of what you are able to offer. Distortion and manipulation are roadblocks you encounter when you let your ego take over. Remember, your evolutionary path is toward Allyship and Advocacy.

The experience of being "the one person people can count on" or not having the ability to say no is not uncommon for you at Point Two. Even if your actions are well-intentioned, you may be unaware of the destruction you leave behind when you create dependencies in which people feel validated in their own toxic behaviors. At the same time, what you consider *helping* may actually be *harming* when you fail to follow through with authentic compassion and truth. Aligning your intent with your impact is just another step to become a whole human being who strives to do better.

If this sounds like you, welcome to the IDEA community. You can be a genuinely valuable Ally for any cause, and I hope you will join us on our path to heal humanity.

As a Two, you have a seemingly endless capacity for compassion, love, and kindness. If Two energy is where you have determined your place resides on the Enneagram map, discover the journey of how you can harness the energy of the gifts from all the different components of the Enneagram: explore your basic desire, basic fear, core motivation, passion/blind spot, fixation/where you get stuck, virtue/your true self, and the Two's connections to Points Eight, Four, One, and Three.

Let's go over a few things to prepare you for your journey.

- The Two blind spot, or passion of pride as it is called in the Enneagram, is the formation of a love-worthy appearance on the outside to mask an internal sense of being unlovable.

- Your Two energy seeks outlets for your boundless love to create a sense of value and a place in other people's lives.

- The connection that your Two energy brings into everything matters and drives you to push the boundaries of integrity and emotional honesty. This conscripted stance is the default to ensure you feel valued and worthy of love, even if it comes at the cost of your true self.

- Your unique way of navigating challenges can lead you into people-pleasing and hollow behaviors, a concept that is taught as the fixation of flattery. This is where you get trapped and your guilt and shame become the guidance for your automatic pilot.

- The manipulations you construct are not only hurting you, they are also fostering environments for toxic beliefs to flourish, unchecked and thriving.

- The invitation to move into activation is attainable when you access the gift of healthy anger and inner strength at Point Eight, moving away from guilt, pride, and flattery, as they are misleading emotions that are blocking your true heart.

- Enter the transformative space of the Heart Center at Point Four where you can cultivate your humility, taught in the Enneagram as the Two's virtue. This is where you will reclaim your strength and emotional honesty as a Love Warrior, Ally, or Advocate.

SUMMARY OF 2s IN THE IDEA SPACE

The images of historical icons in IDEA work, both positive and negative, can easily serve as a visualization for the people who stand at Point Two: Mother Teresa, Maya Angelou, Jimmy Carter, Jennifer Garner, Fred Rogers, Desmond Tutu, Nancy Reagan, Imelda Marcos, Tammy Faye Bakker, Anita Bryant, Marlo Thomas, Ivana Trump, and Dolly Parton.

Working toward a more diverse, inclusive, and compassionate world is often fulfilling and satisfying to people who stand at Point Two on the Enneagram map. People who reside in the Two energy, especially during these tumultuous times, represent our ability to "love thy neighbor" and to lead with a compassionate heart. They have a strong internal experience of caring about others, and they utilize their energy to help and to bring love in whatever form they can manage.

We all have access to the energy at Point Two that encapsulates the ability to see the humanity in everyone just as they are without judgment or bias. The polarity here that must be managed is creating the space for independence and inner strength through accessing the authentic self. Showing compassion and helping others feels natural for people at Point Two, but the challenge is knowing when manipulation and people-pleasing is running the show. When Twos step into Advocacy, they can cut through the paradigm of political correctness and are authentically selfless and genuinely compassionate.

The determination to find a caring approach to conflict avails rich territory for Point Two. When the desire to serve the underserved Love Warriors is matched with a strong sense of self and unconditional love and support,

Two's caring energy is a soothing balm for the soul. You will find Twos in positions of both leadership and support on the front lines of the struggle for civil rights and justice for all people. Twos can be at the heart of positive change-making practices and restorative justice policies. They are the nurturers and caregivers in the communities of the underserved, disenfranchised, marginalized, and all Love Warriors. Twos have an effect on people that makes everyone try a little harder to show compassion and empathy instead of apathy and disdain. Twos can be found leaning in to help, even when those around them are stepping back.

———

Activation is possible when you engage in doing intentional inner work, continue to educate yourself, and create new connections across differences. You can avail yourself of opportunities to choose emotional honesty and strength, allowing your actions to manifest as a reflection of your own true heart rather than an engineered approach to connection. In the next few sections, observe the evolution of a true Two Advocate as we move through the unhealthy, average, and healthy levels of development. You may notice yourself in each of the levels; we are all learning and growing, and it is vital to remain present, grounded, and honest as you allow your inner observer to guide you through this process. As you work your way through the descriptors and examples, pay attention to how you react and respond while you process the information about your attitudes, behaviors, and beliefs. This is a fluid process, and as human beings we are capable of accessing the high road and falling into destructive behaviors and old beliefs, all in the same day. The journey here is being open to a new way of navigating your Enneagram energy to resolve the challenges you face across differences and uncover your hidden implicit biases.

PATH OF ACTIVATION

As we illustrate the path of activation from active othering to passive othering and ultimately to Advocacy, the levels of development (unhealthy, average, healthy) demonstrate how the Two energy manifests in the IDEA space. In our exploration of the various stages of activation, we can uncover the complexities of Two energy by observing the nuances of the evolution of the journey.

THE MANIPULATOR—ACTIVE OTHERING

In the unhealthy levels, we experience active othering, where the *Manipulator* resides—a person who consciously acknowledges and reacts based on a distorted reality that is filtered through the Two's blind spot/passion of pride. The blind spot for the Two manifests as they become overbearing or overly clingy in the search to prove to themselves and to others that they are a compassionate and kind person. In this space, we find highly manipulative, self-serving individuals who play the victim card to pull people into their pity party in the hopes of gaining sympathy and reassurance that they are loved and they are a good person. At this level, the *Manipulator* will justify their actions and beliefs from the unhealthy energy of Point Two, blaming everyone around them for their wrongdoing, all the while never seeing the depth of their own manipulations. Shame, guilt, and manipulation are the primary motivators that distort their reality, resulting in their self-inflicted suffering and a deeply selfish campaign of seeking out validation or sympathy for their efforts.

For Twos at this level who are born with automatic advantage, disengaging from reactionary bias and bigotry in order to activate as an Ally or Advocate can trigger the feelings of deep shame and guilt around the betrayal of their own hearts. The ego-driven agenda fosters a very manipulative and calculating Two who acts and behaves with a selfish approach to connection. When they fail to receive the reciprocal energy they seek, the *Manipulator* will turn against the people with whom they are trying to connect and aggressively remind that person of how much they do for them and that they are owed something in return. This behavior can cause even more disconnects when authenticity is replaced by false flattery, manipulations, and a choreographed approach to connection. They may hold on to the image of being a selfless and caring person by claiming Allyship or being part of book groups, causes, or organizations dedicated to IDEA work. In reality, they have long abandoned these outlets, as they did not fill the hole in their hearts left by low self-esteem and self-image.

Twos who develop positional power at this level of development can become deeply manipulative and possessive. The need to be seen as a genuine and caring human being can distort their own beliefs and needs and cause them to shapeshift to fulfill whatever role they are attempting to cultivate. Many Twos at this level will use their positional power to create dependencies and false connection in the pursuit of martyrdom. At this level, people with positional power oftentimes feel a deep anger and a sense of underappreciation for what they consider to be their unconditionally benevolent nature. They may feel entitled to certain things and demand it from others through coercion, manipulation, and misplacing their own guilt onto others. Dehumanizing behaviors become a fallback for these unhealthy Twos; however, they cannot see the true destructive nature of their actions and beliefs because they still view themselves as kind, caring, and helpful.

In regard to Love Warriors pushed to the margins of society, the *Manipulator* can manifest as a deeply angry, guilt-ridden, maligned individual who manipulates the people in their life to justify their own pain and suffering. They may become aggressive and confrontational, calling out the people closest to them for not reciprocating the amount of energy and love they have given that person. They will lash out at and blame the people around them for not showing up when they needed it, though it's doubtful the Two asked for help at all. They may distort the significance of their trauma or pain to seek out attention for "how much they suffer when they were just trying to help." They may seek out and misplace their anger onto their friends who have automatic advantage as a way of distorting their own pain, and forcing someone to acknowledge their own suffering as a way to turn the tables and fulfill their basic motivation.

Masterful Manipulation

As the wife of an army doctor, I have lived in many countries over the years, and no matter where we are I am eventually asked to teach the Enneagram. My response is always yes, and this time

I should have said no. I was going to teach the Enneagram to a group of church ladies . . . again. Fool me once, shame on you. Fool me twice? You know how that ends.

The day began with the normal niceties: coffee, pastry, a well-thought-out icebreaker. As my teaching got underway, there was a woman who simply would not stay in her seat. She grabbed the coffeepot and started refilling everyone's coffee cups, passed around the pastry trays, and asked each person if they needed more cream and sugar. When I realized that she was not going to stop, I turned to address her. "Excuse me, just a check in. Does anyone need anything else? No? Okay, great. Let's all get settled in our seats now." She turned red as a beet and sat down with a great deal of blustery attention-seeking behavior. I brought the group back to attention and assumed all was well in the land. Now to add a bit more context, I teach the Enneagram as the cornerstone of IDEA work, so people get a lot more than they expected.

We went to break, and I noticed a little crowd forming around our resident helper. I saw tissues being handed to her and realized she was having a meltdown. I approached the little group and asked if there was anything going on that I needed to know about before we started up again. The helper spoke up. "I was just feeling badly because you wouldn't let me take care of the things I'm usually in charge of. I'm not really here for the workshop anyway."

"I'm sorry, I was not aware that you were not a participant," I said.

"I'm supposed to be a participant, but I don't like this stuff that you are teaching, and I'm trying to make it easier for these ladies to be here."

I was totally perplexed. "These ladies invited me here to do the workshop."

She pulled me aside. "I know . . . I probably shouldn't be telling you this, but some of these women are such hypocrites. They are just curious about you, so that's why they invited you to do this. You being colored and educated, some of them think you are...."

I held up my hand. "I think you've said enough."

"I'm just trying to be an honest Christian woman and tell you what's really going on. I tell you what. I'll stay and make sure everything runs smoothly. They depend on me for that, and I can help you."

I said a little prayer and asked for a dose of my mother's strength as I returned to the front of the room. I completed the workshop. The women smiled and nodded, asked questions and took down details about how to continue to learn more. I was ready to move into closing remarks when the helper spoke up. "The Enneagram is only for Christians, right?"

I watched her waiting for my response, as she was well aware that every eye was fixed on me. "No, it's not a dogmatic religious tool. As I explained this morning, the Enneagram is studied by people all over the world. It has universal applicability."

One of the other women picked up on the intent behind her words. "I don't think that should be of concern to us as long as it helps to make us better people," she responded.

I knew I couldn't let things end on that note, so I engaged the group. "Do you have any other questions that I can answer before we have our closing circle?" The women smiled and thanked me while they applauded, and we moved to the center of the room for the closing circle. The helper did not join us. She started putting away chairs and cleaning up the room, all the while being as conspicuous as possible. I could see her stomping her way of the inner line to the low side of Point Eight.

The ladies lingered. We talked and had a good laugh about their conclusions in regard to their spouses' or relatives' types. I glanced over at the helper, who had achieved transmutation into the martyr. She was hard at work. Two of the ladies followed my gaze. "Don't worry about her; she does this all the time. I think she honestly believes she's being helpful, but she is exhausting!

There is always something that she feels like she has done that wasn't appreciated. I think she feels like she was saving us from the devil today. Oh! I'm sorry! That came out wrong." I laughed and told her I understood what she meant.

The president of the women's club thanked me and wanted to share more about the helper's actions. "I've known her for most of my life. She tried really hard to keep this workshop from happening. She's needy and wants to take over everything. She's all over the place, no boundaries at all. She used to be a lovely person. Her son married a Jewish girl, and she won't even see her grandchildren. Can you imagine? The depth of her bigotry is frightening. I hope she didn't say anything offensive to you directly."

"No, she didn't," I lied. *"I hope things get better for her."*

The depth of distortion that bias and bigotry can create in the heart of the kindest of beings is painful to witness.

THE APPEASER—PASSIVE OTHERING

The *Appeaser* resides in the entanglement of passive othering where we experience varying average levels of development. On the unhealthy side of average, we find the Twos who consciously choose to remain in the pattern of behavior, or fixation, of flattery; they seek out connections to feel valued and manipulate their true emotions in the hopes that people will value them for what they offer and not for who they truly are. In this space, Twos are manipulative, domineering, placating, coercive, reticent, self-deceptive, presumptuous, guilt-ridden, and apathetic. When we move to the average levels, we have a space that most people find themselves reverting to as a comfort zone during times of stress: Twos become people-pleasing, emotionally demonstrative, condescending, flattering, and codependent—dehumanizing behaviors resulting from a betrayal of their own true feelings. This area of passive othering is uncomfortable and counterintuitive for most Twos, as they are generally driven by a desire to authentically help in any way possible. However, as we all know, passive othering is the hardest place to move out of in the IDEA space. Most Twos who have been stuck in the role of the *Appeaser* for a long time find it difficult to move past the basic fear of being unloved, unneeded, and unwanted, which ultimately lands them firmly in the pattern of behavior, or fixation, of flattery.

People born into automatic advantage who fall into the space of passive othering are often deeply wounded and insecure individuals who feel that they must give or fill a need to be valued, never disposable or replaced by others. The space of IDEA work feels like an uphill climb with collateral damage everywhere. Twos who are never at a dearth of activity may avoid this work altogether and shift their focus to other areas where there is less intense conflict. This is where we experience the more manipulative and strategic Twos, who may represent themselves as victims who need to be protected and reassured of their worthiness. In this space, the Two looks for validation based on what they have done for others. Twos, when caught in the act of manipulation or attention-seeking behaviors, will blame others for putting them in circumstances that amplify their feelings of low self-worth. If sympathy, validation, and admiration are not forthcoming, the Two will fall into despair, clinging frantically to the victim card. They may attempt to engage in moments of connection and authentic compassion but their guilt, shame, and fear quickly shift them into self-serving behaviors.

Twos who develop positional power and fall into the role of the *Appeaser* can be highly defensive individuals who react and behave in manipulative ways to maintain their self-image of being "good, caring, genuine, and compassionate" people. They have undoubtedly fought hard to get to where they are, oftentimes shapeshifting and people-pleasing along the way. They will use their positional power to prove to others that they are doing their best, being a good person, "fighting the good fight," all while never likely engaging in any real authentic way. These individuals become angry and emotionally demonstrative when faced with challenges across differences in which their character may be called into question. This space is hard for many Twos to accept that they have been stuck in, let alone escape, as they are generally driven by kindness and compassion. The key here is noticing when the actions and behaviors are driven by a hidden agenda.

Love Warriors who fall into the average levels of development, where there is an experience of passive othering, are likely concealing a deep pain that they are unaware of. The desire of the Two is to give love and receive love in return. Dealing with the daily indignities of othering, in whatever form othering takes to push them to the margins, creates a constant state of tension experienced in the Heart Center to retain the sense of being worthy and deserving of experiencing love. Many Twos at this level find themselves working in a field that is not aligned with what they are capable of bringing to the world. The doors may not open easily for them, and their choice in occupation and work location may be affected by some dimension of their diversity. They may settle for what they can get, even if they work considerably harder while holding on to biased beliefs about whatever or whomever is standing in their way. These biases infiltrate every aspect of their lives in their search for love, validation, and acceptance in any form.

The Photograph

During a recent trip to a homecoming event at my husband's alma mater, we arranged to meet with some friends for dinner. We were catching up on life events and having a lovely evening out. I hadn't noticed initially that we were the only Black people in the restaurant until we were intruded upon by a somewhat inebriated but seemingly pleasant White woman. "Would you look at this? Why, y'all look like you need somebody to take your picture! Y'all want a picture, don't you?" We were four Black couples engaged in cross-table conversation about all matters of things who now ceased all conversation. In unison we looked up and stared at her. We were all rendered speechless as she attempted to take our picture with her phone. It wasn't going well, as she obviously didn't know what she was doing.

The person seated closest to where she was standing handed the woman her phone. "Here use mine."

She tried again. "Now y'all smile and say, 'We hate White people!'"

Yes, you are reading this correctly. We were more shocked at that moment than you are right now. I found my voice and responded, "Why would we say that? We don't hate White people."

"But you have to hate us! We have just been awful to y'all. I mean, I just hate myself when I think about it, but there is nothing I can do about it." We made some relatively lame attempts to assure her that we did not harbor any ill will toward her to try to get her to move on. The lament continued, then came the tears, and we did our best to patch her up and get her out the door. When she finally left after her protracted monologue, tears, and a litany of mea culpas, we simultaneously exhaled. Now acutely aware of being the only Black people in the restaurant, we were trying to move past the uncomfortable and unnecessary interruption of our long-awaited evening out. We were also aware now of the sly glances that were coming our way. The manager came over and apologized to us for her behavior. As he walked away he said, chuckling, "You gotta admit that was worth the price of admission." I thought to myself, No, it wasn't.

THE ANGEL—ADVOCACY

The healthy levels of development at Point Two are home to the *Angel*—a strong and independent healer of humanity. These are the people who embrace their authentic selves and understand that they do not need to conform to what they "should be" in order to gain love, have value, or create connection. The *Angel* is unapologetically true to their own beliefs and operates from a pure heart full of compassion and genuine empathy for others in the face of divisiveness, confrontation, and conflict. The force of their inner strength guides them to choose spaces where they can support, lead, or create change from a purely good heart with no hidden agenda. Many *Angels* have developed a warning system using their healthy anger to propel them into right action with tenacity and a strong internal sense of self. They are the healers of humanity, capable of an astonishing amount of fierce compassion and a genuine desire to make the world a better place for everyone.

A Two born with automatic advantage, who has done the inner work necessary to move into the space of the *Angel*, has found humility in the process of providing support and compassion for others without the need to be liked or to receive anything in return. Some *Angels* have embraced healthy anger as a wake-up call to honor their true selves and find the strength to stand up for what they believe in so that they can land on the side of compassion, and humanity. These *Angels* use their automatic advantage, power, and position to create opportunities for the voices of the underrepresented to be heard, valued, and appreciated. They will open doors and fight hard to keep them open; the healthy Eight energy is ever present in a fiercely engaged Two. The boundless and forceful love residing in the Two energy is allowed to flourish, unchained from the underlying need to seek validation.

People who gain positional power at this level of development are capable of being instrumental in creating a sustainable shift toward a more compassionate and empathetic world. There is a healthy anger within these Twos that serves as a catalyst for leading with the heart and finding their own truth. The unique perspective of being present within multiple hierarchies of society allows these *Angels* to connect across all dimensions of our diversity with love, grace, and humility. They have faced the margins of society, found their way back, and know the path to bring "others" along to heal the divides our communities face. Many *Angels* who are in positions of power become the loving and inspirational healers we look up to and try to emulate on our own journey of healing and reconnection.

For the Love Warriors Twos, the *Angel* manifests as a leader for reconnection through humility and compassion. The position of being pushed to the margins allows them to gain perspective and see the whole picture with a clear focus of how to provide support to those who may be suffering. They find positions of leadership with other Love Warriors, often providing the foundation for change and healing. The Love Warriors who step into Advocacy use their healthy anger as a catalyst to find the inner strength in themselves; they become the outspoken champions of compassion, inspiring other people to do better and lead with their hearts. The Love Warrior *Angels* are often the historical icons that lead with a soft heart, a mission to bring compassion anywhere they go, and an underlying fierceness that signals their strength in any fight for justice and peace.

Youth Isn't a Liability

I started Trinity Transition Consultants in the early 1990s, and as a woman entrepreneur I found myself trying to balance life and work, all while carrying the future success of my business on my shoulders. I finally recognized that the only way I was going to be able to maintain my sanity and still do the work was to get some help. The first person I interviewed was a young woman who looked really eager. She was a vision of innocence and hope. She had the youthful exuberance of a person who wanted to make the world a better place.

The interview went very well. She answered all the questions correctly, and she had the right level of decorum and enthusiasm. It was very pleasant to be in her company, and I felt myself beginning to like her before the interview was even over, but she was far too young. I took a deep sigh as we concluded the interview. She put her coat back on, thanked me, and walked down the aisle toward the door. I looked down to see who my next applicant was going to be. When I looked up, the same young woman was standing in front of me again. She looked me directly in the eye with all the sincerity that she had in her being and said these words: "Dr. Egerton, I promise you that if you hire me, I will be the best assistant you will ever have."

I felt my eyes beginning to water a bit as I extended my hand to offer gentle reassurance. I squeezed her hand and said, "I'm quite sure that's true. One way or another I'll be in touch."

I went on to interview at least 10 other individuals, some very qualified, some not so much; however, that first young woman that I interviewed stayed in my mind. There was something about her authentic desire to help that just said volumes about who she was and how she was showing up in the world. Later that evening, I said a little prayer for guidance. I couldn't get this young woman out of my mind. It seemed so unfair to not give someone a chance just because they were young. The guidance came in the form of a soft whisper that affirmed my decision to give her a chance. I checked in with my head, my heart, and my gut. It was a full-body yes for me. And she was as good as her word. She would show up in the mornings with coffee and folders from things that we had been working on and needed for that day. She insisted on doing all the driving to all of our consulting appointments and training so that I could work or rest. When I would speak or conduct a training, there was always a bottle of water lovingly placed on the table so that I could reach it when needed. When my speeches were over, she took the time to answer people's questions to keep them from overwhelming me. She was always the Angel at the gate. The protective and caring nature of her heart served as a shield and a foundation for myself and the other Love Warriors she encountered to be heard, valued, and guarded. Nothing ever seemed to be outside of her capacity to deliver; however, I would notice when she was taking on way too much. I would lovingly take her hand and remove it from the air when it was going to dart up to say, "I got this."

Over the years, I have watched her grow into a competent, capable, highly skilled woman. Upon spending any time with her, the Two energy that resides within her is pretty obvious to most people who know the Enneagram. This young Middle Eastern girl with a heart of gold has worked with me for nearly 15 years. I've experienced the ups and downs of her Two energy. She is warmhearted, caring, compassionate, and fierce. Her kindness shines through in more ways than I can ever write about here, and never make the mistake of confusing her kindness for weakness.

Life as a Brown woman with a last name Mohandessi has sometimes placed her front and center in the space of being dismissed and disrespected, but she chose the road of Advocacy for all people and continues to work with me to bring this message of oneness and connection into the world. When folks step out of line or express messages of hatred, bias, or bigotry, her loyalty

and territorial integrity will come out and she will put them in
their place, or as they say, "rip them a new one."
    Never underestimate the power of the open heart of an Angel
at Point Two, no matter the age.

At Point Two, your greatest strength is your natural combination of compassion, empathy, unconditional love, and a strong drive to help. You use your innate empathy and compassion to serve as healers and integral support systems for social justice and the reconnection of humanity through kindness and integrity.

Consider this prework to practice and explore as you prepare yourself for the path of activation as an Ally, Advocate, or Love Warrior:

- The objective time-out and intentional pause at Point Eight in your Body Center can accelerate your movement with the arrow toward Point Four.

- Take a moment to pause and assess the true reason behind your emotions and actions. Breathe in and embody strength through internal reflection and explore the positive qualities at Point Eight. Explore the healthy anger you may experience at Point Eight, and use it as a warning system to reflect on the reasons behind your reactions, behaviors, and beliefs.

- At Point Four, in the Heart Center, learn to find your true self and see your worth for what is and not what it should be. Allow yourself to reflect on the reasons behind why you feel the need to manipulate yourself to gain value or feel worthy. What is at the core of your intentions?

- Find connections to the Head Center through your wing energy and instead of moving toward pride, manipulative flattery and guilt/shame, allow yourself to reflect on authenticity and inner strength through objective reasoning.

- While there are no direct connections to the energies in the Head Center, Two can pick up the connections in various ways. Point Five can be accessed through your connection to Point Four and Eight. Point Six can be accessed from your wing at Point Three. And Point Seven can be accessed through your wing at Point One or your line to Eight. Explore your connections to the energies at these Points and develop the awareness to access the Head Center Energy in order to align the three centers. Find a way to land in the Head Center and secure your strength in reconnecting to your humanity through honest reflection.

  - Point Five: combining innate emotional intelligence with perceptiveness and objectivity

  - Point Six: truth-seeking capabilities, with a balanced perspective on emotions and rationality

  - Point Seven: freedom to think for yourself and find out what you really want, need, and value

ENNEAGRAM POINT 3

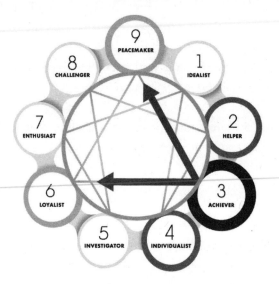

Real integrity is doing the right thing,
knowing that nobody's going to know whether you did it or not.

—OPRAH WINFREY

As we let our light shine, we unconsciously give other
people permission to do the same. As we are liberated from
our own fear, our presence actually liberates others.

—MARIANNE WILLIAMSON

Success comes when people act together; failure tends to happen alone.

—DEEPAK CHOPRA

Each of us is called to do something in the name of love, to make sure that
humanity comes to understand itself and is able to choose love over fear.

—ROBERT HOLDEN

OVERVIEW

The desire to be successful, validated, and valued are not uncommon goals among most people; however, if you stand at Point Three, this is the inner motivation that drives your daily life. Point Three is known in the Enneagram community as the *Achiever,* the *Star,* and the *Performer.* In the IDEA space we experience this extraordinary energy in distinctly different ways. Threes can show up with the energy of the *Champion,* the *Sycophant,* and the *Narcissist.* IDEA work is the place to demonstrate your true potential for greatness as a champion for humanity with strength, inspiration, and authenticity.

If your dominant energy resides at Point Three, you may feel compelled to achieve and to prove your value through how you are perceived by others. Success, hard work, impressiveness, dedication, and ambition are just a few of the many extraordinary characteristics you embody. Like many Threes, you probably have a strong aversion to the word *failure.* Failure in any form is directly opposed to the Three's essence of being. You are driven by a determined and industrious energy, but it comes at a price: stay true to the authentic self or feed the ego. The lens through which you view the world is one of constant ambition, drive, and success in whatever form resonates with you personally. It is important to clarify that success is a relative concept that can look different within Point Three; success could manifest as career advancement or status, education and degrees, material possessions, awards, financial security, self-sufficiency, high social status, and the like. The manifestation of success has a direct correlation with how you find your place of value in the world. While the natural impressiveness associated with the energy at Point Three is almost always front and center, the polarity that must be managed is the way in which you obtained your success.

At your best you are often an evolving Ally, Advocate, and champion for a world in which everyone succeeds and is valued and appreciated. You seem to find a way to get things done and achieve greatness in almost everything you do, at least through your Three lens. The deep fear of being worthless or a failure in some way drives you to fully embody anything that makes you feel worthy and gain acknowledgment and validation. This may cause you to neglect your true emotions, beliefs, and desires as you strive to maintain your paragon status. While radiating an energy that manifests the appearance of a truly astonishing human being capable of incredible things, your failure at Point Three is equally as powerful as your success. At Point Three, you are always aiming for the top—falling or failing is not an option. As you navigate challenges, you may cut corners or bend the truth to make sure you secure your position at the top. But this aversion to failure, in whatever form it may take, deprives you of opportunities to grow and become a whole human being who is authentically exceptional and capable of true greatness. In your search for success and achievement, you often forget to look back and offer a hand to those behind you. You become narcissistic, and your scope of focus narrows; you forget to honor your own humanity, thus negating everyone else's humanity along the way. If this is resonating with you, remember this: an aversion to failure does not guarantee success. It is a counterproductive way of moving through the world and can prevent you from becoming the remarkable human being you were born to be. Remember, your evolutionary path is toward Allyship and Advocacy.

You may feel a constant need to project an impressive exterior, but deep down you are tiptoeing on the line of being truly great and being fearful that you are not, in fact, anything great at all. You may be experiencing impostor syndrome, as do most people who identify with Three energy. You believe that someday someone will see through your shiny exterior and discover that you are a fraud who is empty and undeserving. This fear leads you to conceal your true self and develop an impressive persona to mask whatever shame you are feeling about being loved for what you do instead of who you are. You must overcome this fear and step into your true potential with the confidence and acknowledgment that you do not need to be what others expect of you and that you can honor your authenticity with grace. Stepping into your authentic self requires persistence, but it is just another step to becoming a whole human being who strives to be better.

If this sounds like you, welcome to the IDEA community. You can be an inspirational and authentic Ally for any cause, and I hope you will join us on our path to heal humanity.

At Point Three, you have great perseverance and a strong driving force toward success. If Three energy is where you have determined your place resides on the Enneagram map, discover the journey of how you can harness the gifts from all the different components of the Enneagram: explore your basic desire, basic fear, core motivation, passion/blind spot, fixation/where you get stuck, virtue/your true self, and the Three's connections to Points Six, Nine, Two, and Four.

Let's go over a few things to prepare you for your journey.

- The Three blind spot, or passion of deceit, as it is called in the Enneagram, is a deep desire to manifest an impressive image to mask your true self and prove you are a worthy human being.

- Your Three energy seeks ways to cultivate and develop your image in whatever form serves you best.

- The ambition that your Three energy brings into everything matters and drives you to push the limits in your life and in your integrity. This conscripted stance is the default to project and adapt an image that will garner respect, validation, and admiration.

- Your unique way of navigating challenges can lead you to repress your authentic self and leave you projecting a fraudulent image of yourself, a concept that is taught as the fixation of vanity. This is where you get trapped and your shame and the preservation of your self-image becomes the guidance for your automatic pilot.

- The deep desire to project a superior and impressive image to others leads you to believe that you must avoid failure at all costs. *If you fail, you are not worthy; if you are not worthy, what are you?*

- The projection of an impressive exterior is your way of masking your Achilles' heel: *self-worth.* You have built an impressive exterior but underneath you are a bundle of insecurities and a repression of your true self. You may believe that if people don't see you for what you do, then they will have to judge you for who you are, and deep down you may be afraid of being undeserving of love.

- The invitation to move into activation is attainable when you access the gift of stillness at Point Nine, moving away from shame, deceit, and vanity as these are false emotions that are blocking your true heart.

- Enter the transformative space of true self-awareness and authenticity at Point Six, where you can cultivate your ability for authenticity and truthfulness, taught in the Enneagram as the Three's virtue. This is where you will reclaim your balance and the grace to be your authentic self as a Love Warrior, Ally, or Advocate.

SUMMARY OF 3s IN THE IDEA SPACE

The images of historical icons in IDEA work, both positive and negative, can easily serve as a visualization for the people who stand at Point Three: Oprah Winfrey, Will Smith, Deepak Chopra, Bill Clinton, Mitt Romney, Bernie Madoff, Jesse Jackson, Marianne Williamson, Candace Owens, Tony Robbins, Lady Gaga, Beyoncé Knowles, Muhammad Ali, Meghan Markle, Brené Brown, O. J. Simpson, and Kevin Spacey.

The work necessary to create a more inclusive and equitable global community is well aligned with the drive and ambitious nature of people who stand at Point Three on the Enneagram map. Point Three represents the persistence and relentless work ethic needed to endure the ongoing work of social justice. Healthy Threes can be found on the front lines, making changes, serving as the faces of causes and the motivating and charismatic leaders we aspire to be. The energy that we can access at Point Three is the strong internal desire to succeed. Failure is not an option. Threes have little patience with the flawed efforts of bureaucracy and will cut through the red tape when possible to advance a social justice agenda. Racial injustice, gender disparities, socioeconomic disadvantages, and various inequities caused by othering can sometimes be difficult for Threes to process. The challenge here is that Threes see life through the lens of image-based decision making and oftentimes do not honor their authentic selves or true emotions in the hope of maintaining the self-image they've constructed. Additionally, many Threes' strong inner drive for hard work and persistence leads them to believe that another person's circumstance could be improved if they just worked a little harder, rather than the person's circumstances being beyond their control or a direct result of systemic inequities. This is a common disconnect for many Threes when communicating across differences and can lead to actions, beliefs, and behaviors steeped in bias, bigotry, and stereotyping.

People who possess the dominant energy at Point Three can be champions for social justice causes, leaders of movements, and the people who make things happen. The desire to succeed in all things translates into a motivated and inspirational spokesperson for removing and overturning obstacles while healing the wounds caused by racial and social divisions. Threes have a profound effect on those around them; their natural tendency to strive for being the best they can be inspires others to do better or be better. They can be natural sources of charisma and paragons of any social justice movement.

———

Activation is possible when you engage in doing intentional inner work, continue to educate yourself, and create authentic connections across differences. You can avail yourself of opportunities to choose love and authenticity, allowing your actions to manifest as genuine behaviors free from ego. In the next few sections, observe the evolution of a true Three Advocate as we move through the unhealthy, average, and healthy levels of development. You may notice yourself in each of the levels; we are all learning and growing, and it is vital to remain present, grounded, and honest as you allow your inner observer to guide you through this process. As you work your way through the descriptors and examples, pay attention to how you react and respond while you process the information about your attitudes, behaviors, and beliefs. This is a fluid process, and as human beings we are capable of accessing the high road and falling into destructive behaviors and old beliefs, all in the same day. The journey here is being open to a new way of navigating your Enneagram energy to resolve the challenges you face across differences and uncover your hidden implicit biases.

PATH OF ACTIVATION

As we illustrate the path of activation from active othering to passive othering and ultimately to Advocacy, the levels of development (unhealthy, average, healthy) demonstrate how the Three energy manifests in the IDEA space. In our exploration of the various stages of activation, we can uncover the complexities of Three energy by observing the nuances of the evolution of the journey.

THE NARCISSIST—ACTIVE OTHERING

In the unhealthy levels of development, we find active othering where the *Narcissist* lives—a person who consciously acknowledges and reacts based on a distorted reality that is filtered through the Three's blind spot/passion of deceit. The blind spot for the Three manifests as a constant drive to present themselves in a way that does not reflect their authentic self but instead creates a mask of "value." In this space, we find the extremely egotistical, self-centered, dishonest, vindictive, and duplicitous individuals who justify their actions and beliefs from the unhealthy energy of Point Three. Fear, shame, and low self-worth are the primary motivators that distort reality, resulting in a destructive arrogance that facilitates the dehumanization of anyone who challenges their value or position in this world.

For Threes born into automatic advantage, disengaging from reactionary bias and bigotry in order to activate as an Ally or Advocate can feel like failure; deep down they recognize that someone has seen through their facade and knows how much shame they are holding on to. This can trigger the feelings of deep guilt and worthlessness, and reinforce the aversion to failure, which will further fuel deceitful and narcissistic behaviors. The need to project a certain image that conceals their true self is so strong that the *Narcissist* will actually justify their actions as "who they are." They become performers of true dehumanization and apathy aimed toward other humans. These are the individuals unwilling to engage in the work because of self-serving patterns of behavior; they may even find a place leading groups of people rooted in bias and bigotry as long as they are somehow in the spotlight.

Threes who have developed positional power and fall into the unhealthy levels of development can become incredibly conceited and arrogant, consciously rejecting the people, the circumstances, and the details of their journey. An internal distortion of reality creates an "I did it all myself, and I should be acknowledged for what I have overcome" attitude, which serves as the justification for the dehumanization of anyone who challenges their position, value, or success, or serves as a reminder of their origin. We can experience the concept of horizontal bias at this level, where people who share similar dimensions of diversity can dehumanize other people within the same "category" in order to validate themselves. Many unhealthy Threes with positional power can become the "token" spokesperson for furthering bias, bigotry, and hatred; they betray themselves, their identity, and their humanity by finding value in a hollow position of recognition.

Love Warriors at this unhealthy level can be the literal embodiment of the title of the *Narcissist*. It is uncommon to find a Three who does not work hard, strive to do great things, or make themselves appear successful. Even within the Love Warriors you will likely experience these Threes with some degree of positional power; it is not in their nature to accept their place on the margins of society. Believing that they achieved their position solely as a result of their hard work and perseverance, they conceal the high probability that their success was choreographed from deceit and untruthfulness. The climb to the top, or middle, emboldens them with the mentality of "I am better than you, and I deserve this more because you are less than me." They become hollow shells of achievement who repress a deep shame and worthlessness that they refuse to acknowledge. They dehumanize anyone who represents their origins of struggle and oftentimes justify their actions as a means to maintain their false sense of entitlement. Horizontal bias is a common occurrence at this level within the Three energy: the dehumanization of people who fall into similar categories of diversity as a way of lowering the value of others to elevate their own value. They often find it difficult to address their own internal wounds or trauma; fearing that people will see through the shiny exterior of the persona they've constructed, they shift the guilt outward and hold on to their achievements and success in order to conceal their real pain.

The Harder They Fall

In the U.S., successful Threes in the workplace are fairly ubiqui-tous. The U.S. admires and respects the relentless ambition of the Three, and this country most certainly has a collective Three cul-ture. In my work as an executive coach, I frequently draw what I call hospice duty. Hospice duty for me is defined as having a client who needs to retire or resign, not necessarily because of their age but rather because their age combined with their biases render them no longer compatible with the workplace culture. And they are not willing to change. These are always sad situ-ations as the people trapped in these circumstances often lack the ability to separate who they are from what they do. When you add in the subtleties of IDEA work, it makes a complicated situation much more volatile.

I was called in to help one client in a particularly difficult situation. It was clearly time for this regional director to retire or resign. Her outspoken disdain for what she termed "multicul-tural bullshit" was beyond offensive. It was reprehensible. I had worked with her direct reports for several years before she was promoted as the interim acting director into the job. She came up through the ranks of the organization and worked her way to the top. She had taken several Enneagram tests, and every time the results pointed her in the direction of the Enneagram Three. I ar-ranged for our first meeting, and it did not take long to discover that she did in fact possess many of the Three attributes. She was ambitious with an impressive resume of accomplishments. Obvi-ously, she was much too busy to invest any time in our meeting; she had been putting off scheduling with me for weeks because of her tight schedule.

An impeccably dressed White woman who carried herself with a false air of confidence walked into the room. Her energy was low, and she seemed distant and checked out. I could see that I was not what she expected. "So you are the coach they've been telling me about. I'm not sure why."

A strange way to start the conversation, but I'd certainly heard worse. I explained to her that coaching was contingent upon client and coach determining that they could work well together. "If either of us does not feel like we are a good fit for one another, I will make sure that you get a different coach."

"You will do what?"

I wasn't sure what she was questioning, but I figured it out. "The coaches that work with this organization are contracted by my company."

She started to laugh. "Isn't this rich! The only obstacle in my path to getting this promotion was the CEO wasn't sure how well I would do with his pet diversity project. So they went out and got ..."

I stopped her from finishing her sentence; I knew the next words out of her mouth were likely to be offensive given what I had heard from her employees. "I would choose the next words that you speak very carefully. I am not going to allow you to disrespect me. Your next words will say more about who you are than they will about who you think I am."

She looked puzzled, as if I were speaking to her in a language that she couldn't comprehend. "Okay. Then, here's what I have to say," she responded. "I don't give a shit about any diversity crap. I've worked my ass off for this place. I'll hire who I want, and I'll fire who I want. If that means that I have to run out all the [at this point she let out the most unrelenting stream of derogatory ethnic, cultural, sexual diversity, and religious terms that I have ever heard put together in one sentence]."

"This meeting was definitely interesting and informative," I said. I got up, left her office, and went to see the CEO. I told him to send for the HR director. On this woman's watch, no one was going to get ahead if they did not fit her narrow classification

of who deserved to be in the workplace. As a woman, it was obvious she had to overcome many obstacles to get promoted into her current position, but she had no awareness of her discriminatory beliefs and abuse of privilege, and felt entitled to dehumanize the entire workforce. Unfortunately, her reputation of bias and bigotry preceded her, and the CEO was wise enough to only put her in as an interim director. When narcissism, automatic advantage, arrogance, and burnout collide at Point Three, the sullen and unpredictable behaviors can and do destroy careers. Fortunately for her direct reports, she wasn't in place long enough to take them down with her.

THE SYCOPHANT—PASSIVE OTHERING

The *Sycophant* resides in the destructive limbo of passive othering, where we experience the average levels of development. In the unhealthy level of average, we find Threes who consciously choose to remain in the pattern of behavior, or fixation of vanity; they seek out outlets to justify or validate their self-worth by constantly promoting the image of success and value. In this space, Threes are projecting a fraudulent self-image, unwilling to engage authentically; they become shape-shifting, stubborn, self-absorbed, shameful, and apathetic toward other people. In the average levels of development, we have a space that most people find themselves reverting to as a comfort zone during times of stress: Threes become conceited and self-serving, they are emotionally dishonest in deflecting their authentic self, and repress their capacity for humility. These are the people that are apprehensive of forward progress or sacrifice without the guarantee of success; their apathy is caused by fear of failure. This area of passive othering is uncomfortable and counterintuitive for most Threes, as they are generally driven by achievement and being at the front of pack. However, as we all know, passive othering is the hardest place to move out of in the IDEA space. Most Threes who have been stuck in the role of the *Sycophant* for a long time find it difficult to move past their basic fear of being seen as a failure or feeling worthless and caught in a lost cause, which ultimately lands them firmly in a pattern of vanity, the fixation of an Enneagram Three.

People born into automatic advantage who fall into the space of passive othering are often deeply hurt or insecure individuals who feel that they must be on top to be valued, never overshadowed or outdone by others. The space of IDEA work feels like a no-win situation where they cannot maintain their image of a high achiever; they may avoid the work altogether and shift their focus to other areas where they know they will shine. This is where we experience the detached, cold, indifferent, often deeply narcissistic Three, who may only care about themselves, their self-image, and doing what is most advantageous for themselves in the moment. When confronted with this perspective, many Threes are heartbroken to realize that they have failed to live up to their full potential. They retreat inward and become detached and disappointed in themselves. They believe they have become the very thing they fear: a worthless failure. This can serve as the wakeup call for some Threes, pushing them to engage in the inner work necessary to move into Advocacy. On the other hand, it can paralyze some and lead them down a dark path of self-serving and destructive behaviors and actions aimed at devaluing others.

Threes who develop positional power and fall into the role of the *Sycophant* can be defensive individuals who react and behave in deceitful and conceited ways out of fear of being seen as not worthy of their position or place in this world. They have undoubtedly fought hard to get to where they are, oftentimes leaving a path of deep divides caused by their outward narcissistic tendencies and self-promoting behaviors. They are not likely to let go of their position for any reason, believing their position or success represents who they are and without it they are nothing. These individuals become cruel and emotionally demonstrative when faced with challenges across differences especially in regard to their own struggle; they may experience a moment of empathy toward people in similar situations but the fear of giving up their self-image or position of engineered value quickly shifts them into a pattern of self-serving justification. Instead of using their position of power for good and to advocate for equity and social justice, they will conceal their true emotions to maintain the persona they have constructed. Many people in this position are concealing their true selves; never really knowing who they are or what they truly stand for, they adapt their image to become whatever serves them best in the moment.

Love Warriors who fall into the average levels of development, where we experience passive othering, are likely concealing a deep pain that they refuse to acknowledge. Threes strive for success and achievement in some form or another, and they truly aspire to do great things. Dealing with the daily indignities of othering—in whatever form othering takes to push them to the margins—is a constant burden and obstacle that they must work to overcome. Many Threes at this level are in positions they are over-qualified for and find it difficult to advance due to some dimension of their diversity. They may use this as an excuse to work even harder while holding on to biased beliefs about whatever or whomever is standing in their way. These biases infiltrate every aspect of their lives, as their drive for success in any form is usually their main concern. The ability to differentiate between the persona they project to the world and the person they truly are becomes extremely difficult, and can lead to complications when addressing the implicit biases, unhealed wounds, and ability to engage in inner work.

The Demotion

Charlottesville, Virginia, was my first experience living in the South. It took many years for me to even travel south as I wanted to believe that things were better up North. Eventually, as army life goes, I found myself living in Virginia and looking for a job, day care, and enrolling back in school. I was hired at a local travel agency. I enjoyed working there, making new friends with the other employees, and gaining quite an impressive cache of clients. One day, the owner of the travel agency called me into his office and asked me to close the door behind me. He was wearing his usual velvet blazer adorned with a flawlessly knotted ascot, every hair perfectly slicked down. His cigarette holder in his hand was the final touch for this Southern gentleman.

"I'm going to replace you as an agent, but the receptionist job is yours if you want it."

I was speechless. "Why?" I asked.

After a short pause he sighed deeply and said, "I have no choice. I have to be mindful of the image of my agency."

"What are you talking about?" I asked, hoping that this was not going in the direction that I had experienced so many times before.

"Surely you understand that things are different here. You do excellent work; in fact, I could let the other two girls go and you could save me quite a bit of money. But some of the clients are concerned about you being here." I got it. It was happening again. I could be a receptionist, but an actual agent . . . well, I was definitely rising above my station, and this man was about to put me in my place. I left his office without saying a word. At lunch time I went to the University of Virginia Medical Center and applied for a job. On my way back from my break I received a call from the university and was offered the position over the phone.

The next morning when I returned to work at the travel agency, a small, red-headed White woman was sitting in the owner's office. After about an hour the two of them strolled into the agent area and made the announcement that this woman would be replacing me and I would be moved down to fulfill the receptionist position. He walked her over to my desk, introduced her to me, and with a smug smile told me to train her well. Well to hell with that, I thought. On my lunch break I asked him when she would be starting. He told me that she would start full time the next day and that he expected me to split my duties between training her and attending to the receptionist desk. I had planned to transition slowly into my new job and train whoever was taking my position at the agency. However, it was clear at this point that the owner had been planning to replace me with a person he deemed better for his image for a few weeks.

I went back to my desk, gathered my things, and walked back into his office. I laid the keys to the building on his desk and told him that this was my last day. "I had every intention of giving you two weeks' notice but seeing that you had a replacement for me before you demoted me, I don't think that applies."

"You can't possibly have found a job. I haven't given you a recommendation, and believe me, I know everyone in this town." I recognized that as a thinly veiled threat of power and control, though I'm sure he did know everyone in the small town. He assumed he could open or close any door based on a recommendation, but the university I applied to hadn't asked for it, possibly because I had told them exactly why I was leaving. Two weeks later he called me and asked if I would accept my job back.

"At the receptionist desk?" I asked.

"No, your travel agent position. This woman is a disaster, and the clients are complaining." I told him I was happy in my new job and I would not be coming back to work for him. He offered me more money, explaining that no one had actually complained but he knew how people could be, and he was only trying to protect his image and his business. Surely I could understand that. Once again, I was on the receiving end of the insular words from someone who was protecting their image and well-being but had absolutely no regard for mine. "I'm certain you'll reconsider. I'm offering you more money, and you actually make my place look better. You are well-groomed, intelligent, and articulate." What he meant was "You are well-groomed, intelligent, and articulate . . . for a Black woman." These are words we hear all too often; we are expected to take them as a compliment instead of hollow words concealing racist and sexist messages.

At this level of passive othering, it is very easy to see how one's self-interest comes before all else. When the preservation of one person's image comes at the cost of another person's humanity, we can only question the character behind the image. Not only was this individual not interested in equity, but his lenses were formed by a racist culture and served as a mirror that reflected back to him whatever would make him shine.

THE CHAMPION—ADVOCACY

The healthy energy of Point Three is home to the *Champion*—an inspiring and formidable leader for the honoring and advancement of our collective humanity. These are the people willing to face failure and truth with principled strength and resilience, leading with kindness and selflessness in the face of division, confrontation, and conflict. A Three who has done the inner work necessary to move into the space of the *Champion* has found truthfulness in the ability to access the authentic self and take right action with a collective awareness rather than a self-centered approach. They find worthy causes and channel their energy into making the cause successful and impactful, sometimes finding supporting roles without needing to be front and center. The need to project a desirable identity in order to maintain validation transforms into the emotional awareness for growth over progress and a value in service. These *Champions* are capable of truly astonishing transformations; they are selfless in seeking outlets for their abundance of ambitious energy, often serving as role models who bring out the best in everyone who experiences their inspirational energy.

People born into automatic advantage who have done the inner work necessary to activate as an Ally or Advocate have stepped into the power of their authentic selves. They become self-confident and develop themselves authentically with an awareness for who they really want to be and find balance in their value and their feelings. The need for projecting a false image to impress others falls away and makes space for their boundless compassion and benevolent ambition to flourish. *Champions* will use their position or power to make space for the Love Warriors and the people pushed to the margins to be brought in with dignity and respect. Standing with the Love Warriors, they let go of the need to be front and center and instead serve as foundational support to make sure everyone can have the opportunity to achieve—in whatever form that may take. The ability to speak out against bias, bigotry, and hatred becomes a weapon for love and connection that the *Champions* can harness.

Love Warriors who step into their true potential as *Champions* become extraordinary humans who create, inspire, and sustain anything and everything good in the IDEA world. They become leaders of causes, role models for other Love Warriors, motivational speakers, and paragons of societal change. These are the humans who let go of ego and find their authentic selves with grace, compassion, and truth. They embody the human ideal for achievement, success, benevolence, altruism, and strength. Using their position of power, they lift up other Love Warriors and create space for people to be brought back in from the margins. These *Champions* are often the historical paragons who fight for equity across all dimensions of diversity and lend their ambition, compassion, and motivational energy to the betterment of all of humanity.

Allies across the Pond

You can find beautiful humans filled with love and light at all nine Points of the Enneagram. When this particular human who happens to stand at Point Three came into my life, I remember experiencing an instant connection with his spirit. An invitation appeared to attend a workshop that he was conducting with another dear friend of mine. The workshop was in London, which meant an opportunity to enjoy some traveling. It sounded glorious; a real change from some of the heavier inner work retreats and workshops that I was normally drawn to explore. I signed my husband and I up, and off we went.

Did I say something about thinking this was not the normal heavier inner work workshops that I usually attend? Well, I was mistaken. The difference here was that, while the content was in fact quite heavy, the facilitator had an unusual capacity for doing this work from the place of a truly joyful heart. I was filled with love and gratitude. The week we spent working with him (and our other brother from another mother) was one of the most fulfilling experiences that my husband and I have ever shared. During this week-long study, we were gifted with the experience of these two wonderful humans weaving a beautiful tapestry of love, enlightenment, and joy into and around our spirits. It was amazing. The energy of this Three was intoxicating and sobering at the same time. He showed up authentically. Reverent and funny, sometimes messy and playful, and all of it is who he is. There was purity and generosity of spirit that resonated with us in that room. We all left somehow changed for the better. It was a magical Point Three experience, one that I will never forget.

Not long after, we became friends and have gone on to do some really good work together. Now I have not mentioned that this is a British White male. This may seem irrelevant, but it's not. It's entirely relevant because this authentic spirit-filled British White male has become one of my strongest Allies and Advocates in my love battle against racism and all forms of othering. He has used his platform to promote my work around the world. He has sat with me in times when I have felt discouraged and carefully and lovingly reminded me of the many words of Maya or Martin or Howard, encouraging me to stay the course. His Advocacy has meant so much to me, not just because of the many opportunities he has provided, but for the authenticity of his efforts. He spotlights the issues of race, inequity, justice, and diversity on his platform, recognizing full well that some of his followers might not be on board with this message. His courage and his love for all of humanity demonstrates the caring heart of the Three in its most beautiful form. We've become family now. His children are our God-grandchildren.

The open heart of the Three can create miracles across differences and will bring a charismatic energy to any cause.

At Point Three, your greatest strengths are your passion for success, enthusiasm, charming energy, and strong drive as a natural Advocate. You use your innate charm and motivational energy to serve as unexpectedly kindhearted and selfless healers and the leaders for championing social justice causes.

Consider this prework to practice and explore as you prepare yourself for the path of activation as an Ally, Advocate, or Love Warrior:

- The objective time-out and intentional pause at Point Nine in your Body Center can accelerate your movement with the arrow toward Point Six. Take a moment to find presence and be still. Breathe in and embody peace through internal reflection and explore the positive qualities at Point Nine.

- In the Body Center, instead of moving toward vanity, allow yourself to reflect on truthful action and the honoring of humanity in others and place this practice over your own self-serving needs. This grounding energy at Point Nine can allow for the stillness you need to find a harmonious and balanced approach to your actions and beliefs.

- As you move to access the energy at Point Six in the Head Center, learn to acknowledge when you are repressing your shame and engaging in self-serving behaviors as a way of hiding your true self. Think about the real reasons behind why you feel the need to project a false self-image and what you are compensating for within your heart.

- Allow yourself to reflect on who you really are. Uncover your hurt, pain, and suffering with compassion and patience. You can heal these holes within your heart by unearthing your true self and learning that you are worthy and valuable exactly as you are.

- Find the strength in yourself and be the amazing human being you were created to be. When you step into the power of your full presence, you can find truthfulness in everything you do, including standing as an authentic Ally, Advocate, or Love Warrior.

ENNEAGRAM POINT 4

Grief can be the garden of compassion. If you keep
your heart open through everything, your pain can become your
greatest ally in your life's search for love and wisdom.

—RUMI

One must not let oneself be overwhelmed by sadness.

—JACKIE KENNEDY ONASSIS

At the end of the day, we can endure much more than we think we can.

—FRIDA KAHLO

It is in our idleness, in our dreams,
that the submerged truth sometimes comes to the top.

—VIRGINIA WOOLF

OVERVIEW

If Point Four is where you stand on the Enneagram map, you have a deep appreciation for finding beauty in an ugly world through honoring the depth of emotion and the complexities of life. Emotional intelligence, empathy, and a deep connection to humanity are a few of the unique traits you embody at a molecular level. The Four is known in the Enneagram community as the *Individualist* or the *Romantic.* In the IDEA space we experience this unique energy in distinctly different ways. Fours can show up with the energy of the *Companion,* the *Pretender*, and the *Victim.*

If the dominant energy you experience resides at Point Four, you may feel compelled to honor your authentic self and stay true to who you are and what you stand for. You may even describe your experience as a deep appreciation and awareness for the wide spectrum of human emotions, oftentimes aligning it to a transformation of pain and suffering. The gift of your energy at Point Four is a double-edged sword: understanding the broad spectrum of emotion and finding the light in the darkest moments, while at the same time naturally gravitating toward and absorbing the darkness. This energy can sometimes manifest as creative or artistic in one way or another. The metamorphosis of pain and suffering into something poetic, beautiful, transformative, or cathartic is a common theme among all Fours. Your gaze is often drawn to honoring the emotional intelligence within any given situation. While there is a deep connection to emotional responses, the polarity that must be managed is maintaining a present awareness of emotional honesty without dropping into a state of unhealthy emotional fatigue or destructive fantasies. The lens through which you view the world is one of deep empathy, collective human emotion, and poetic and transformative experiences. A common experience among Four energy is the construction of an alternate reality where emotions and feelings can be played out and cause the subsequent entrapment of emotional distortion to fulfill some hidden fantasy. While you do have the capacity for an enormous amount of healing energy, the challenge is knowing when you are falling into unhealthy internalization of emotion instead of engaging in genuine emotional honesty with yourself and other humans.

At your best you are often an evolving Ally, Advocate, and healer of the downtrodden and the Love Warriors. You seem to find a way to stand in spaces of deep suffering and pain with a healing presence, when most people are running in the opposite direction. The strong connection to your own emotions allows you to honor the emotions of others and acknowledge the validity of what is happening, even when it may not be physically tangible. However, the deep fear of being ordinary or not having a unique identity may cause you to compete in "pain Olympics"—comparing the severity of your suffering to others and becoming envious in a toxic and contrived way. While radiating an energy that manifests the appearance of a truly unique and special individual, your heartbreak at Point Four is equally as powerful as your gifts. When you let your guard down, there is a lovable, kind, and worthy human sometimes hidden under a projection of neediness and melodrama. If this is resonating with you, remember this: your emotions do not define who you are. You are capable of being a whole human being without living through sensationalized and tortuous emotional fantasies. Your tendency to get trapped in your emotions is a counterproductive way of moving through the world and can prevent you from revealing your authentic self. You have an enormous capacity for healing and human connection as long as you get out of the fantasies in your head and live your life authentically. Remember, your evolutionary path is toward Allyship and Advocacy.

The experience of being overly dramatic, moody, and emotional may not be an uncommon experience for you at Point Four. You may even thrive on the fact that people consider you outside of "normal," thinking that being a unique human somehow gives you value. Deep down you just want to be accepted for who you are, but do you actually know your authentic self? The fantasies you have constructed to try to explain yourself do not actually define you. You are a whole human being, capable of amazing things; just let go of the persistent search for something inside of you that you believe is missing. Whatever it is, it has always been there; you just need to unearth it.

If this sounds like you, welcome to the IDEA community. You can be an unparalleled Ally for any cause, and I hope you will join us on our path to heal humanity.

At Point Four, you have great emotional intelligence and a unique healing energy that the world is desperate to feel. If Four energy is where you have determined your place resides on the Enneagram map, discover the journey of how you can harness the gifts from all the different components of the Enneagram: explore your basic desire, basic fear, core motivation, passion/blind spot, fixation/where you get stuck, virtue/your true self, and the Four's connections to Points One, Two, Three, and Five.

Let's go over a few things to prepare you for your journey.

- The Four blind spot, or passion of envy as it is called in the Enneagram, is a toxic pattern of comparing your struggles to the ease at which everyone else seems to exist.

- Your Four energy feels incomplete or lacking in some way and seeks ways to point it out to yourself and live within your own melodramatic despair.

- The intensity that your Four energy brings into everything matters and drives you to create distortions of reality in which you can live out your fears and pain while you try to figure it out. This conscripted stance is the default to live in your emotions rather than act on them.

- Your unique way of navigating challenges can lead you to a dark downward spiral of despair, a concept that is taught as the fixation of melancholy. This is where you get trapped and your shame and low self-worth become the guidance for your automatic pilot.

- The internalization and rejection/transformation of your shame is your way of masking your Achilles' heel: *being ordinary.*

- The invitation to move into activation is attainable when you access the gift of emotional honesty and compassionate and focused balance at Point Two, moving away from narcissism, envy, and melancholy, as these are toxic emotions that are blocking your true heart.

- Enter the transformative space at Point One in the Body Center, where you can establish your equanimity, taught in the Enneagram as the Four's virtue. This is where you will reclaim your balance, presence, and ability to take action as a Love Warrior, Ally, or Advocate.

SUMMARY OF 4s IN THE IDEA SPACE

The images of historical icons in IDEA work, both positive and negative, can easily serve as a visualization for the people who stand at Point Four: Frida Kahlo, Billie Eilish, Angelina Jolie, Anne Frank, Virginia Woolf, Kat Von D, Jackie Kennedy Onassis, Rumi, Prince, Sylvia Plath, Rihanna, Joni Mitchell, Amy Winehouse, Meryl Streep, Marilyn Manson, and Prince Charles.

The healing space held by the Four energy is an integral part of this work. Point Four represents the warm embrace of the freedom for psychological safety in the face of pain and suffering. Historically, the Fours are the people we find front and center in moments of deep trauma and healing. The energy we all have access to at Point Four is the ability to connect to others with a compassionate and deep understanding of emotional honesty. The polarity here that must be managed is creating the space for emotional balance and receptive compassion while not falling into the trap of self-serving emotional distortion. Emotional honesty is an asset the Fours can gift to the rest of us through engaging in the inner work.

People who possess the dominant energy at Point Four can be authentic, genuine, and true to who they are with a profound awareness for the importance of honoring all aspects of diversity. The desire to honor emotions and experiences as valuable and important is the stepping stone of holding the space for global healing. You will find Fours in positions of foundational support systems and in the creation of healing spaces for marginalized communities and those with unhealed internal wounds. Fours have an effect on people that signals a safe space for them to express emotions and lets them know that someone is genuinely listening with an empathetic heart—a distinguishing characteristic unlike any other Enneagram energy.

Activation is possible when you engage in doing intentional inner work, continue to educate yourself, and create new connections across differences. You can avail yourself of opportunities to choose love and compassion, allowing your actions to manifest as tangible and principled solutions rather than internalized fantasies and emotional distortions. In the next few sections, observe the evolution of a true Four Advocate as we move through the unhealthy, average, and healthy levels of development. You may notice yourself in each of the levels; we are all learning and growing, and it is vital to remain present, grounded, and honest as you allow your inner observer to guide you through this process. As you work your way through the descriptors and examples, pay attention to how you react and respond while you process the information about your attitudes, behaviors, and beliefs. This is a fluid process, and as human beings we are capable of accessing the high road and falling into destructive behaviors and old beliefs, all in the same day. The journey here is being open to a new way of navigating your Enneagram energy to resolve the challenges you face across differences and uncover your hidden implicit biases.

PATH OF ACTIVATION

As we illustrate the path of activation from active othering to passive othering and ultimately to Advocacy, the levels of development (unhealthy, average, healthy) demonstrate how the Four energy manifests in the IDEA space. In our exploration of the various stages of activation, we can uncover the complexities of Four energy by observing the nuances of the evolution of the journey.

THE VICTIM—ACTIVE OTHERING

In the unhealthy levels we find active othering, home to the *Victim*—a person who consciously acknowledges and reacts based on a distorted reality that is filtered through the Four's blind spot/passion of envy. The blind spot for the Four manifests as a shame-filled comparison of other people to themselves in order to highlight or construct an outlet for emotional

194

fulfillment. In this space, we find the angry, dramatic, judgmental, self-destructive, emotionally tormented, and isolated individuals who justify their actions and beliefs from the unhealthy energy of Point Four. They become deeply narcissistic and self-absorbed, creating a unique persona that they believe makes them better than "ordinary" people. Shame, fear, and emotional manipulation are the primary motivators that distort reality, resulting in a disdain for other humans who seem to live with ease. This disconnect may trigger the Four's deep resentment and envy, which masks their own unhealed wounds that they refuse to truly acknowledge.

For Fours born into automatic advantage who fall into the space of active othering, disengaging from reactionary bias and bigotry in order to activate as an Ally or Advocate can trigger the feelings of deep shame and guilt around their own identities. In search of whatever they believe is missing within them, the *Victim* with automatic advantage becomes a self-absorbed vessel for collecting pain and suffering. They live in their emotions and feel that their own suffering is more than they can bear, so the thought of dealing with other people's suffering is unimaginable. They absorb experiences and distort their reality to victimize themselves, believing that their pain and suffering is all that they are; they have nothing else if they do not hold on to these feelings. Their long-term suffering and internal fantasy world leaves them little room to find compassion or empathy for other people, which leads them to selfish and dehumanizing behaviors. In an attempt to live authentically and be themselves, they believe the rules don't apply to them; they are unlike anyone else and thus do not need to live by anyone's constraints. They reject social norms and believe that because they are unique they deserve unique treatment. This leads to a deeply narcissistic and delusional individual who can easily dehumanize other people.

Fours who develop positional power and fall into the unhealthy levels of development can become truly tormented individuals who live in a constant state of despair. The chaos and suffering in the world blankets them in darkness and fuels their envy. Reality becomes too much to handle at times, and fosters their justification for living in their internalized fantasy world. Many Fours at this level refuse to engage and will avoid news outlets, social media, and conversations around difficult topics. They can even experience a dual reality as if they were watching the world's pain and suffering from behind a curtain. The constant state of despair becomes a natural state and enables them to justify their dehumanizing behaviors, beliefs, and actions. The Fours who find themselves in the role of the *Victim* will find enemies in anyone who differs from them, has an easier time moving through the world, or mirrors their own struggle. We can experience the concept of horizontal bias at this level, where people who share similar dimensions of diversity can dehumanize other people within the same "category" in order to deflect the envy they have been holding on to.

Love Warriors who fall into unhealthy levels of development become truly overwhelmed by the pain and suffering of everything and everyone around them. They become depressed and lost at the sheer volume of suffering in the world and absorb this pain so deeply that they can't fathom how anyone manages to live their lives without feeling the same amount of despair. While they may understand the disconnects at a deep level, they become paralyzed by the self-inflicted torment that comes with the burden of this amount of emotional connection. They return to a state of despair over and over and are usually unable to address their own internal wounds and trauma; feeling overwhelmed by sadness and pain, they will lash out and perpetually push people away and hold on to the deep and paralyzing emotional torment.

The Blog

When I realized that leading in the IDEA space was a permanent part of my life journey, I recognized that I needed to get clear about what I believed to be true and what was the actual truth. I grew up in what many would consider a "typical home," raised by a cisgender mother and a cisgender father in a family environment where no one talked about sexual diversity as it pertained to LGBTQ+ and the gender and sexual diversity community. I had to educate myself, enter into deep inquiry, and recognize that I really didn't know what I didn't know. I was standing in front of groups of people encouraging, teaching, and supporting the journey of those who were trying to embrace one another exactly as they are, and I knew I had more work to do to understand how the gender and sexual diversity community showed up in this world. There are people in my life who identify as gay, queer, lesbian, and bisexual. My middle child, who identifies as nonbinary, has been a Godsend in helping me to understand the nuances of their journey.

I was contracted to work with a team where one of the employees read a book about the Enneagram and decided to share what he had learned with his co-workers. They ridiculed him, and they took his effort to share the Enneagram, turned it around, and weaponized it against him. Ronald, a self-identified Four is compassionate, creatively gifted far beyond his colleagues, and also identifies as a gay man. He immigrated from Spain to the U.S. hoping to find a more welcoming and inclusive environment. He was hired as a graphic artist and was miserable at his workplace. He eventually began to call in sick for weeks at a time. When I met him, it was not difficult to see that he was operating from a dangerously unhealthy place. He was grateful that I knew the Enneagram and we connected in that place, but he had little to no energy for anything.

When I interviewed his co-workers, I was surprised to discover that they thought well of him and appreciated his contributions to the team. They did find him to be a bit fragile and definitely quirky, but he wasn't the only gay person on the team; as he had previously assumed, he was excluded from his team because of his "unique" gender and sexual diversity.

I met with Ronald regularly and listened to his assessment of his colleagues. They were exceedingly damning. He had created stories about all of them, some of which I would have believed except the distortions were outside of the realm of reality. He articulated that he was right back in the same circumstances that led him to leave Spain. He had labeled all of his colleagues as being biased against him because of his gender and sexual identity and status as an immigrant. Ronald was really stuck in a place of self-loathing, where he felt broken because of his indulgence of vivid storytelling. He began to share his stories as actual experiences and eventually went to HR to demand that action be taken to protect him from a hostile workplace.

After an investigation was done and Ronald's claims were not found to be valid, he took matters into his own hands and started a blog, calling out his colleagues by name. He was released from his job, and he eventually returned to Spain, where the cycle of active othering would likely begin again. Ronald is a Love Warrior by definition as a person who has experienced actual othering during his lifetime. He has wounds that have never been addressed. Falling to the unhealthy level at Point Four, his unhealed wounds began to bleed out, leaving him incapable of seeing or believing that anyone had any level of compassion or respect for him. He did quite a bit of damage before he left. The blog destroyed the reputations of many of his co-workers because the accusations were so heinous in nature. Love Warriors acting outside of the energy of love at unhealthy levels inflict deep wounds on themselves in an attempt to decimate others.

THE PRETENDER—PASSIVE OTHERING

The *Pretender* lurks in the valley of passive othering, where we experience varying average levels of development. In the unhealthy levels of average, we find Fours who consciously choose to remain in the pattern of behavior, or fixation, of melancholy; they seek out outlets for their fantasies and the realities they have constructed to live out their pain and suffering. They hold on to their emotions believing that this is the only thing that makes them who they are. In this space, Fours are unwilling to accept reality, emotionally paralyzed, overly judgmental, self-indulgent, depressed, and apathetic. In the average level we have a space that most people find themselves reverting to as a comfort zone during times of stress: Fours become emotionally manipulative, internally motivated without the commitment to step into action, tormented and uncomfortable, and apathy is caused by hopelessness. Passive othering is the hardest place to move out of in the IDEA space, and Fours are very likely to return to this space frequently. They unintentionally (or intentionally) occupy a space designed to torment themselves by the seemingly endless pain and suffering in the world, not because they are choosing to be passive racists or "other-ers" but because they are paralyzed by the burden of carrying the pain of everyone around them. Most Fours who have been stuck in the role of the *Pretender* for a long time find it difficult to move past their basic fear of being ordinary or lacking personal significance, which ultimately lands them firmly in the fixation of envy, adding to the disconnection of authentic self.

For people born into automatic advantage, the energy at this level fosters a deeply disconnected and apathetic human being who lives in an internal fantasy world of despair and hopelessness where they may create imaginary situations to live out their pain through other people's experiences. For some unhealthy Fours, this enables them to get trapped in an internalization and distortion of reality, fantasizing about the world and falling into the trap of comparing their pain to the pain of others. They become truly apathetic at the sheer volume of suffering in the world and absorb this pain so deeply that they can't fathom how other people live their lives so normally. The *Pretender* can have a hard time acknowledging their automatic advantage and may even deny that they have any privilege at all. This can become the default setting when the melancholy begins to take over. While they may understand the disconnects at a deep level, they become paralyzed by the self-inflicted torment that comes with the burden of this amount of emotional connection. They return to a state of despair over and over while they experience fleeting moments of hope and healing.

Fours who develop positional power and find themselves in the role of the *Pretender* can experience extreme emotional swings from deep despair to moments of true Advocacy. The inability to stay in the space of Advocacy is fostered by the Fours conscious choice to live in their emotional distortions. Instead of acknowledging their position and using it to move into a healing space and develop connections to help other people, they remain tormented by the deep pain and suffering they absorb. They will experience fleeting moments of hope and clear opportunities to engage in an authentic and compassionate way, but the fear, shame, and low self-worth quickly shift them into a state of hopelessness, defeat, and anguish. The *Pretender* can rob themselves of the ability to acknowledge and heal their own wounds when they choose to live in the darkness instead of finding the light.

Love Warriors who fall into these levels of development allow the need to be seen as having a unique and authentic identity push them into a constant state of envious behaviors that ultimately drops them into a melodramatic spiral of emotional distortion. The Love Warriors who get stuck in this space of passive othering find faults in everyone and everything; their judgmental actions, implicit biases, and strong emotional connections foster a deeply resentful individual who may find it difficult to see the light at the end of the tunnel. Facing reality becomes too difficult to even consider at this level, but deep down these individuals want to engage in healing the world. The ability to engage is stifled when they lean too far into the pain and suffering and become trapped by their internalized fantasies of self-inflicted torment.

The Bucket That Didn't Get Kicked Over

Whether or not we surface our own stereotypes about Enneagram types, we develop them over time and have to be mindful of the harm that any stereotype can cause. This was work that I had to do based on my own relationship with my line to Four as the stress point of Point One. I know many self-typed, claim-to-be Fours and a few friends who are doing their inner work at Point Four. As they would all agree, the struggle is real, and the inner work is crucial. I was talking with a dear friend one day about her "Fourness" and she shared that she would never be a healthy Four. "It's too hard to get there, and I've become accustomed to my relationship with my melancholy." I countered with an inquiry as to whether or not she was serious about being an Ally in the IDEA space, or whether she felt that was also too difficult. She answered honestly, saying, "I care about you and your family because I know you and love you. The world is completely out of control, and you know as well as I do that we are all doomed to totally self-destruct. No great empire has ever escaped it and we won't either. I can't put my energy into something that will only be a drop in a bucket that is only going to be kicked over once filled anyway; but I will love you and yours with all my heart." I felt the gravitational pull of her melancholy and had to catch myself before I went to the bottom of the well with her. It was a somber moment. She gave voice to the feelings that surface for me when a not-guilty verdict comes in after another Black body has been destroyed.

I turned to face her, wiping tears from her eyes and mine, and I spoke a name. "Ahmaud Arbery. The bucket didn't get kicked over."

She smiled and responded, "Not yet, Deborah. This story is not over with this one. We will celebrate after the endless cycles of appeals."

I left her home that day feeling somewhat defeated. She is locked in the passive othering space, where she cannot see any hope for justice or a new path forward. I shook it off, remembering that I can't go to that space with her. Once again, the sadness returned as I thought about how common this mindset is for many, if not most, people. I hear the same words usually spoken with much less empathy: "There is nothing I can do about it! I didn't create this mess." The paralysis induced by pain and suffering is a space well-known to those who stand at Point Four. The Four energy at this level is very emblematic of the state of mind of the masses who stand frozen at all nine points. Fours recognize the suffering for what it is: a part of the human condition.

THE COMPANION—ADVOCACY

The healthy energy of Point Four is home to the *Companion*—a genuinely empathetic and selfless human capable of holding space for the world to heal. These are the people willing to be the gentle guardians of another person's humanity. They are kind and emotionally aware, balanced in their ability to hold space without falling into the pain. A Four who has done the inner work necessary to move into the space of the *Companion* has found equanimity in the balance of emotional intelligence and rational reasoning.

The need to create the experience of a deep emotional state in order to maintain a false sense of identity fades away and allows for activation. *Companions* will walk the path with a hurt individual and provide a sacred space for true compassion and healing energy. The space created and sustained by these individuals is vital to all social justice work and can be the deciding factor in whether or not we move toward healing and connection or into chaos and destruction. The world needs more *Companions* right now.

Fours born into automatic advantage who move into the space of true Allyship and Advocacy become authentic healers and essential figures in the IDEA space. These are the people who are capable of being the unique Enneagram energy that can effortlessly serve as the connections to our humanity. They let go of self-serving emotional distortions and internalized fantasies that used to paralyze them from taking action or seeing clearly, and they become authentic and share their gifts with grace and humility. Using their position of power, a *Companion* with automatic advantage becomes the foundation for elevating Love Warriors and anyone who is suffering or in pain. They will stand with people who have been pushed to the margins and people who have experienced and held on to deep trauma, and find a way to be the source of love and healing energy needed in any given situation. This unique energy is a much-needed addition to the Love Warrior arsenal.

Companions who develop positional power at this level are amazing sources of healing energy and a wonder to behold. They have faced the darkness, acknowledged the abyss of pain and suffering in the world, and found a way to heal themselves and extend that gift to everyone they encounter. These are the individuals who do not allow emotions to define or trap them, instead they use their emotional intelligence as a barometer to maintain their equanimity. They consciously choose to use their position and power as a gift rather than a burden and embrace their unique ability to elevate other Love Warriors and everyone who is in pain or suffering to help them heal with grace and genuine empathy.

Love Warriors who have done the inner work necessary to address their trauma and heal their wounds move into a unique space of healing energy. They are capable of being able to create a healing space for other Love Warriors and also cultivate the strength to become guardians for everyone else to feel safe. Being fully aware of the broad spectrum of human emotions and the highs and lows that are inherent in everyone makes them experts in knowing how to behave, react, and offer support in whatever form is necessary for the person who needs healing. They can serve as bridges between Love Warriors and Allies when difficult conversations arise, holding a safe space for processing and emotional honesty. Many Love Warriors who step into the role of the *Companion* create lasting legacies of beautiful healing works of art, social justice causes, and inspirational messages of connection that span generations.

Four-Ever Angel

The deeply personal story that I share here is one that will live in my heart forever.

We were all in Montserrat for a retreat, where we spent some time visiting with the Black Madonna. This was a very sacred journey for me, and I was happy to be a part of this experience. The Black Madonna, like all good Madonnas, had visiting hours. Unfortunately, I don't like crowds of people, so I decided to skip the visiting hours and make my way over to the chapel at a quieter time. When I got there, I discovered that others had the same idea, but I was not to be trifled with on my mission to visit with her. I stepped over the guardrail (yes, I know I'm a One, but I broke the dang rule) and made my way to the back of the chapel behind the Black Madonna. There sat my new friend who I had just met the day before. I slipped in next to her, and she leaned in to ask, "Have you visited with her yet?"

"No, not yet," I responded. "They still have another guardrail up, and I'm not sure exactly where the entrance is."

"Come with me," she said. She led me to the bottom of the steps at the entryway up to the Black Madonna. When I finally reached the altar where the Black Madonna was positioned, I immediately fell to my knees. There was no way that my legs would hold me up, as I was so overcome in that moment with the power of spirit, love, grace, joy, and gratitude. The tears fell hard

and fast. The kind of tears that come from deep in your belly and leave your body shuddering. I had no awareness of what was going on around me, I just knew that this was a reverent moment that I wanted to be fully present for; and so I let it be what it was. I have no idea how long this lasted, and I did not try to understand it. I am powerless to explain it, but I know that something profound happened on that day. When the tears subsided, I tested my legs, and I said a prayer of thanks. I placed my hand upon the Black Madonna again, bid her farewell, and promised that all of the messages that were being downloaded into my being at that time would be honored.

I descended the stairs opposite from the entrance, and I looked around the room. At that moment I realized that my friend had never left her post at the bottom of the stairs. We laugh when we speak of it now because I refer to her as my guardian angel who held back the Red Sea, parted the waters, and wouldn't let anyone pass until she knew whatever was happening for me in that moment was completed. She didn't ask any questions; she just sat by my side. She hasn't asked me to relive or explain what was going on, even all these years later. As an Ally at Point Four, she has an uncanny, extraordinary way of just being with a hurting human in a loving and comforting way and providing a safe space for healing. It doesn't escape me that God gave her the voice of an angel. I hear it every time she speaks or sings or laughs. I have developed such a love in my heart for her. There are times I want to reach out to her because I know how healing her energy can be in any space where I find myself struggling. However, I know how deeply she is affected by my pain. Her compassion and empathy allow her to access something that many of us struggle to maintain: presence. It is clear she knows the terrain of the heart. I know that on any given day this lovely human would stand up, part the Red Sea, take on the gladiators, and arrive at my side with a legion of angels beside her—no questions asked. This is what it feels like for me personally to have an Ally, an Advocate, and a true friend.

Our friendship blossomed into the creation of workshops to bring people together across differences. My friend, who I now call my sister, demonstrates her love for all of humanity with the actions of an Advocate.

She finds creative ways to comfort, to teach, and to be a presence that actively stands on the side of the Love Warriors as an Ally. She is like a whisper in the wind; kind, gentle, unexpected, and unforgettable. Her Advocacy at Point Four has brought to fruition connections in spaces and places for comfort, healing, and wise counsel. Once again, I find a White British human willing to do her inner work who steps up and allows her gentle voice to be heard. There is always a different level of depth and beauty in any workshop where she is present. In those moments, you can truly feel the shifting of the heart. She has a gentle but effective way of being in the world. She is a true healer because she recognizes and gives space and time to her own healing. She comes to others with an open heart and outstretched hands. You can almost hear her saying without words, "I understand, we all hurt, and I am here with you."

The healing heart at Point Four brings a level of comfort, empathy, and compassion to the world that is a soothing balm for the soul.

At Point Four, your greatest strength is your ability to maintain a safe space for people to express their emotions with the reassurance that someone is genuinely listening with an empathetic heart; a distinguishing characteristic unlike any other Enneagram energy. You use your innate ability for emotional intelligence and transformative response to serve as healers and Advocates for the collective reconnection of our global community.

Consider this prework to practice and explore as you prepare yourself for the path of activation as an Ally, Advocate, or Love Warrior:

- The objective time-out and intentional pause at Point Two in your Heart Center can accelerate your movement with the arrow toward Point One. Take a moment to pause and find compassion for yourself and others through honest, emotional reflection.

- With the extended access to your Heart Center, instead of moving toward envy, allow yourself to reflect on what is behind your emotional response and develop emotional equanimity. Focus your emotions outward instead of holding them tightly as if they defined and determined your existence.

- As you move to Point One in the Body Center, learn to still the emotional flurry that you have created and get grounded in the present. Connect to your body and pay attention to the sensations to establish your strength as a balanced human being.

- While there are no direct connections to the energies in the Head Center, Fours can pick up the connections in various ways. Point Five can be accessed through your wing connection. Point Six can be accessed from your wing at Point Three. And Point Seven can be accessed through your line to Point One. Explore your connections to the energies at these Points and develop the awareness to access the Head Center energy in order to align the three centers. Find a way to land in the Head Center and secure your strength in reconnecting to your humanity through honest reflection.

  - Point Five: combining innate emotional intelligence with perceptiveness and objectivity

  - Point Six: truth seeking capabilities, with a balanced perspective on emotions and rationality

  - Point Seven: emotional honesty to escape the internal fantasies and find balance in hope, joy, and optimism

Chapter 7

THE BRIDGE BUILDERS— HEAD CENTER: 5-6-7

The Head Center, or Thinking Triad, is home to Points Five, Six, and Seven. These three energies have a wisdom that comes from internalization and reflection. This group is centered around inner guidance—a persistent state of "getting stuck in their head"—and expressing their fear in different ways. Many people who identify with the Head Center Points (Five-Six-Seven) have a distinct experience with the emotion of fear or anxiety, more so than the other centers. All humans experience fear, as it is a basic human emotion; however, for the Five-Six-Seven fear is the paralytic behind many of their patterns of behavior.

During times of pain and suffering, either internally or externally, Five-Six-Sevens experience an uncomfortable cognitive dissonance that often transforms into internalized anxiety and redirected fear. This pattern consequently connects Five-Six-Seven to the capacity for reflection and guided action. The Head Center is concerned with looking to the future as a way of finding solutions, support, and guidance for addressing their fears. The management of fear and anxiety is dependent on how the Point in question is attempting to reassure themselves, fulfill the core motivation, and avoid the basic fear.

We call the Head Center the *Bridge Builders*, because that is exactly what they do—find or create the bridges between people and themselves for reconnection and collective healing or protection. Each Point *builds bridges* in its own way, which we dive into in each section, but they all take action based on how they internalize their anxiety and fear. The capacity for honest reflection during times of conflict without reacting impulsively or instinctually resides within the Head Center. When operating from a healthy space, Five-Six-Sevens are wise observers of how to secure justice, equity, and fairness and will find pathways for reconnection through kindness, courage, and objectivity. They are the center that can see the big picture and access a multiperspective balance because they are wired to make space for reflection and intentional presence more readily than most.

On the other side, the internalization and fear residing in the Head Center can lead to deep disconnection and destructive patterns. When operating from an unhealthy space, Five-Six-Sevens can be neurotic, selfish, unfeeling, insecure, and nihilistic, and ultimately fall into a toxic pattern of rationalizing and acting upon their own internal narrative for the wrong reasons. Many people within the Head Center experience a paralyzing wall of fear and anxiety surrounding a particular unhealed or unexplored internal wound. This wall can be brought down by diving into the inner work necessary to move through the passion, fixation, and virtue.

We all have access to the Head Center energy, and sometimes the fear we pick up from these Points can serve as a wake-up call or a catalyst for helping us land in our virtue. Not all fear needs to be paralytic in nature.

HEAD CENTER STRENGTHS

Objective analysis, astute insight, productive planning, wisdom, dedication, loyalty, independence, observation without judgment, productivity, neutrality, decision making free from emotional manipulation, truthfulness, visionary, advocacy for truth and justice, ability to see "big picture" and connect others across differences.

HEAD CENTER CHALLENGES

Fear, anxiety, direction, overanalysis, inability to take authentic action, projection, security, safety of self, authentic connection to others, isolation of self, selfishness, feeling genuine compassion, discomfort with conflict, insecurity, guidance, value, trust, stillness, emotional honesty

ENNEAGRAM
POINT 5

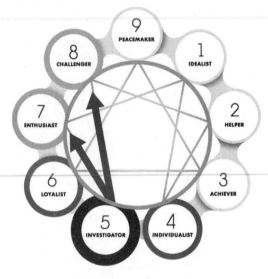

*One thing studying the Enneagram has done for me
has been to liberate me from all my ideas
of what "normal" looks like.*

— RUSS HUDSON

*We cannot solve our problems with the
same thinking we used when we created them.*

— ALBERT EINSTEIN

*Prejudice of any kind implies that you are identified with
the thinking mind. It means you don't see the other human being
anymore, but only your own concept of that human being.*

— ECKHART TOLLE

OVERVIEW

In a world where knowledge is at the click of a button, the desire to consume data quickly is a common theme among most people. Generally a superficial or fleeting action for most, for people who resonate with Point Five, the intake of knowledge is as vital as breathing. If Point Five is where you stand on the Enneagram map, you are more than likely a truly knowledgeable, wise, and capable person. The Fives are known in the Enneagram community as the *Investigator*, the *Observer*, and the *Thinker.* In the IDEA space, we experience this complex energy in distinctly different ways. Fives can show you with the energy of the *Pathfinder*, the *Misanthrope*, and the *Nihilist.* If Point Five is your dominant Enneagram energy, IDEA work is the place to put your wisdom and deep understanding of how the world works to good use.

At Point Five, you may feel compelled by a constant need to consume information and add to your already impressive arsenal of wisdom, knowledge, and resources. This drive is fueled by the Fives' basic fear of being incapable, overwhelmed by helplessness, or feeling depleted. Most Fives are masters of finding out how things work, researching every facet of the inner mechanisms of a system, and developing a cache of knowledge as an unconscious security blanket. As a Five, you are the vault keepers of a broad spectrum of knowledge, expertise, and valuable resources. Those who identify themselves with this energy share a common aversion to readily sharing their wisdom or resources with others, or of being seen as valuable only for what they know. The innovative thought processes, internalization and isolation of self, and a strong drive to figure things out create the comfort zone for you at Point Five. The polarity here is managing the need for more information and resources in order to prevent yourself from feeling incapable or overwhelmed while not hoarding or taking on so much to the point of retreating into yourself, feeling depleted, and becoming a withdrawn recluse. If you are an Investigator or Observer, you can automatically see the big picture and easily access the information needed to make sense out of a situation. The lens through which you view the world is one of internalization of external stimuli in order to understand and find order in chaos.

At your best you are often an evolving Ally, Advocate, and a pathfinder for the connections needed to reunite our global communities. You seem to find a way to become objective and impartial, even during deep disconnects, and search for the road back to reconnection with wisdom and innovative vision. The deep fear of being incapable or underprepared, often aligned with the anxiety around being depleted of resources, can cause you to hoard your knowledge and resources and retreat inward. While radiating an energy that manifests the appearance of a knowledgeable and proficient human being who can take on anything, your fear at Point Five is equally as powerful as your strength. When you let your guard down and allow people to share in your gifts, there is a lovable, kind, and generous human sometimes hidden under a cold and callous exterior. If this is resonating with you, remember this: your strength and wisdom are not sustainable if you disconnect from your humanity and the humanity of others. It is a counterproductive way of moving through the world and can be considered insensitive and apathetic to some, which can amplify disconnects across differences. Remember, your evolutionary path is toward Allyship and Advocacy.

The experience of being misunderstood or of being underestimated in your wisdom and capability may be a common experience for you at Point Five. You deny people the opportunity to connect with you out of fear and insecurity, and in turn you deprive yourself of true wisdom and opportunities for growth and compassion. An intentional shift to find presence and connection will allow you to grow as a true visionary and is just another step to becoming a whole human being who strives to do better.

If this sounds like you, welcome to the IDEA community. You can be an essential and wise Ally for any cause, and I hope you will join us on our path to heal humanity.

At Point Five, you have great innovation and generosity hidden away in your giant arsenal of wisdom and knowledge. If Five energy is where you have determined your place resides on the Enneagram map, discover the journey of how you can harness the gifts from all the different components of the Enneagram: explore your basic desire, basic fear, core motivation, passion/blind spot, fixation/where you get stuck, virtue/your true self, and the Five's connections to Points Seven, Eight, Six, and Four.

Let's go over a few things to prepare you for your journey.

- The Five blind spot, or passion of avarice as it is called in the Enneagram, is a deep desire to locate and acquire any and all resources that will ensure you are knowledgeable, competent, and prepared.

- Your Five energy seeks more knowledge, more books, more sources, more answers, more of everything.

- The intensity that your Five energy brings into everything matters and fuels your fear around losing what resources you have collected, which may render you incapable of functioning. This conscripted stance is the default to justify your thirst to acquire more and retreat inward.

- Your unique way of navigating challenges can lead you to an unwillingness to share your knowledge and resources or to connect with other humans, a concept that is taught as the fixation of stinginess. This is where you get trapped, and your fear and anxiety become the guidance for your automatic pilot.

- The hoarding and isolation you allow is your way of masking your Achilles' heel: *fear.*

- The invitation to move into activation is attainable when you access the gift of freedom and balance at Point Seven, moving away from fear, avarice, and stinginess as these are toxic emotions that are blocking your true heart.

- Enter a transformative space at Point Eight where you can reclaim your strength and courage to take your wisdom out into the world, taught in the Enneagram as the Five's virtue of nonattachment. This is where you will find your balance and connectivity as a Love Warrior, Ally, or Advocate.

SUMMARY OF 5s IN THE IDEA SPACE

The images of historical icons in IDEA work, both positive and negative, can easily serve as a visualization for the people who stand at Point Five: Buddha, Albert Einstein, Bill Gates, Bob Dylan, Diane Sawyer, Ben Carson, Eckhart Tolle, Anita Hill, Ted Kaczynski, Jane Goodall, Stephen Hawking, Garrett Morgan, Katherine Johnson, John Walker Lindh, Timothy McVeigh, Phil Spector, and Mark Zuckerberg.

In IDEA work we experience a mixed bag of supporters: we have the "go out there with the people" activist, and then we have the people who make it possible for the work to actually get done—often a space occupied by people who stand at Point Five. The behind-the-scenes systems of social justice work is where we typically find the wisdom and innovation of people who stand at Point Five. If this is where your dominant energy resides, then it is likely you are a person capable of constructing the consummate inquiry to uncover inequities through research, data collection (often more than we ask for, but relevant nonetheless), and a thirst for genuine knowledge. People at Point Five are consistent in their efforts to connect the dots across systems and they dive into the deep waters of historical context. In their quest for knowledge and truth, the energy that radiates from Point Five allows us to gaze upon the uncovering of facts and to reject fabrications and generalizations that too often dehumanize the experiences of Love Warriors and people who have been pushed to the margins of society. Fives help us to reconstruct our history from objective reflection and implement the practices necessary to address inequities and injustices. The energy that we all have access to at Point Five is an introspective but curious and kindhearted perspective grounded in fairness and neutrality. The polarity here that must be managed is creating the space to honor the need for internal inquiry while maintaining presence, openness, and a willingness to share freely.

People who possess the dominant healthy energy at Point Five are incredibly knowledgeable and capable of seeing multiple perspectives. They possess a beautifully intricate appreciation for all aspects of diversity; we all become credible as Love Warriors, Advocates, and Allies at Point Five. We can find Fives as the keepers of the documented path that allows us to put the pieces of history back together. They are often the historical and institutional sources of wisdom and narratives of their communities. Fives have an effect on people that is reassuring when a situation is starting to look overwhelming or unmanageable and can serve as the pathfinder when things are heading downhill. People who identify with Point Five generally have a natural ability to make decisions free of biased emotion or prejudice; they are calm and collected on the outside, but deeply engaged internally.

Activation is possible when you engage in doing intentional inner work, continue to educate yourself, and create new connections across differences. You can avail yourselves of opportunities to choose love and connection, allowing your actions to manifest as courage over fear, and connectedness over withdrawal. In the next few sections, observe the evolution of a true Five Advocate as we move through the unhealthy, average, and healthy levels of development. You may notice yourself in each of the levels; we are all learning and growing, and it is vital to remain present, grounded, and honest as you allow your inner observer to guide you through this process. As you work your way through the descriptors and examples, pay attention to how you react and respond while you process the information about your attitudes, behaviors, and beliefs. This is a fluid process, and as human beings we are capable of accessing the high road and falling into destructive behaviors and old beliefs, all in the same day. The journey here is being open to a new way of navigating your Enneagram energy to resolve the challenges you face across differences and uncover your hidden implicit biases.

PATH OF ACTIVATION

As we illustrate the path of activation from active othering to passive othering and ultimately to Advocacy, the levels of development (unhealthy, average, healthy) demonstrate how the Five energy manifests in the IDEA space. In our exploration of the various stages of activation, we can uncover the complexities of Five energy by observing the nuances of the evolution of the journey.

THE NIHILIST—ACTIVE OTHERING

In the unhealthy levels of development, we find active othering where the *Nihilist* hides—a person who consciously acknowledges and reacts based on a distorted reality that is filtered through the Five's blind spot/passion of avarice. The blind spot for the Five manifests as a relentless search for more resources and more knowledge in order to calm their fears. In this space, we find the highly unstable, obsessive, isolated, arrogant, detached, and egotistical individuals who justify their actions and beliefs from the unhealthy energy of Point Five. These are the people who can use their vast knowledge for ill gain, sometimes out of spite or misdirected anxiety. Fear, greed, and insecurity are the primary motivators that distort reality, resulting in disdain for anyone or anything that may compromise or challenge their existence.

For Fives who are born into automatic advantage, disengaging from reactionary bias and bigotry in order to activate as an Ally or Advocate can trigger deep feelings of fear and anxiety, and cause some to spiral into a skewed justification for their behaviors and beliefs. At this level, we experience the deeply detached and extremist individuals who isolate and submerge themselves in whatever resources they have collected to sustain their biased perspectives. These are the people who become deeply arrogant and narcissistic in their behaviors aimed at belittling other people. Deep down they are trying to cover the reality that they are a bundle of fear and anxiety.

Fives who develop positional power at this level of development can become deeply resentful and oppressive, consciously rejecting the people, the circumstances, and the details of their journey. A distortion of reality creates an "I'm not connected to you because I know more than you" attitude that serves as the justification for the dehumanization of anyone who challenges their position or competency or anyone who serves as a reminder of their origin. We can experience the concept of horizontal bias at this level, where people who share similar dimensions of diversity can dehumanize other people within the same category in order to justify their behaviors rooted in insecurity and arrogance. The fear of being pushed back to the margins for any reason fuels the insecurity of the Five at this level and can cause them to withhold their support, knowledge, and solutions to engage in social justice work.

Love Warriors at this level of development become isolated and detached from their communities. They may dive into an unhealthy level of research into systemic inequities, laws, history, practices, and policies; they have a deep understanding of the conditions that caused the divides we currently face, but their fear and anxiety are the controlling factors that prevent them from connecting to other people. They withdraw and become detached from finding real solutions and continue to exist isolated in their bubbles. Many Love Warriors at this level understand the depth of othering and the trauma that has been inflicted upon people who have been pushed to the margins, causing them to hold on to deeply ingrained biases against "dominant culture." They often find it difficult to address their own internal wounds and trauma; fearing being overwhelm by their anxieties, they will lash out and perpetually push people away and continue to retreat inward.

Frankenstein's Enneagram

I have taught the Enneagram to many scientists, researchers, and IT specialists. While Fives reside everywhere, I have found these career paths to be more Five-heavy. Individuals who stand at Point Five want to check out the validity of the Enneagram. Once they have done their own research, they are either all in or all out. At this unhealthy level of active othering, I experienced the actions of a mid-level manager who used his dime-store knowledge of the Enneagram to single-handedly destroy an organization. I witnessed ultimate levels of demonization of people across differences, armed with an erudite predilection for his own intellect and the flawed assumption that he was always right. He decided that he was going to create the perfect team using the Enneagram as the ultimate decision matrix. He embedded facets of his own making into the utilization of the Enneagram in the IDEA space that undermined the integrity of its application.

In his version of the Enneagram, women were Twos, except Black women; they were all angry Eights (Michelle Obama was his archetype). Black men were Sixes because they were not good decision-makers. He decided that what he called "gay/queer" (all members of the gender and sexual diversity community) people were Fours. When he got to the Fives, he declared that all Fives were White males. Part of his "research," which he demonstrated right in front of me, was to Google famous Enneagram Fives. He had a pigeonhole for every type that he cataloged by their sphere of universal placement on the Humanity Mosaic. It was reckless, irresponsible, and denigrating. He thought it was genius and he wanted me to validate and condone his Frankenstein version of the Enneagram. What he had really accomplished with his deeply destructive project was a widespread discriminatory practice that ultimately unraveled the very fabric of this organization. I knew people who worked there and needless to say if they could find jobs elsewhere, they did. The Enneagram should be used to build bridges, not to further the divides.

A mere sampling and selection of research used to justify a distorted system of beliefs can illuminate the flawed ego structure of those who believe they are the brightest and the best.

THE MISANTHROPE—PASSIVE OTHERING

The *Misanthrope* isolates themselves in the darkness of passive othering, where we experience the average levels of development. At the unhealthy level of average, some Fives consciously choose to remain in the pattern of retention, often referred to as the fixation of stinginess. They seek out ways to avoid connection and believe they must hold on to their resources to survive, whether it is time, knowledge, groups, books, or anything that they may have acquired. In this space, Fives are unwilling to connect, stubborn and intellectually arrogant, cold and angry, fearful and apathetic. The thought of connection to others is exhausting, so they stay isolated in fear of becoming depleted and thus rendered incapacitated or underprepared. At the average level we have a space where most people find themselves reverting to as a comfort zone during times of stress: Fives are emotionally stunted, internally motivated without external motion, stuck in their heads trying to make sense of things, and apathy is generally caused by hopelessness. The area of passive othering is unfortunately common for people who identify with the Five energy; isolation, separation, and the hoarding of resources is a natural state for Fives. Passive othering is especially difficult to escape for Point Five in the IDEA space. Most Fives who have been stuck in the role of the *Misanthrope* for a long time find it difficult to move past their basic fear of feeling incapable or helpless, which ultimately lands them firmly in a pattern of stinginess, the fixation of the Five.

A Five born into automatic advantage who falls into the limbo of passive othering becomes a withdrawn and intellectually arrogant person who carelessly neglects the humanity of others. They hoard their knowledge, wisdom, and the innate ability to find answers as a way of addressing their core motivation of remaining capable and competent. Many unhealthy Fives feel as though if they share their knowledge and resources, the demand from others will deplete them and render them incapable or underprepared for challenges. They may have flickers of connectedness and see the value in sharing their wisdom, but the fear of becoming depleted or incapacitated quickly shifts them into self-isolation. These Fives may offer bullet points to a solution, but they withhold the full picture, just in case. Instead of using their position to serve as a pathfinder for hope, connection, and growth, they become paranoid and defensive of their power and position.

Fives who develop positional power and fall into the role of the *Misanthrope* can be highly detached individuals who retreat into their minds and get trapped in finding solutions and answers without having the motivation to act upon them. They have a deep fear of losing their position or power as an innovative problem solver and a valuable source of wisdom. They have undoubtedly fought hard to get to where they are, oftentimes leaving a path of deep divides caused by their cold exterior and unwillingness to connect with other humans. These individuals become calculated and emotionally stunted when faced with challenges across differences; they may experience a moment of empathy toward people in similar situations, but the fear of giving up their valuable resources or knowledge quickly shifts them into a defensive stance. Many Fives in this position have connected the dots and exhaustively researched the systems and practices used to create disparities, but they are fearful of acting or engaging in an authentic way.

The Love Warrior Fives who reside within the levels of passive othering are usually deeply wounded and fearful humans who are just trying to figure it out. They are doing the research, finding resources, and attempting to make sense of their pain and trauma. But they often collect so much and become so scattered that the real inner work is never allowed to surface. These are the humans that need connection, now more than ever. The internalization of their trauma and the causes behind them are lost in a sea of knowledge, facts, figures, and historical context. They become unfocused and revert to isolation during conflict or challenges; when a moment of connection presents itself, they may connect the dots and offer a path to connection, but the fear can overwhelm them.

Too Exhausted to Engage

It is actually painful for me to teach the Enneagram to a very small, disinterested group. More often than not, small can be good. After an afternoon session where this was not my experience (three people in the room who had never heard of the Enneagram and slept through the class), I ended the class after one hour and went in search of the individual who had requested the workshop. She was a rather diminutive woman tucked in behind her desk in such a way as to be barely visible. I knocked. She looked up, and I entered the room. She knew who I was immediately and began speaking before I could share why I was there. "This isn't on me. I don't think we should have these offerings in public spaces." Apparently, this workshop was requested by members of the local community who wanted to learn about how the Enneagram could strengthen their presence in social justice work. She was the supervisor of the center and knew that she stood at Point Five.

She continued. "I told management that we were putting in-formation out there that was way over these people's heads." Did she say "these" people or "those" people? Definitely not "you" people. Either way, I braced myself for what would come next. *"I laid it all out for them as to how this should be done. They didn't listen, so this is what you ended up with. As I said, it's not on me." I took a breath, recognizing that I was speaking with an individual who stood at Point Five and had somehow felt unheard and disrespected. I asked her to share with me what happened and why she felt as she did. "These people (there it was again) come in here making demands, and when they don't get what they want they go over my head. I did a presentation for the leadership team and showed them why the Enneagram was far too advanced for these people. Most of them barely have a high school education. I've studied the Enneagram for a while— you probably have as well (probably?)—and there is no way to teach this to them, and it has nothing to do with social justice work!" As I was sitting there listening to her quiet and matter-of-fact rant, the faces of the custodians, factory workers, school aides, hotel maids, and grounds maintenance workers flashed before my eyes—just as they do now. This woman's passive oth-ering in the name of "they couldn't possibly understand" was preventing people from gaining access to the Enneagram. At that moment, I was filled with self-righteous indignation. She wasn't White. She wasn't Black. She was Brown. I am not one to make assumptions about anyone's ethnicity. Her last name gave me a clue, but one never knows if that name is by marriage or from birth.*

Divide and conquer, *I thought to myself. You are working here to "help" a largely impoverished community, but you block their access to knowledge. I asked her if she had advertised the workshop. She looked up and sheepishly answered no. "So who were the three people in the room?" I asked.*

"They clean up after the center closes," she said.

"You never put any information out for the community about the workshop, so how do you plan on explaining why it never happened?" I asked.

"I'll tell them that we had the workshop and no one signed up." She looked smug and self-satisfied.

"What are you afraid will happen if they come to the workshop?" I asked. I saw her eyes soften just a bit.

"They will be embarrassed, and they will expect me to explain things to them after you are not here. The entire thought of this is exhausting. This conversation is exhausting!" I recognized that I had overstayed my welcome and left. I had the workshop rebooked at a different community center and returned there many times. There was never an empty seat in the room.

When the competency of a Five is questioned and their recommendations are rebuked, the passive othering is often played out in the form of subtle sabotage or complete detachment.

THE PATHFINDER—ADVOCACY

At Point Five, the healthy levels of development are where the *Pathfinder* lives—an innovative and open-minded visionary on the path to healing humanity. These are the people willing to connect to others in the hopes of finding subject matter experts in the IDEA world. They actively seek out people who are Love Warriors or people who experience the daily indignities caused by systemic oppression and develop personal relationships in order to establish valid sources for trying to figure out how to dismantle systemic inequities. The *Pathfinder* is a valuable and flexible leader in the search to rebuild the bridges across differences, and has stepped into their virtue of nonattachment by openly sharing their wealth of knowldge and resources. They are experts in true Allyship and Advocacy, never wavering in the face of adversity. The emergence of their true spirit allows them to overcome their basic fear of being depleted or overwhelmed to the point of feeling incapable; they surrender to the reality that they must maintain connections to feel truly capable and step into their real power as an innovative visionary. These *Pathfinders* help us to reconstruct our history from objective reflection and implement the practices necessary to address and dismantle inequities and injustices.

Fives with automatic advantage at this level have done the inner work necessary to move into the space of the *Pathfinder*; they have found non-attachment in the search to use their knowledge for themselves and uncovered a path for bringing knowledge and solutions to all of humanity. The scattered accumulation and hoarding of resources are replaced with a fair and objective perspective of finding, transforming, and sharing wisdom. These *Pathfinders* use their positions of power to become trustworthy sources of information for anyone who challenges the validity of othering. For people born into automatic advantage, activation and Advocacy take the form of formidable power and strength to support and reconnect the work of achieving equity, equality, and justice.

Fives who gain positional power at this level of development are capable of being instrumental in creating sustainable change. The unique perspective of being present within multiple hierarchies of society allows these *Pathfinders* to not only open doors but to also know which doors to open and the reasons behind why they were shut in the first place. They have faced the margins of society, found their way back, and developed a path to bring "others" along to reconnect the divides our community faces. Many *Pathfinders* who are in positions of power become the historical humanitarians who establish the systems for true change.

Love Warriors who move into the space of the *Pathfinder* become the leaders who establish credibility and sustainability for whatever cause or movement they are fighting for, oftentimes behind the scenes or in fundamental positions of power. They are true experts and keepers of truth when it comes to Advocacy and social justice work; they can cut through the falsities of any argument with precision and strength. The Love Warrior *Pathfinders* at this level are beacons of inspiration and hope for people who cannot see the path back to justice and peace. These *Pathfinders* are usually the reason we are able to continue to fight injustices day in and day out.

The Wisdom of the Pathfinder

One of my Enneagram teachers seemed to have a warning system that informed him when I was particularly perplexed, struggling with a new concept, or challenging my own personal assumptions and beliefs. He appeared to be a person who spent a lot of time analyzing thoughts, concepts, mental models, and spiritual beliefs. I would approach him from time to time with questions, and he always left me with something to deepen my own process of inner work.

Nearly two decades have passed since I encountered this human who, during the course of my journey, has become a cherished and beloved friend to me and my family. This is a man whose way of being in the world centers around understanding and accepting what is, without judgment. This human who stands at Point Five has walked beside me in good times and in bad, helping me to make sense of the senseless when no one else could find the words. He understands, without words, the loneliness that I experienced in this love battle for the soul of our humanity. Most importantly, he voluntarily joined me when he began to see very clearly that the battle required all hands on deck and a deep cache of knowledge and resources. We have worked together guiding people in their exploration of how to become effective Allies. Together we have taken on the tough conversations in the "race space," guiding them through the gnarly terrain of understanding and respecting differences. Black, White, Brown, Asian, queer, straight, nonbinary people have sat with us to learn and grow as we try to guide them forward onto a new path.

During the years that our friendship was growing, we would have occasional chats, non-Enneagram related, and enjoy conversations just about our daily lives. We took the time to establish a level of relationship that makes us credible working together as Enneagram teachers in the IDEA space. We can authentically demonstrate what working together looks like as I stand in place as a Love Warrior and he stands with me as an Ally and also my

Advocate. We have laughed, cried, and even colluded together in an attempt to get my granddaughter to choose Columbia University so that she would be in my home of origin in New York City. Despite our best efforts, she decided to go to Harvard.

My relationship with this human has taught me many things over the years—each experience and shared moment adding to our journey. When he had a health crisis, I realized how different life would be without this lovely human in our lives. This lovely being at Point Five is deeply connected to us in the heart space. Somewhere on our journey together and in our relationship, it went from head to heart to gut. It was the alignment of the three centers of our being that created the depth of the relationship, allowing for the trust, the camaraderie, the love, and the shared connection. A cherished connection that extended from him to me, to my spouse, to my children and grandchildren, and to my friends. The connection is what we share, and it is what keeps the relationship and the work that we do together solid, precious, and tangible. I have watched his heart open and open and open. His love for humanity is not buried deep inside of him; it is out and fully on display. I have watched how his teaching has transitioned and how he serves as an example of what it looks like to be on the journey at Point Five while walking the path of justice with the Love Warriors.

There have been perceptible shifts along his journey—the warmth that comes from his eyes, his joy and genuine compassion that guides his being, the love that is communicated when he speaks to people who hang on his every word. And while every word is precious, it is also his being, his presence that pulls us all in and creates a space where we can bring our innocence and listen to words of wisdom. We feel nurtured, empowered, and enlightened because he chooses to share certain truths, usually exactly what we needed to hear on that day. The playfulness, the knowledge, the messiness, and the love at Point Five sometimes gets lost as Fives get relegated to being appreciated only for the knowledge that they have. Through the process of inner work, I have learned how those who stand at Point Five have a capacity for so much more than they are given credit for or sometimes allow us to see. I'm grateful for my Five Ally and Advocate. He has become an architect and cartographer in rebuilding the bridges that differences broke, by openly sharing and offering different paths for people to connect and heal.

When willing to share valued resources like knowledge and time, the capacity for emotional connection and awareness is truly priceless at Point Five.

At Point Five, your greatest strength is your ability to make sense out of chaos and find ways to truly impact and transform systems to benefit all of humankind. Using your inner drive for acquiring wisdom and knowledge, you are able to find ways to reconnect across differences and become the guides for people from all walks of life to shift into new perspectives.

Consider this prework to practice and explore as you prepare yourself for the path of activation as an Ally, Advocate, or Love Warrior:

- The objective time-out and intentional pause at Point Seven in your Head Center can accelerate your movement with the arrow toward Point Eight.

- Take a moment to pause and address your fears. Going against the arrow to Point Seven first gives you the opportunity to create additional space for reflection and processing with the courage and wisdom to find connection. Stay with the Seven energy, embrace the outward curiosity and appreciation for freedom of thought, and try not to give into the forceful pull inward when things seem overwhelming.

- Breathe in and embody peace through internal reflection and explore the positive qualities at Point Eight. In the Body Center, learn to ground yourself in your body and get out of your head.

You can find perspective with objectivity and a curious spirit while remaining present with others.

- Enter a transformative space at Point Eight where you can reclaim your strength and courage to take your wisdom out into the world, taught in the Enneagram as the Five's virtue of nonattachment. This is where you will find your balance, power, and connectivity as a Love Warrior, Ally, or Advocate.

- While there are no direct connections to the energies in the Heart Center, Fives can pick up the connections in various ways. Point Two can be accessed from your line to Point Eight. Point Three can be accessed from your wing at Point Six. And Point Four can be accessed from your wing connection. Explore your connections to the energies at these Points and develop the awareness to access the Heart Center energy in order to align the three centers. Find a way to land in the Heart Center when you are faced with challenges and secure your strength in reconnecting to your humanity. The connection to your heart allows people to see the real you and appreciate your intensity, power, and capacity for influence. You can connect with others across the differences with compassion, kindness, and generosity.

  • Point Two: compassion and empathy for yourself and others

  • Point Three: inner drive to accomplish great things with an appreciation for emotional truthfulness

  • Point Four: emotional honesty to manage your inner wounds and find compassion for yourself to heal

ENNEAGRAM POINT 6

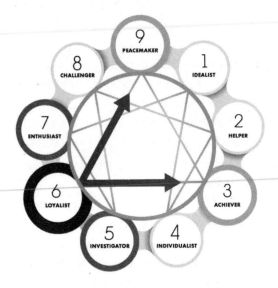

In oneself lies the whole world and if you know how to look and learn, the door is there and the key is in your hand. Nobody on earth can give you either the key or the door to open, except yourself.

—JIDDU KRISHNAMURTI

You have to do the research. If you don't know about something, then you ask the right people who do.

—SPIKE LEE

Truth is, I'll never know all there is to know about you just as you will never know all there is to know about me. Humans are by nature too complicated to be understood fully. So, we can choose either to approach our fellow human beings with suspicion or to approach them with an open mind, a dash of optimism, and a great deal of candor.

—TOM HANKS

OVERVIEW

In a world where things are rapidly changing and problems seem to be piling up, most of us can find a way to integrate these changes and transitions into our lives without great angst. If you stand at Point Six, the capacity to envision all the ways that things can go wrong creates a constant sense of overwhelming anxiety. The Six is known in the Enneagram community as the *Loyalist,* the *Guardian,* or the *Skeptic.* In the IDEA space we experience this powerful energy in distinctly different ways. Sixes can show up with the energy of the *Hero,* the *Pessimist,* and the *Loose Cannon.* IDEA work is the place to showcase your capacity for truth and courage and show up as a devoted hero for the protection and guidance of our humanity.

If the dominant energy you experience is at Point Six, you may feel compelled by a need for security, stability, and support. Loyalty, commitment, and the incessant internal chatter of a worrying mind create the comfort zone for this particular energy. The appearance of problems without clear solutions creates anxiety and frustration for the loyal, steadfast, dutiful individuals that stand at Point Six. There is always something to be prepared for in today's world, and you take that responsibility to a molecular level; backup plans for the backup plans, preparing for worst-case scenarios, consulting the "committee in the head" before even considering taking action. The "committee in the head" is a common theme among people who identify with the energy at Point Six. This is not a mental health issue or anything to be considered negative; for a Six the "committee" is how you consider every possible option and outcome before making a decision. Playing out scenarios and weighing the benefits and risks associated with whatever decision needs to be made, whether big or small, is a way of navigating daily life, but it can also become an incapacitating pattern. The need for security in all things stems from the fear and anxiety associated with the self-doubt around the ability to function without guidance. You often find it difficult to trust; this is true in regard to trusting other people, but it also applies to trusting yourself.

At your best you are often an evolving Ally, Advocate, and a valiant seeker of truth and justice. You seem to find a way to envision the big picture, cut through the red tape, and find clear solutions to any challenge, at least through your Six lens. The deep fear of losing guidance, support, and stability may cause you to become trapped in your head, paralyzed by fear and anxiety. While radiating an energy that manifests the appearance of a prepared and considerate human, your fear at Point Six is equally as powerful as your courage. When you let your inner strength serve as your guide, you become a grounded, trustworthy, confident human sometimes hidden under an anxious and scattered exterior. If this is resonating with you, remember this: there is no need to allow your fear to paralyze you in your search for guidance. It is a counterproductive way of moving through the world and can be uninviting and disheartening to people around you, which can amplify disconnects across differences. Remember, your evolutionary path is toward Allyship and Advocacy.

The experience of being seen as scattered, fearful, indecisive, and cynical may not be an uncommon experience for you at Point Six. Your inner narrative may be preventing you from connecting to other people and deprive you of the opportunity to find actual stability and guidance. Addressing your fears and anxiety in order to contribute to your growth is just another step to becoming a whole human being who strives to do better.

If this sounds like you, welcome to the IDEA community. You can be an essential and trustworthy Ally for any cause, and I hope you will join us on our path to heal humanity.

At Point Six, you have a great commitment to truth and courage in your search for connection. If Six energy is where you have determined your place resides on the Enneagram map, discover the journey of how you can harness the gifts from all the different components of the Enneagram: explore your basic desire, basic fear, core motivation, passion/blind spot, fixation/where you get stuck, virtue/your true self, and the Six's connections to Points Three, Nine, Five, and Seven.

Let's go over a few things to prepare you for your journey.

- The Six blind spot, or passion of fear, as it is called in the Enneagram, is a deep distrust of all things: self, people, information, authority, actions, beliefs, behaviors.

- Your Six energy seeks out anything that may render you vulnerable, unstable, or without guidance and support. You look for the worst-case scenario and see all possible outcomes, positive and negative—but you are mainly focused on the negative.

- The intensity that your Six energy brings into everything matters and drives you to fall into a cynical and pessimistic space, which only fuels your fear and anxiety. This conscripted stance is the default to redirect your fears and attempt to remain in your comfort zone, refusing to be open to new ideas and perspectives or to trust anyone who challenges your comfort zone.

- Your unique way of navigating challenges can lead you to a paralyzing pattern of panic, distrust, and helplessness, a concept that is taught as the fixation of cowardice. This is where you get trapped and your fear becomes the guidance for your automatic pilot.

- The outbursts of paranoia and fear to project your anxiety on others is your way of masking your Achilles' heel: *trust.*

- The invitation to move into activation is attainable when you access the gift of inner strength and trust in yourself at Point Three, moving away from fear, anxiety, and cowardice as they are virulent emotions that are blocking your true heart.

- Enter the transformative space of the Body Center at Point Nine, where you can reclaim your focus and courage, taught in the Enneagram as the Six's virtue. This is where you will find your balance and confidence as a Love Warrior, Ally, or Advocate.

SUMMARY OF 6s IN THE IDEA SPACE

The images of historical icons in IDEA work, both positive and negative, can easily serve as a visualization for the people who stand at Point Six: John Lewis, Mindy Kaling, Michael Moore, Jimmy Kimmel, Bono, Spike Lee, J. Edgar Hoover, Jon Stewart, Rush Limbaugh, Prince Harry, Ellen

DeGeneres, Lewis Black, Tom Hanks, Mel Gibson, Joe Biden, George H. W. Bush, and Richard Nixon.

The people who stand at Point Six are the unsung heroes of the IDEA space, but they can also be the shockingly destructive fanatics who sow the seeds of bigotry and bias. The Six energy has distinct variations depending on how the person navigates life through their lens of fear. Point Six represents the courageous voice grounded in truth seeking and sacrifice. These are the people capable of asking the right questions in order to address and solve real problems. The energy we all have access to at Point Six is a courageous reasoning grounded in hard-earned trust, truth, and self-awareness. The polarity that must be managed is allowing space for truth seeking and internalization while remaining present and finding the courage to allow for this trust through connection to the Body, Heart, and Head.

People who possess the dominant energy at Point Six are capable of internalizing multiple perspectives simultaneously and then accessing the solution for the best possible way to proceed. You will find Sixes positioned at the pinnacle of true positive social change, leading with a courageous spirit and an authentically genuine heart. Sixes have an effect on people that is reassuring in regard to social safety and cooperation. People who identify with Point Six are steeped in anxious energy and when they remain present this anxious energy transforms into an engaged process of enacting right action with reflection and persistence. Sixes are the people actively searching for solutions through a multiperspective approach, bridging the divides we face across our differences.

————————

Activation is possible when you engage in doing intentional inner work, continue to educate yourself, and create new connections across differences. You can avail yourself of opportunities to choose love and courage, allowing your actions to manifest as a connection to trust and truth rather than fear and anxiety. In the next few sections, observe the evolution of a true Six Advocate as we move through the unhealthy, average, and healthy levels of development. You may notice yourself in each of the levels; we are all learning and growing, and it is vital to remain present, grounded, and honest as you allow your inner observer to guide you through this process. As you work your way through the descriptors and examples, pay attention to how you react and respond while you process the information about your attitudes, behaviors, and beliefs. This is a fluid process, and as human beings we are capable of accessing the high road and falling into destructive behaviors and old beliefs, all in the same day. The journey here is being open to a new way of navigating your Enneagram energy to resolve the challenges you face across differences and uncover your hidden implicit biases.

PATH OF ACTIVATION

As we illustrate the path of activation from active othering to passive othering and ultimately to Advocacy, the levels of development (unhealthy, average, healthy) demonstrate how the Six energy manifests in the IDEA space. In our exploration of the various stages of activation, we can uncover the complexities of Six energy by observing the nuances of the evolution of the journey.

THE LOOSE CANNON—ACTIVE OTHERING

In the unhealthy levels of development, we find active othering, home to the *Loose Cannon*—a person who consciously acknowledges and reacts based on a distorted reality that is filtered through the Six's blind spot/passion of fear. The blind spot for the Six manifests as a deep distrust in all things: self, people, information, systems, and authority, among other things. In this space we find the incredibly unstable, nihilistic, irrationally belligerent, self-destructive individuals who justify their actions and beliefs from the unhealthy energy of Point Six. Fear, distrust, and paranoia are the primary motivators that distort reality, resulting in disdain for humans who may be perceived as a threat or challenge to their way of life.

For Sixes who reside within the automatic advantage groups of society, disengaging from reactionary bias and bigotry in order to move toward activation as an Advocate or Ally can seem like a threat to the very existence of a Six, and may trigger deeper fear and anxiety—directly opposing the necessary path for growth. At this level, people born into automatic advantage become fearful that their stability or position of perceived power is under threat by the very existence of anyone who appears different from them. These are the people whose toxic anxiety, paranoia, and fear run the agenda. Many unhealthy Sixes hold on to an unquestioned loyalty in favor of unfair and biased systems already in place out of fear of being left on uncertain or shaky ground. Fearful, unstable, delusional, and blindly loyal, these individuals cause deeper divides with their authentic selves and other people. They become irrational and are prone to outbursts of truly detestable behaviors toward "others," spewing vitriol in every direction. They lose control of their inner narrative and allow their fears to pour out through biased, bigoted, and deeply hateful remarks.

People who have developed positional power and fall into the unhealthy levels of development can become paranoid and unsettled, consciously rejecting the people, the circumstances, and the details of their journey. An internal distortion of reality intended to redirect their fears creates an "I know the truth and I trust the system" attitude, which serves as the justification for the dehumanization of anyone who challenges their position or serves as a reminder of their irrational fears. We can experience the concept of horizontal bias at this level, where people who share similar dimensions of diversity can dehumanize other people within the same "category" in order to reaffirm to themselves that they can find stability and security in what they believe to be true and trustworthy. Many Sixes at this level are deeply entrenched in their insecurities and may even hold on to biased, bigoted, and discriminatory beliefs as a way of proving to themselves that they have the answers to "how things should be."

Love Warriors who fall into the role of the *Loose Cannon* become deeply distrustful of anyone who does not share similar dimensions of diversity; they see threats to their existence in everyone and everything. They often find it difficult to address their own internal wounds and trauma; fearing everything that comes their way, they will lash out and perpetually project their fears in every direction. This space is heartbreaking to witness as anger, fear, and a complete lack of trust take over a person's ability to heal or to find compassion for themselves and others.

Fear and Loathing in the Workplace

There are moments in life that we would all like to forget. This story illustrates one of those moments for me. I share it to demonstrate how much damage unbridled fear and anxiety can create.

While going about my daily duties of keeping track of students, I was startled by a knock on my door and the forceful intrusion of an extremely angry man. He was one of my colleagues, so I recognized him immediately, but this was a new side of him I had not experienced. He hesitated, as if he were trying to put order to his words before speaking. When he finally spoke, it was difficult to follow his stream of consciousness discourse. He was telling me that I had no right to be working in a position that was not designated for people like me. "You have stolen my friend's job and there will be hell to pay for this." He went on to say many things that I choose not to write, but I can tell you this: there was hell to pay. I had disturbed the order of things, and someone born into automatic advantage and positional power had been displaced by the unwelcome intrusion of my being. A campaign to have me removed from my position persisted from the moment I entered the building until the day I left. The palpable fear that I had instilled in this group of White-bodied men was beyond anything I had ever experienced, a fact that remains true to this day. I loved the job and cherished the students I worked with, but the environment became increasingly more toxic and dangerous. When I realized that a move and a new assignment was on the horizon, I resigned. It took a great deal of healing to get beyond the pain of living through that much hatred, hostility, and direct bigotry, a process that took me deep into my inner work and into the healing heart of God.

The vengeful actions fueled by anxiety and fear that arise based on a real or perceived threat of loss of stability is truly astonishing to witness. When acted upon at this unhealthy level at Point Six, this caustic force leaves a deep path of destruction in its wake.

THE PESSIMIST—PASSIVE OTHERING

In the state of passive othering, where we experience the varying average levels of development, we find the *Pessimist*. At the unhealthy level of average, some Sixes consciously choose to remain in the pattern of behavior, or fixation of cowardice; they may have the capacity for seeing solutions or accessing the challenges in front of them, but their fear quickly takes over. In this space Sixes are highly suspicious of others and their beliefs. They become reactive and unpredictable, continuously focusing on the threats to their own security. These are the deeply fearful and apathetic humans who refuse to acknowledge opportunities for hope or humanity. In the average levels, we have a space that most people find themselves reverting to as a comfort zone during times of stress—Sixes become critical, panicky, passive-aggressive and sarcastic, fearful of change, and apathy is caused by ambiguity. This area of passive othering is unfortunately a default setting for a lot of Sixes who do not engage in the inner work necessary to gain presence. Most Sixes who find themselves stuck in the role of the *Pessimist* for a long time have difficulty moving past their basic fear of being without support or guidance, which ultimately lands them firmly in a pattern of cowardice, the fixation of an Enneagram Six.

People with automatic advantage who fall into the space of passive othering are oftentimes wounded individuals attempting to conceal their true fears by lashing out with distrustful and irrational beliefs and hollow acts of hatred aimed at anyone who threatens their perception of stability and security. Despite having the innate ability to see the big picture and access all perspectives in question, these *Pessimists* choose to select whatever data supports them in their quest for justifying their own fear. They may become blindly loyal to systems of oppression or authority figures who perpetually enable othering in one form or another; maintaining the status quo seems like a better option than the uncertainty that is inherent with all forms of change. Sometimes they will engage in social justice work, seeking out sources of truth and trust, but they can become paralyzed by the fear of not knowing what to do or who to trust. They may experience moments in which trust and emotional honesty seem like viable options, but their unresolved fear quickly shifts them into a dehumanizing state of paranoia and anxiety.

Sixes who develop positional power and fall into the role of the *Pessimist* can be highly defensive individuals who react and behave in fearful and cynical ways out of fear of losing trust in themselves and their security or having their belief systems questioned. They have undoubtedly fought hard to get to where they are, oftentimes leaving a path of deep divides caused by their distrustful demeanor and the cynical outlook they hold on to as a mask for their own insecurities. By finding stability in certain causes, organizations, or authority figures, these *Pessimists* will try to engage in social justice work but have an unresolved fear of jumping in too far and not being able to return to their comfort zone. These individuals become dismissive and distrustful when faced with challenges across differences where their choices and stability become uncertain. They may experience a moment of truth and courage to step into action, but the fear and cowardice quickly shift them into a deep internalization of their fear and leave them stuck in their heads.

For the Love Warrior who stands at Point Six, this space of inaction and cynicism leads to complications when addressing and healing the internal trauma and wounds caused by fear and cowardice. They can fall into patterns of self-betrayal and painful indifference when the anger and fear take over their hearts. They become enablers in their own dehumanization by ignoring their problems and reverting to a state of helplessness and hopelessness in the face of challenges. The fleeting moments of presence they may experience are quickly replaced with the pessimistic approach of allowing their fear to prevent them from taking action. They may begin to engage in social justice work, seeking answers and uncovering the truth to find a path toward peace and reconnection, but when they neglect to do their inner work the fear of what could happen if they step out of their comfort zone become too much to handle and leaves them paralyzed by uncertainty.

Intrusively Curious and Paralyzed by Cowardice
The earlier a person develops a comfort level with people who have different dimensions of diversity in the sphere of universal

placement, the easier it is to release the fear. In all the years that I've spent doing IDEA work, I have noticed a pattern around fearful responses across differences aligned with late life exposure and the anxiety that rises at Point Six.

My husband and I were on vacation recently and met a couple that seemed to gravitate toward us from the moment we arrived. We chatted for a while, exchanging pleasantries and eventually we set up a dinner date so that we could get to know one another. It was just dinner after all, and I was looking forward to engaging in conversation with some potential new friends who shared our love of traveling. Before my husband and I were even seated, we were inundated with an onslaught of questions. I noticed that this couple appeared a bit anxious and fidgety. The husband quickly chose a seat at the table, sharing that he never sat with his back to the door. The questions continued, and they were all over the place. Not the normal "how many children do you have?" questions, rather they were far more personal, intrusive, and inappropriate. To my surprise they knew the Enneagram and I thought I could use this commonality to steer the conversation back into safe territory. They shared that they both stood at Point Six and played the "you know we ask a lot of questions" card. It was clear that they did not have any Black friends and had not spent very much time outside of their own racial comfort zone. They were curious about my social justice work and even asked if I was a founder of the Black Lives Matter movement. I was polite and understanding in my responses, but I couldn't wait for the evening to end. The icing on this unpalatable cake was the closing comment as we parted ways: "Good luck with that stuff that you do. I just can't imagine being involved with something like that." There were many indications during the course of the evening that we were not socially, politically, or spiritually aligned, but the dismissive "good luck with that" has become a red flag moment for me.

Stuck in the comfort zone of what works to keep the world secure and manageable at this level for the Six, there is very little hope of stepping outside of a comfort zone to extend a helping hand toward healing humanity.

THE HERO—ADVOCACY

The healthy levels of development of Point Six are home to the *Hero*—a courageous and bold advocate for reconnecting the fractures within our global society. These are the people who honor the value in truth and duty; they stand up to destructive forces and challenge the systems designed to create disparities and inequities, all while managing the polarity of fear and integrity. Their courageous spirit and the true force of their inner strength begins to guide them on their journey of becoming a leader in the fight for reconnecting humanity. The anxiety and fear that once paralyzed the Six's activation evolves and makes space for a decisive and truth-seeking champion who recognizes their fear as a wake-up call to take action. They will stand up and fight against any challenge to the stability and security of any human or group; cutting through the false narratives and the negativity with courage and compassion they stand with Love Warriors and anyone who finds themselves pushed to the margins of society.

People who are born into automatic advantage, when operating within the levels of activation and Advocacy, can lead the world to find reconnection, safety, protection, and stability through a deep awareness and a sense of responsibility and trust. A Six who has done the inner work necessary to move into the space of the *Hero* has found courage that comes from challenging the inner narrative and trusting their own inner wisdom. They recognize the power of their discernment in facing challenges across differences and serve as the truth tellers who seek out the reconnections of humanity. Using their position as an Ally, they stand firmly in spaces with Love Warriors and other Allies, rarely backing down from a challenge to justice. The surprising capacity for courage and strength residing in the Six energy can catch people off guard, and encourage them to take action alongside the Six in whatever battle they may be fighting.

The *Heroes* who gain positional power at this level of development are inspiring leaders on the front lines of true historical change in the social justice arena. The unique perspective of facing the margins of society and actively seeking out solutions to regain their power allows these bridge builders of humanity to become inspirations for people who find themselves feeling helpless and paralyzed by fear. These *Heroes* use their position of power to fight for the truth and dismantle the systems causing the obstacles other Love Warriors may be facing. They are courageous and powerful; they will even catch people off guard with their decisive action and take-charge attitude. Many of these Sixes go on to become the notable figures responsible for calling out the forces of destruction by standing on the front lines of the path back to justice and peace.

The Love Warrior who has done the inner work necessary to move into true Advocacy has found a balance in the polarity of fear and integrity. They have addressed their trauma and the true cause of their fear, healed their inner wounds, and found strength in their ability to trust themselves and find trust in others. These Love Warriors can actively seek out solutions to communicate across differences during conflict. They can internalize the challenges in order to find right action and courageously enable dialogue and conflict resolution, which allows them to create a stable foundation for sustainable growth. Oftentimes these Love Warriors can become the fierce and inspirational humans who create mutually beneficial systemic change, leading with a clear focus and a valiant spirit during difficult challenges.

Inner Work and Recipients of Grace

During the immersion phase of my formal education process of the Enneagram, I would make frequent trips to retreat centers for workshops and training sessions. Sometimes in the middle of the woods, most times off the beaten path, but never any place that was well-suited for my stiletto heels—which I still refuse to give up. Familiar faces started showing up; some of us would bond, keep in touch with each other between workshops, and go on to sustain the relationships over many years. One of those relationships for me was with a beautiful Southern woman who stands at Point Six. She has a peaceful, comforting, and loving way about her that actually drew me in. During those years, I had no idea that she and I shared a common passion. Our shared passion manifested as a desire to do something—anything—to not only learn about racism and othering but to be a part of the actual education, healing, and dismantling process of this painful scourge on society. I always enjoy talking to her because she radiates kindness and compassion.

She is courageous, fierce, and unrelenting. I recognize so many of the characteristics of Point Six when I think of her. In all of our interactions, I can feel how powerful and meaningful her presence is to the cause of restoring our connections. Her commitment and loyalty to truth and duty are astounding. She literally makes me weep. She has shown me what White-bodied people are capable of in the role of Ally and Advocate when they tap into their empathy, compassion, and love. She is also an example of what one person's commitment, dedication, loyalty, and love can do to change the environment where they happen to reside. She invited me to her home state and into one of her groups to speak. I discovered that she has managed to be a magnet for others who wanted to "go there" in the discussions that we all need to be having, and she is always able to bring people to the table. Yes, she is an Ally and an Advocate—not self-proclaimed but designated by those of us who society has pushed to the margins. She is that force for good that can sometimes be seen through the fog reaching out her hand to help pull us forward.

The loyalty, love, and Advocacy of a human who stands at Point Six is unparalleled.

At Point Six your greatest strength is your commitment to truth and duty and the ability to sustain a multiperspective balance. You use your innate ability for seeking out the truth to honor and repair the fractures within communities and serve as bridge builders across the collective divides we face as a human race. You become invested in all humans gaining the capacity to know justice and peace, and you are essential for the security, safety, and protection of all humans across the wide spectrum of diversity.

Consider this prework to practice and explore as you prepare yourself for the path of activation as an Ally, Advocate, or Love Warrior:

- The objective time-out and intentional pause at the Three energy in your Heart Center can accelerate your movement with the arrow toward Point Nine.

- Take a moment to pause and breathe in compassion and empathy. Allow the spirited energy of Point Three to serve as a catalyst for your movement into the virtue of courage.

- Going against the arrow to Point Three first gives you the opportunity to quiet your Head Center and drop into your heart to create additional space for emotional honesty.

- As you move to Point Nine in the Body Center, learn to still the "committee in your head" and get grounded in the present. Connect to your body and pay attention to the sensations to establish your strength as a balanced human being.

- In the Body Center, begin to address the underlying cause of your fear and anxiety. Stay present in the moment and have the strength to stand in the uncertainty; only then will you find a path to move through it and find your courage.

- Allow yourself to find trust and inner guidance in your own being and step into your true power as a fierce visionary for truth seeking paths back to justice and equity.

ENNEAGRAM
POINT 7

Too much self-centered attitude brings isolation.
Result: loneliness, fear, anger. The extreme self-centered attitude
is the source of suffering.

—DALAI LAMA

I discovered that joy is not the negation of pain, but rather
acknowledging the presence of pain and feeling happiness in spite of it.

—LUPITA NYONG'O

We have the tendency to run away from suffering
and to look for happiness. But, in fact, if you have not suffered,
you have no chance to experience real happiness.

—THICH NHAT HANH

OVERVIEW

Humans strive to find happiness, to have the freedom of choice in most situations, and to have the ability to access joy and hopefulness. These are things that seem to be basic human attributes, but for people who stand at Point Seven, these attributes live at the very core of your being. The Seven is known in the Enneagram community as the *Enthusiast* or the *Optimist*. In the IDEA space we experience this unique energy in distinctly different ways. Sevens can show up with the energy of the *Campaigner*, the *Escapist*, and the *Hedonist*. IDEA work is the place to utilize your optimistic perspective and visionary capabilities to bring people together across differences with love, compassion, and natural charisma.

If the dominant energy you experience is at Point Seven, you may feel compelled by a need to seek out fulfillment and satisfaction in whatever form that may take for you personally. You often experience a forward motion that keeps you from falling too deep into any uncomfortable emotional state. This progressive outlook on life can be a double-edged sword: an enterprising vision or an avoidance tactic. Optimism, curiosity, versatility, freedom, and a general appreciation for seeking out experiences, create the comfort zone for you. Many people who stand at Point Seven navigate life by avoiding pain and suffering, oftentimes feeling the need to redirect their attention as a way of maintaining their freedom of choice. If you resonate with this concept, you may have a deep desire to stay positive and take in all that life has to offer by overindulging and bouncing from experience to experience, never actually becoming present to the reality of what you are experiencing. Despite your constant momentum and planning for future experiences, you may still be able to find joy in or bring joy to almost anything you do.

Point Seven exemplifies the desire we all have to be happy or find happiness and contentment in our lives and in the lives of others. At Point Seven, your gaze is automatically drawn to finding an optimistic perspective in any situation. If you are an *Enthusiast* or an *Optimist*, you can usually sense negativity or suffering from a distance and either shift the situation for a positive outcome through vision and innovation or avoid it completely and remove yourself from the equation. The lens through which you view the world is one of constant opportunity and freedom, an inspiring gift you unknowingly bestow upon the rest of us. Sevens are capable of bringing an enthusiastic energy to life and leading with a "first-responder mentality": they are the first through the door, ready to tackle the tough stuff or at least attempt to bring hope and joy in some form or another.

At your best you are often an evolving Ally, Advocate, and an optimistic and motivational energy for all humans to appreciate. You seem to find the good in anything, even when others may not be able to. However, the deep fear of being deprived of your freedom or trapped in pain and suffering may cause you to avoid dealing with conflict, situations, or people who challenge your freedom of choice. While radiating an energy that manifests the appearance of a truly happy and joyful human being, your fear and pain at Point Seven is equally as powerful as your joy. When you begin to look inward and deal with your real pain and trauma, there can be a deeply wounded and repressed human sometimes hidden under a buoyant exterior. If this is resonating with you, remember this: your search for happiness and contentment will be a hollow victory if you never become still enough to acknowledge what you have buried deep down and are now trying to conceal. It is a counterproductive way of moving through the world that can lead you to develop a strong aversion to anything even remotely uncomfortable, which only amplifies your disconnects across differences. Remember, your evolutionary path is toward Allyship and Advocacy.

The experience of being considered a person who lacks compassion, sensitivity, or consideration may be a common experience for you at Point Seven. Your aversion to suffering may lead you to sidestep true compassion and empathy, a maneuver that many find cold and heartless. This is a disconnect that can be addressed and reestablished through presence and stillness. Even if your actions are well-intentioned, you may be unaware of the true impact of your words and behaviors when you try to remove yourself from discomfort or conflict. Aligning your intent with your impact is just another step to become a whole human being who strives to do better.

If this sounds like you, welcome to the IDEA community. You can be an essential Ally for any cause, and I hope you will join us on our path to heal humanity.

You have a tremendous capacity for versatility and optimism. If Seven energy is where you have determined your place resides on the Enneagram map, discover the journey of how you can harness the gifts from all the different components of the Enneagram: explore your basic desire, basic fear, core motivation, passion/blind spot, fixation/where you get stuck, virtue/your true self, and the Seven's connections to Points One, Five, Six, and Eight.

Let's go over a few things to prepare you for your journey.

- The Seven blind spot, or passion of gluttony as it is called in the Enneagram, is a deep desire to take on life and experience anything and everything it has to offer.

- Your Seven energy seeks more experiences, more fun, more distractions, more of everything.

- The intensity that your Seven energy brings into everything matters and drives you to push the limits in your life, never actually committing to one thing at a time or letting yourself experience something fully. This conscripted stance is the default to never let anything trap you or take away your freedom of choice.

- Your unique way of navigating challenges can lead you to deflection of the authentic self and a redirection of focus on anything that allows you to feel satisfied, a concept that is taught as the fixation of planning. This is where you get trapped and your fear becomes the guidance for your automatic pilot.

- The hyperactivity, perpetual motion forward, and the refusal to remain present or still for too long is your way of masking your Achilles' heel: *addressing your deeply repressed internal trauma.*

- The invitation to move into activation is attainable when you access the gift of grounded energy at Point One, moving away from fear, gluttony, and planning as they are distractions that are blocking access to your true heart and authentic self.

- Enter the transformative space at Point Five, where you can reclaim your sobriety, taught in the Enneagram as the Seven's virtue. This is where you will find your balance and focus as a Love Warrior, Ally, or Advocate.

SUMMARY OF 7s IN THE IDEA SPACE

The images of historical icons in IDEA work, both positive and negative, can easily serve as a visualization for the people who stand at Point Seven: the Dalai Lama, John F. Kennedy, Eddie Murphy, Elton John, Nas X, Jim Carrey, Ram Dass, Leonardo DiCaprio, Howard Stern, Jeff Bezos, George W. Bush, Leni Riefenstahl, Lily Tomlin, Betty White, and Edward VIII, Duke of Windsor.

As in all aspects of life, the IDEA space is brought to life by people who stand at Point Seven. These are the people capable of using their infectiously positive outlook on life to enable others to seek happiness and joy, even when things are looking hopeless. The energy we all have access to at Point Seven is an optimistic approach to tackling the tough stuff. Though Sevens generally avoid pain and suffering at all costs, when they remain present, they are capable of using their stillness to advocate for the acknowledgment of others' pain, suffering, and experiences. The polarity here that must be managed is honoring the need for freedom (a freedom of choice) while staying grounded in stillness through internal reflection and inquiry.

People who possess the dominant energy at Point Seven are sometimes capable of gracefully using humor to defuse a situation (though they often tiptoe the line of alleviating humor and tactless humor) and often bring a spark of joy to others in their time of need. You can find Sevens at the front lines of the battle for reclaiming and rebuilding the connections to our humanity. When operating from a healthy and grounded space through slowing down and remaining present, Sevens can serve as the connections across diverse communities, bringing all different types of people together in light, joy, and love. Sevens have an effect on people that is uplifting, inspiring, and optimistic. People who identify with Point Seven are the campaigners and first responders in the IDEA world, a position for which we should all be deeply grateful.

———

Activation is possible when you engage in doing intentional inner work, continue to educate yourself, and create new connections across differences. You can avail yourselves of opportunities to choose love and presence, allowing your actions to manifest as engagement and connection instead of deflection and avoidance. In the next few sections, observe the evolution of a true Seven Advocate as we move through the unhealthy, average, and healthy levels of development. You may notice yourself in each of the levels; we are all learning and growing, and it is vital to remain present, grounded, and honest as you allow your inner observer to guide you through this process. At Point Seven, this journey can be especially "triggering" if you have deeply repressed wounds; it is important to remain present to your emotions and allow yourself the grace and compassion to heal. As you work your way through the descriptors and examples, pay attention to how you react and respond while you process the information about your attitudes, behaviors, and beliefs. This is a fluid process, and as human beings we are capable of accessing the high road and falling into destructive behaviors and old beliefs, all in the same day. The journey here is being open to a new way of navigating your Enneagram energy to resolve the challenges you face across differences and uncover your hidden implicit biases.

PATH OF ACTIVATION

As we illustrate the path of activation from active othering to passive othering and ultimately to Advocacy, the levels of development (unhealthy, average, healthy) demonstrate how the Seven energy manifests in the IDEA space. In our exploration of the various stages of activation, we can uncover the complexities of Seven energy by observing the nuances of the evolution of the journey.

THE HEDONIST—ACTIVE OTHERING

In the unhealthy levels of development, we find active othering, where the *Hedonist* lurks—a person who consciously acknowledges and reacts based on a distorted reality that is filtered through the Seven's blind spot/passion of gluttony. The blind spot for the Seven manifests as a deep desire to take on more of whatever life has to offer in order to avoid conflict, pain, or feeling trapped. In this space we find the extremely narcissistic, unstable, insensitive, cynical, vindictive, and delusional individuals who justify their actions and beliefs from the unhealthy energy of Point Seven. They often inadvertently become trapped in their self-inflicted unhappiness and pain, and feeling helpless they react impulsively and erratically to avoid any real emotional honesty. Fear, denial, and the repression of unhealed wounds are the primary motivators that distort reality, resulting in a disdain for anything that feels like a challenge to their happiness or freedom. This disconnect may trigger the Seven's deep fear of becoming present to themselves, leading to an irresponsible pattern of acting out in panic and heedlessness, which is only masking their own unhealed wounds that they refuse to truly acknowledge.

For Sevens born into automatic advantage who fall into the space of active othering, disengaging from reactionary bias and bigotry in order to activate as an Ally or Advocate can trigger deep fear and anxiety around feeling trapped or deprived. In search of whatever they believe will bring them happiness and satisfaction, the *Hedonist* with automatic advantage becomes a self-absorbed vessel for consuming anything that will serve as a distraction for the deeply repressed pain they refuse to acknowledge. When presented with the pain of others who face being pushed to the margins of society, the Seven can become triggered and use their unhealthy energy to dismiss, demean, and dehumanize anyone or anything that forces them to brush up against the darkness lurking inside of them. They may make jokes and point out the pain of others as a way to deflect the responsibility. They have to access true compassion as a decent human being, a considerable challenge for unhealthy Sevens at this level.

People who develop positional power at this level of development can become deeply repressed and cruel to other humans. They forget their own struggle and often dehumanize others on the same path, making tactless jokes at the expense of others. Their tendency toward indifference and apathy increases as they drop deeper into the unhealthy levels. The callousness and detachment create a hotbed for hatred, bigotry, and bias to flourish unchecked. The "not my problem" mentality sets in and becomes the justification for the indifference they harbor toward the struggle of other humans. At this level, *Hedonists* with positional power oftentimes feel a deep anger and misdirected fear around the injustices they had to overcome in order to get to wherever they may be, and they misdirect these emotions onto others who mirror their own struggle. Dehumanizing behaviors become second nature and pollute the Sevens ability to find compassion for themselves and others. These are the individuals completely unwilling to admit that they have held on to some very painful memories and trauma around their experiences of being othered. The wounds they hold on to fester from within and allow them to misdirect this pain and suffering outward as a way of denying and repressing their truth.

Love Warriors who fall into these unhealthy levels of development are more than likely deeply traumatized individuals who, by their very nature of being a Seven and facing oppression, live in a constant state of denial around the amount of trauma they are holding within their bodies. They deflect their pain with self-deprecating humor, never allowing themselves to drop too deep into their pain. They become deeply apathetic at the sheer volume of suffering in the world, theirs included, and they completely reject any opportunity to deal with any of it. They often find it nearly impossible to address their own internal wounds or trauma when they consciously choose to remain in the unhealthy levels of development. This space is utterly heartbreaking to witness as anger, hopelessness, apathy, and fear take over a person's ability to heal or find compassion for themselves and others. The fun-loving, joyful human the world was lucky to have is now a shell of themselves, knocked down by the onslaught of daily indignities.

Freedom, Fear, and Collateral Damage

After 9/11 I found myself doing a lot of work with a nonprofit that worked with AIDS patients. I was working with this organization to help their team become more respectful of one another's differences. The director stood at Point Seven. This group really had a lot to hold up under a heavy load. The energy of the entire city was affected, and those who were subjected to marginalization were recipients of more intense levels of discrimination. People struggling with mental illness and homelessness were characteristically invisible as they were not the priority. The same was true of AIDS patients and many other disenfranchised groups. 9/11 brought out the best of my city and the worst simultaneously.

The team I was brought in to help was working tirelessly to create space for their clients in a city that was overwhelmed with grief. I spent many long hours encouraging and helping the team to continue to fight for resources to keep their work alive. Then the director threw a grenade into the team dynamic. After 9/11 he made some truly horrific comments about the Muslim community. It began with little comments aimed at a few of the team members who had Middle Eastern surnames. The comments were floated in a jocular manner, but their intent could not be overlooked. He took every opportunity to remind the team that Muslims had destroyed the city and they could not be trusted. The team was a rich and diverse mixture of human beings, and the director's comments were not aligned with the core values of the team and the organization.

They turned to me for help to intervene in this particularly difficult situation. We participated in a circling discussion intervention. No matter how many times we gave him the opportunity to view his reactions from a different perspective, he wouldn't budge. During our attempts to try to help him see how his actions and beliefs were harmful and how they were being received by the rest of the team, he would consistently make excuses. "You guys know I'm a Seven, I don't mean any harm. You know that right?"

Many people left that organization because of his blatant othering. He never stopped the behavior, and when he was eventually held accountable, he had no empathy for the team members that he targeted daily. They were already facing blatant othering from people who judged them only by their names. The dynamic tore the team apart. He eventually bounced on to a leadership role with an emergency response organization. On his way out the door he told the remaining team members that he wouldn't miss them because they had become a real drag to work with.

At the core of this unhealthy behavior is fear and anxiety. Fear that the actions of one group of people represented the ultimate fear of the Seven: loss of freedom. This core fear ultimately destroyed the benevolent and positive work of an entire team.

At the unhealthy level of Point Seven, there is a rigidity and insensitivity that comes from the energy fueled by anxiety and fear. It is from this stance that they seek vengeance without remorse for collateral damage.

THE ESCAPIST—PASSIVE OTHERING

The *Escapist* resides in the toxic atmosphere of passive othering where we experience varying average levels of development. In the unhealthy levels of average, we find a space where some Sevens consciously choose to remain in the pattern of behavior, or fixation, of planning; constantly looking for the next best thing, they are always moving forward, never looking back in their search for whatever they believe may bring them happiness. In this space Sevens are scattered and tactless, unwilling to engage authentically in any real emotional honesty, disengaged and dismissive, self-absorbed, fearful and apathetic. When we move to the average level of development, we have a space that most people find themselves reverting to as a comfort zone during times of stress—Sevens become emotionally stunted; in deflecting their authentic self, they are now self-seeking and uncomfortable with engaging or remaining present in any space that has conflict, and apathy is caused by the anxiety of feeling trapped. This area of passive othering is unfortunately a default setting for a lot of Sevens who haven't engaged in the inner work. Sevens who have been stuck in the role of the *Escapist* for a long time find it difficult to move past their basic fear of feeling trapped or deprived of freedom, which ultimately lands them firmly in their fixation of planning.

For people born into automatic advantage, the energy at this level fosters a deeply disconnected and apathetic human being who is constantly looking for any distraction from the pain they witness or endure on a daily basis. They detach from actively engaging in communicating across differences, oftentimes avoiding spaces where there may be conversations around race, religion, politics, or discrimination. They may have a tendency to use inappropriate humor to deflect emotional honesty or connection and, more often than not, will completely cut out anyone or anything that causes them to confront challenging or difficult situations. They become truly apathetic at the sheer volume of suffering in the world and feel helpless and hopeless. During fleeting moments of presence, the *Escapist* may experience a calming sensation and find a clear focus on how to engage in the work, but the fear of getting trapped and not being able to escape the pain and suffering involved in this kind of work quickly shifts them back into their deflection and evasion tactics.

People who develop positional power at this level of development can become deeply repressed and cruel to other humans. They forget their own struggle and often dehumanize others on the same path. Their tendency toward detachment and apathy increases as they drop deeper into the unhealthy levels. The callousness and indifference create a hotbed for hatred, bigotry, and bias to flourish unchecked. The "not my problem" mentality sets in and becomes the justification for dehumanizing behaviors they use to support their aversion to emotional honesty. They may experience a flicker of hope and focus on how to engage in this work when they begin to find presence, but it is short-lived as they become still enough to see the pain they have caused themselves and others by being detached and self-absorbed.

When operating from this space, the Love Warrior *Escapist* can become disconnected from their emotional capability and use their optimism and innovative vision for self-serving purposes. They find it difficult to address their own internal wounds and trauma; fearing the mere thought of waking up to the true cause of the deep pain they revert to a state of denial. The fleeting moments of presence they may experience are quickly replaced with the pessimistic approach of "numbing out" with distractions and diversions from their authentic self. Just as with the unhealthy levels of Seven, the average levels also deflect their pain with self-deprecating humor, never allowing themselves to drop too deep into their pain.

Feet to the Fire

As I reflect on my journey with my ride or die friend, I recognize that we have seen each other through some really tough times. We are two friends who are very different if you look at us from our spheres of universal placement. If the world had its say, we shouldn't be friends, much less have the bond that we share. Despite our differences, we have stayed true to our friendship and usually try to meet at least annually and spend some quality time together.

This last decade in the world of IDEA has been a very heavy lift for me personally. Through it all my friend and I still try to connect a few times a year. We have had more discussions about race, religion, spirituality, and gender and sexual diversity in the past two years than ever before. Ever the optimist, looking forward to our next trip together she would make all the plans and for a few days we would leave our family, other friends, responsibilities, and the weight of the world behind. No guilt, no shame. It worked beautifully, until it didn't. The weight of the world got heavier for both of us, just in different ways. We met during one of the darkest periods of my life, and I can honestly say she was the person who helped me through it. She would lighten my mood with laughter and optimism, bringing me back in from the darkness. When the proverbial shit hit the fan in her life, it was no laughing matter. I was there for her. No questions asked. That's what we do. We show up for each other.

As the years passed, the reality that I had not yet come to terms with was beginning to surface. In my life it wasn't about one day or one event, but rather an accumulation of daily indignities that were grinding me down. There had been multiple occasions where things had occurred and we talked it out on the phone, but somewhere between 2016 and 2020 something changed. There was undeniable anger, hurt, and pain that was trapped in my body. In 2020, when we got together for our annual girls trip I was exhausted, discouraged, and angry. This time there was no escaping. I brought the full weight of my pain, my disappointment, and my anger. My dear friend was about to have a very different experience with me, one where I held her feet to the fire.

We had some really hard conversations as she shared how she couldn't bear to look at the "race stuff." I shared that I couldn't bear to live it. When the killing of George Floyd made its way into our homes, I received calls from friends and acquaintances all over the world. They were check-ins. Some wanted to know if there was a missing piece to the story while others just wanted to know if my family and I were okay. My BFF was not one of those callers, and I suddenly realized how much that hurt me. I shared those feelings with her. I told her that I expected more from her and that if our friendship really mattered, then I needed to know that she actually had my back across the racial divide, that she would stand with me across differences in the same way she stood by when life brought "normal" challenges to my door. There were some very intense moments during our conversations that week. I let her see the full extent of the pain that I had kept locked away for years.

We have a friendship that is built on love, support, common ground, and disparate viewpoints. Our conversations have never been just fluff or superficial nonsense. We have been a port in the storm for one another. I suffered many storms in silence until they became hurricanes. It was hard. She was uncomfortable and wanted to understand, and I could sense her trying to gain solid footing on what was rapidly turning into very slippery ground.

I hoped with all my heart that I had gotten through to her. This is where the ride or die is determined. Recognition of her own passive othering (that I had to own some level of culpability for) was followed by her words: "I just didn't know."

Of all the things that I share in this book, this may be one of the most important takeaways: People who love you need to be willing to stand with you in this Love War for the soul of humanity. What happens to those of us who are placed in categories of being less than, known as othering, affects everyone. While it may have been created by a dominant white male societal norm, it is not just affecting the groups of people who are targeted. The apathy, entitlement, numbness, self-absorption, and hypocrisy that invades the beings who are part of the dominant norm erodes the very core of their humanity. It was from this place of love that I spoke my unfiltered truth to my friend, and hopefully when you access this within yourself, you will do the same. Those of us who were born into the status of Love Warriors don't always choose to share our pain with everyone. We also need places to go and people we can talk to where we can breathe and feel safe.

Many people get stuck at this level at every Point on the Enneagram. At Point Seven the challenge is waking up in the middle of the love battle and choosing to engage . . . or not.

THE CAMPAIGNER—ADVOCACY

The healthy energy of Point Seven is home to the *Campaigner*—an inspiring and optimistic leader of the movement toward equity and justice for all humans. These are the people willing to face difficult situations and stand firmly as Allies and Advocates with principled focus and resilience, leading with presence and profound vision in the face of divisiveness, confrontation, and conflict. A Seven who has done the inner work necessary to move into the space of the *Campaigner* has found stillness and sobriety in the ability to access the authentic self and take right action with laser focus rather than a scattered approach to avoiding pain. The need to find outlets for deflecting pain in the hopes of maintaining a false sense of freedom is transformed into a warning system for the Seven to wake up and become present in order to achieve activation as an authentic Advocate. The extraordinary ability to find common ground and connections across differences with grace and consideration is truly astonishing when a Seven steps in the role of the *Campaigner.*

People who are born into automatic advantage, when operating within the levels of activation and Advocacy, can lead the world together through the remembering of connection, unity, and oneness. This requires a deep awareness and a sense of responsibility and accountability. A Seven who has done the inner work necessary to move into the space of the *Campaigner* has found the ability to take right action and remain present without the fear of being trapped by disruptive influences. They recognize the power of their presence in facing challenges across differences and serve as the unifying crusader of the reconnections to humanity. Using their position as an Ally, they stand firmly in spaces with Love Warriors and other Allies, rarely backing down from anything. The capacity for grounded presence and strength residing in the Seven energy can catch people off guard, and encourage them to take action alongside the Seven in whatever battle they may be fighting. Having a *Campaigner* as an Ally and an Advocate on this journey can bring hope and encouragement to those feeling lost and hopeless; they have a reassuring presence that makes people feel connected and hopeful.

The *Campaigners* who gain positional power at this level of development are inspiring leaders on the front lines of true historical change in the social justice arena. The unique perspective of facing the margins of society and using their impactful presence to regain their power makes these individuals the inspirational and outspoken crusaders for justice and equity. The healing energy they begin to embody can connect them to other Love Warriors who need healing and allow them to serve as a guide for transformative experiences. They become motivational role models and paragons for people who find themselves feeling hopeless and abandoned by bringing love, light, and joy even in the darkest of times.

The Love Warrior who has done the inner work necessary to move into true Advocacy, has woken up to reality, addressed their trauma, begun to heal their inner wounds, and found strength in their ability to remain present as a *Campaigner* of humanity. When Sevens have done the inner work, they can begin to heal the inner wounds that prevent presence. They become self-aware of the real reasons behind why they avoid pain, and they can let go of the fear of the tough stuff. These Love Warriors are capable of bringing an enthusiastic energy to life, leading with an open heart and a laser focus on creating real change. Many of the *Campaigner* Love Warriors who go down in history as icons in the social justice world are the light we cling to in the darkest moments. Their presence sends ripples out into the world, bringing joy and hope to millions of people.

Offspring

As we journey through life there is one thing we can be certain of: some things will change. The small changes we learn to expect and roll with, but the bigger ones require time, patience, and sometimes Divine intervention to keep us grounded and steady.

I am a mother of three. My oldest and youngest children are male, and my middle child who was identified as female at birth, formerly my daughter, is nonbinary.

Tiffany has kept the name given at birth, however their pronouns are no longer "she/her/hers," but rather "they/them/theirs." My child, now an adult who jokes that they are my "offspring," is one of the great loves of my life. It's really hard to put all that they are into a few paragraphs in a book, but I don't have to as they have authored five books on the topic of Diversity, Inclusion, and Equity (DEI), and implicit bias.

They came into the world quite ceremoniously as it was only by the grace of God that we both survived. Inquisitive, full of life, and with white lightning coming out of their head, this humxn has forged a path of innovation, equity, and inclusion that has brought them squarely into the full power of Love Warrior, Ally, and Advocate. Standing firmly and proudly at Point Seven, they began their journey into the DEI world working beside me. A quick study and natural fit for the work, it became clear that they were ready to take the world to task.

There was a passion that drove my offspring to make space for people who could hear the beat of a different drum. Recognizing the many areas of marginalization that exist, they made it a mission to use their positional power to transform workplace culture. Tiffany is fearless, persistent, funny, and fierce. Their TedX Talk on the power of privilege is still a go-to resource for millions of people. If you haven't seen it, I suggest you look it up.

I have watched Tiffany focus the abundant energy at Point Seven to bring intentional presence and show up in a hurting world with spirit, perseverance, and vivacity. They do not step away from the painful spaces for fear of being trapped, but rather they harness their God-given ability to bring light to the darkness.

The spontaneous pull toward joy and freedom with the authentic goal of honoring all of humanity is a beacon to follow at Point Seven. It is a reminder that life is not intended to only be suffering and pain, but rather growth and joy.

At Point Seven your greatest strengths are your optimism and your inner drive to find joy and light in any situation. You use your infectious positive energy and natural tenacity to advocate for the acknowledgment of others' pain and suffering and serve as bridge builders for people from all different backgrounds. The extraordinary ability to find common ground and connections across differences with grace and consideration is truly astonishing when a Seven steps into the full power of their presence.

Consider this prework to practice and explore as you prepare yourself for the path of activation as an Ally, Advocate, or Love Warrior:

- The objective time-out and intentional pause at Point One in your Body Center allows you to move toward an objective grounded perspective and can accelerate your movement with the arrow toward Point Five, where you can remain present, focused and productive.

- Take a moment to pause and slow down. Find a method of reflection, meditation, or mindfulness that works for you.

- Breathe in and embody peace through internal reflection and explore the positive qualities at Point One. You can begin to unravel your unexplored wounds and trauma in a safe and grounded space where the fear of becoming trapped in the pain will dissipate and allow you to move through your emotions with perseverance and profound clarity.

- In the Head Center learn to still the rumination about "what is to come" and take stock of "what is here now." At Point Five reflect on what you can do where you are and find a way to stay in this space. You have an abundance of wisdom and capability to become a truly effective Advocate for reconnection.

- While there are no direct connections to the energies in the Heart Center, Sevens can pick up the connections in various ways. Point Two can be accessed from your wing at Point Eight or your connection to Point One. Point Three can be accessed from your wing at Point Six. And Point Four can be accessed from your line to Points One and Five. Explore your connections to the energies at these Points and develop the awareness to access the Heart Center energy in order to align the three centers.

  - Point Two: compassion and empathy for yourself and others

  - Point Three: inner drive to accomplish great things with an appreciation for emotional truthfulness

  - Point Four: emotional honesty to manage your inner wounds and find compassion for yourself to heal

Part III

THE
ACTIVATION

Chapter 8

CONNECTING
THE CENTERS FOR
ACTIVATION

Every Point of the Enneagram is contained within our own being. We lead with a single dominant Enneagram energy that is identifiable based on the unmistakable connection that we have to the basic desire, basic fear, passion, fixation, and the virtues of our personality structures. Additionally, the movement between the lines and arrows of our Point or type allows us to see more clearly; that is, to engage our inner observer in uncovering what we are really up to.

In our lifelong quest to become balanced beings, we learn the necessity of the unfolding of layers and legacies that help us gain access to our full authentic selves. An essential factor in that unfolding is to be able to recognize and align all three centers: Body, Heart, Head. When we fail to do the inner work necessary to become the person we were created to be, to remember when we were whole, we are out of alignment with one or more of these centers. Without the balance of our three centers, we exist as incomplete beings navigating life without embodying the fullness of what it means to be alive and fully present. If we only have the experience of one, or even just two, of our centers we perceive life through a biased and skewed lens. Activation of our three centers is part of our inner work as Love Warriors, Allies, and Advocates; when we do not have the experience of being fully present, we are not living but rather existing as fractured incomplete beings who cannot defend, protect, or heal ourselves or humanity.

ACTIVATION DOES NOT GUARANTEE ALLYSHIP

In order to activate as an authentic Ally and Advocate for all of humanity, we must engage in our own ongoing journey of inner work and personal healing. This journey is not an overnight process. You cannot just pick up a few books on inclusion, diversity, equity, and anti-racism and pin on your Ally badge. Additional exploration into the historical evolution of othering, bias, and bigotry, and the global nature of the marginalization of people may empower you to say, "I get it; now I'm an Ally." *You are not qualified to give yourself that designation.* When you declare yourself an Ally, you are using the term as an indication of your place in this work as it pertains to feelings of anger, shame, and fear. When self-proclaimed, the title "Ally" can become a thinly veiled self-promoting moniker that serves as a false internalized identifier rather than the action it represents. Allyship is not a permanent state of being, it is not a self-appointed title, and it is not a fixed reward for any one action. You temporarily fulfill authentic Allyship for marginalized groups based on the actions you take in the moment and the choices you make to utilize your position to dismantle systemic othering. To be an Ally requires maintaining a delicate balance between persistent and intentional effort in order to uphold the valuable responsibility it represents. A true Ally is a person who does not strive to maintain the title but rather endeavors to remove the very need for the title.

We must collectively dismantle systemic racism, sexism, ableism, and all forms of discrimination, to include the overarching practices put in place to keep people pushed to the margins of society. It begins with people acting in solidarity and taking one action at a time to address the ingrained inequities within our cultures. These actions build upon each other and foster the progress toward growth and equity. You become an Ally when the results of your intentional efforts keep you moving forward for the Love Warriors.

The people who are affected and lifted up by your efforts will recognize you as an Ally. As you strengthen your resolve in Allyship, you move closer to true Advocacy. Becoming an Advocate for people in the margins is to step fully into your power as an Ally; to use your privilege and positional power in society to bring the people pushed to the margins back into a position of equal power and privilege, allow space for everyone's voices to be heard, and strive to dismantle the systems of oppression. If we aspire to become Allies and step into true Advocacy, we must be willing to make mistakes, to fail and admit it, to grow, to educate ourselves, and to do better. We must engage in the difficult conversations with grace and respect and learn how to do better from the people whom our actions affect, without tokenizing people or distorting the process to satiate feelings of internal guilt or shame.

If you are ready and willing, your growth and journey toward authentic Advocacy begins with the intentional alignment of your three centers.

CONNECTING THE PIECES OF THE ENNEAGRAM + IDEA WORK

As we continue on the journey through the Enneagram, we can achieve temporary alignment of the Body, Heart, and Head Centers, and then experience a tangible sense of enlightenment that defies articulation. We begin to understand the inner workings that are hard-wired and reveal the motivation behind our actions, beliefs, and behaviors. In some cases, the wisdom gained is used to become more conscious of our own self-awareness and cultivates a deeper experience of our personal spirituality. While useful, this work can become overly self-serving and limited in its capacity to bring true connection. This is where inner work requires expansion.

It is necessary for us to go deeper to unravel the biases interwoven within our unique being and our own dominant Enneagram Point. When we allow ourselves to look at how each of us holds on to specific messages from our early influences around value and othering, we can explore whether or not these messages are aligned with honoring the humanity of each individual. The retention of these messages or the inquiry into them, when linked to the core motivation and basic fear of our dominant Enneagram Point, reveals a different level of understanding around what our ego agendas are up to. This is where we have the opportunity to examine whether or not we have alignment of our three centers.

The confrontations and occurrences of bias, bigotry, and hatred are where we often experience the disconnect within a self-proclaimed "enlightened" individual. The wisdom of the Enneagram is used to gain a deeper level of the perspective of self, but what is lacking is the wisdom that needs to be employed within us when we are in relationship with others. We can learn from our Enneagram work to change our behaviors and beliefs toward other humans. The deep understanding anyone gains about themselves is very limited in its utility if it does not extend to how we treat other humans, or to address what gets in the way of accessing compassion and kindness when trapped by the passion and fixation of personality.

There are certainly circumstances where any of us can be triggered by particular actions, behaviors, and beliefs. If we engage and allow our inner observer to show us how internalized messages and familial biases and bigotries have crept their way into our psyche, we can call upon compassion and empathy for ourselves and others. These conflicts and challenges filtered through the heart can provide us the opportunity to pause for reflection and true emotional honesty. Most of us are stuck in our heads or ready to spring into action based on the unconscious biases and messages that affect how our brains and bodies process and then react. We often bypass our hearts when dealing with challenges—especially across our differences.

We have all seen contentious scenarios of heated conflict played out by individuals in public; for instance, the relentless dehumanizing actions and beliefs aimed at the gender and sexual diversity community. Many of these occurrences have infiltrated our political and social systems and reinforced the divisions we face in regard to the wide spectrum of our gender and sexual diversity. Unfortunately, many people focus on these differences as a way to demean, objectify, and dismiss anyone who differs from what they consider to be "normal." The underlying lesson in all of these instances is the reason behind why people treat others the way they do.

Additionally, we have witnessed the recent phenomenon, by way of social media and cell phones, of instances of calling the police on a Black family for being at a community pool, being in a neighborhood that some-one has deemed "not theirs to be in," or having a family barbeque in a park. Over the years, the use of certain names to describe these individuals and unfortunate circumstances have evolved as a way to address the rampant bigotry perpetrated against people of color. The terms "Miss Ann," "Becky," and "Karen" have been adopted to put a universal label on racist and big-oted actions of countless individuals. These terms, most recently "Karen," are used to call out the actions, typically of White-bodied females who have created, fabricated, or reacted to a situation where the immediate response was to accuse, report, demean, and disrespect another person or people based on their skin color. While the terms "Miss Ann," "Becky," and "Karen" have become offensive and disparaging names for White-bodied women, we can still use these situations as a learning opportunity for growth and reconnection.

This phenomenon of calling out individuals for feeling entitled or al-lowed to devalue another human being based on a dimension of their di-versity is merely the tip of the iceberg.

We have all heard a racial slur, sexist name, or derogatory term hurled at someone who falls into the category of "other" in some way. Many of these terms fade with time or with the persistence of people who have the power to remove the stigma from the name in some form or fashion. The manner in which labels and stereotypes evolve over time is deeply embedded in the social construct of race. This is a topic that could fill another book.

While many of these derogatory terms have changed over time, one in particular has unfortunately endured and continues to wound, insult, and disrespect Black-bodied people. The well-known and too often used word is *nigger*. It is a word that I heard directed toward me as a child, and on any given day it may return with the same venomous impact. I personally do not use the word, hoping to halt the devastating effect that it has on my spirit. I refuse to contribute to perpetuating this vile term because it has lasted for centuries and it seems to never change, go away, or be-come any less damaging. Just this morning, I woke up to a video shared with me by multiple people. It was taken at the 2022 Olympics in Bei-jing, China. There was a crowd of people heckling Black athletes as they were getting out of a vehicle. The crowds got louder as each Black athlete stepped off the bus. The intensity with which the word spewed from their mouths escalated with each footstep. The enunciation of the word from the local crowd in Beijing made it sound somewhat unfamiliar, and yet it was still recognizable. The hatred and violence entangled in the word was clear. The crowd screamed it over and over again, demanding that these Black-bodied athletes get out of their country. Anyone who does not recognize the global nature of bias, bigotry, and hatred is residing in a deep state of slumber.

When we approach conflicts around our different dimensions of diversity, many people revert to an "us versus them" or a "me versus you" perspective. The predisposition toward disconnection has become a natural way of navigating challenges for most of us, and if we are to evolve as a species we must be willing to acknowledge our connectedness as a single human race. Did the crowd of local people in China recognize the sanctimonious nature of denigrating Black athletes? Where did the motivation come from to disrespect these particular athletes coming to compete in the 2022 Olympics?

I experienced a moment where the pieces came together in a disheartening but very clear way. We witnessed hatred and bigotry directed toward Asian people, which can easily be traced back to American politicians at the highest levels of our government, blaming China and the Chinese people for the COVID-19 pandemic. No one wants to occupy the lowest rung of the ladder, and so we find horizontal bias among people who have been marginalized. People who have been pushed to the margins of society can use this knowledge as a guide, and can cultivate the awareness needed to move past disconnection and into the warmth of the heart space.

SHIFTING OUR FOCUS

At some point along the Enneagram journey, we are all presented with the opportunity to access the wisdom of connection through understanding how each energy resides within us. Many people claim to be a certain "type" and focus their efforts on discovering everything there is to know about how this specific energy manifests. What many of us fail to remember is that our dominant energy is also affected by our wings, lines to other Points, and our levels of development. We focus so much of our time on understanding a single Point on the Enneagram that we miss opportunities to access all nine energies and fail to pick up the gifts offered at each Point. We overlook our connections to the other Centers of Intelligence and bypass the work necessary to align our Body, Heart, and Head.

Engaging in our own personal Enneagram journey is essential to becoming an authentic Ally, Advocate, and Love Warrior, but we must all remember that the work doesn't stop once we acquire the knowledge; we must do something with it. We must be willing to look in the mirror and see ourselves, accept our warts, foibles, and all, and acknowledge that we are all works in progress. However, the work must also include how our beings are received by the outside world. *Are we kind? Are we judgmental? Are we dismissive? Are we able to admit when we make mistakes and try to do better next time? Are we willing to uncover the biases and stereotypes that are hidden behind elements of our personality?* These are the questions we must ask ourselves as we move toward finding alignment of our three centers and unearthing our authentic selves. We all need to step into our place in order to bring hope and healing out into the world.

ACKNOWLEDGE THE HEAD

The Head Center, which consists of Points Five, Six, and Seven, holds our ability to rationalize and process information. The energy we all have access to within the Head Center provides us with the opportunity to gather and analyze information, create new ways of thinking, and manage how we process our fears and anxiety. One of the main obstacles we all face in the Head Center, regardless of our dominant Enneagram energy, is our ability to physically take action based on what is going on in our head. The trap of the Head Center energy can either leave us stuck in our head or provide the opportunity to connect our bodies for action and our hearts for compassion.

We filter the messages we receive from our early influences around othering and the way we are preprogrammed to treat other humans through our

Head Center. It is in this space that we are able to reinforce or challenge our preconceived notions around what factors inform our implicit biases. If left unchallenged, these biases affect how we respond and react to cross-cultural communications and conflict in our Body and Heart Centers. When we engage in the IDEA space and our inner work, many of us remain stuck in our heads and forget to engage our other two centers to create a balanced approach to growth and awareness. As stated before in Chapter Three:

> The cycle of anger, shame, blame, guilt, and fear is a constant way of being for some; unconsciously reverting to a default of 'justified' behaviors based on unhealthy early messages and influences. If you experience bias, bigotry, or harmful actions (physical or psychological) inflicted upon you or people that you are connected to, this negative experience can create a mental and somatic blueprint that activates when you navigate all future interactions in similar situations with similar groups of people.

When our minds are unbalanced and we find ourselves stuck in internal chatter during difficult or challenging situations, the fear of taking the next step can leave us paralyzed in inaction and unable to connect to our Body and Heart Centers. The work we do in the IDEA space is difficult by nature and a fair amount of people who engage on the journey never really move out of the Head Center.

Many people believe the process of activation is solely developed in a head space, through reading articles and books, watching videos, and engaging in surface conversations with people who often already share the same perspectives. Most of the work around inclusion, diversity, equity, and anti-racism has been filtered through this cognitive experience. While this is one step on the path to dismantling the systems created to disenfranchise and marginalize certain groups of people, it is not the only.

Some people who reside within positions of power and automatic advantage believe they can complete the work and become Allies and Advocates through this one-dimensional process. There is the belief that if we can acquire enough knowledge and understand how othering manifests in the world, then we have achieved activation; however, the process is never allowed to move past our brains. This is how we end up with well-intentioned people who are unprepared and unequipped to deal with the true nature of this work. You can have all of the correct information, but without the proper tools and a balanced approach you cannot truly activate or heal. This flawed theory of achieving activation through cognitive analysis is a key reason why many people never truly engage in the work and cannot become consistent and authentic Allies and Advocates for social justice.

For the Love Warriors, reading the books, watching the documentaries, and engaging in surface conversations without going further into the inner work may trigger some unexplored trauma and leave them with more pain and disconnection than before. The process of activation for Love Warriors is blocked by an unbalanced connection from our heads to our bodies and heart. This is where we find the Love Warriors frustrated and incapacitated by the fear and anger around their inability to create sustainable change or engage in tangible solutions to dismantle the systems of oppression. Additionally, the unhealed or unexplored trauma and the root causes of these wounds are never truly uncovered and oftentimes prevent Love Warriors from facing their biases and healing their inner wounds.

Activation is only attainable when we develop the capacity to align and occupy our three Centers of Intelligence. What occurs outside of this alignment can be called "flurries of activity and activism"—like snowflakes, flurries do not accumulate and become substantive. If we are truly present in our minds, with strong and consistent access to our hearts, and the acceptance of the wisdom held in our bodies, we can engage with the entirety of what grace allows us to access. While we begin this work in the head space, we encourage you to evolve and adapt your process into an aligned approach within the Centers of Intelligence.

LISTEN TO THE BODY

Let's consider the energy we have access to in our Body Center, where Points Eight, Nine, and One reside, and explore the importance of paying attention to the physical sensations when doing inner work. Our Body

Center affects our abilities to take action, exert our energy to control our environment, and holds our awareness of boundaries and our instinctual or gut reactions. One of the main obstacles we all face in the Body Center, regardless of our dominant Enneagram energy, is our ability to filter our actions through our Head and Heart Centers. The trap of the Body Center can either create an overactive and instinctual response to challenges or provide us the opportunity to feel the sensations in our physical form and use it as a warning system for activation.

There is intuitive wisdom in our bodies. Resmaa Menakem illustrates this significance of somatic awareness in *My Grandmother's Hands*—a book we encourage all to read while on their own journey of racial healing. In his book, Menakem explores the body's role in processing trauma.

> *Unhealed trauma acts like a rock thrown into a pond; it causes ripples that move outward, affecting many other bodies over time. After months or years, unhealed trauma can appear to become part of someone's personality. Over even longer periods of time, as it is passed on and gets compounded through other bodies in a household, it can become a family norm. And if it gets transmitted and compounded through multiple families and generations, it can start to look like culture.*
>
> *But it isn't culture. It's a traumatic retention that has lost its context over time.*

He continues by explaining that trauma is embedded into our bodies as well as our brains, which in turn creates the unconscious lens through which we interpret all of our current experiences. This is how we form unconscious biases. In light of these discoveries, it is clear that in order to address our unconscious biases embedded in our brains and to heal our own trauma stored in our bodies, we must explore the mind-body connection.

When we experience something traumatic or painful, our bodies naturally have a response: fight-flight-freeze-fawn. This response is established in our bodies from early exposure to a situation that causes pain, suffering, or trauma, and/or poses a perceived threat; it develops and strengthens over time as we experience similar situations. The response is etched into our bodies becoming part of our nervous system and affects us at an unconscious level. The fight-flight-freeze-fawn response, from a physiological stance, is our body's way of protecting itself from continued harm or trauma, real or perceived.

A *fight* response manifests as an intentional defensive reaction to the threat, fighting back and expelling our energy outward to oppose the threat. The *flight* response, sometimes referred to as "flee," manifests as an evasive maneuver to avoid any danger that may cause us harm. The *freeze* response renders us paralyzed in fear and unable to act against the threat in question. The *fawn* response is usually a last-ditch effort when fight, flight, or freeze has failed or worsened the threat; we act in a nonthreatening way to acquiesce or surrender to avoid further danger. The fawn response is not a commonly known factor in what is normally called the "fight-or-flight" response. This fawn response typically manifests in people who have experienced chronic abuse or persistent threats to their being. The fawn response can be observed in bodies of color who have repeatedly found themselves in situations where the danger was imminent. Sadly, this fawn response and the subsequent agreeableness and compliance is often considered the only hope for survival when a person has held on to a lifetime of trauma within their body. Many people of color have the fawn response ingrained in their DNA and ingrained into their bodies from centuries of ancestral trauma.

It is important to be mindful of the fact that there is no automatic human response that is correct or guarantees psychological or physical safety in any given situation; there are many factors at play when considering how to navigate a potentially traumatic experience.

In order to demonstrate how this concept of fight-flight-freeze-fawn manifests from a racialized lens, let's look at the way in which bodies of color and White bodies may experience the response differently.

For bodies of color, the response is usually a culmination of personal racial trauma, daily micro- and macro-aggressions, environmental, external, and ancestral trauma. For some bodies of color, the response begins with fight or flight: resisting and confronting the threat or escaping the threat. But what is important to note here are the physiological effects that reside in and alter the body from the repetitiveness of the fight-or-flight response through continued exposure to traumatic events.

We can expand upon this concept through the events surrounding the murder of George Floyd. After witnessing the death of George Floyd at the hands of Derek Chauvin, many people of color were forced to revisit the grim reality of continued devaluing of Black and Brown bodies in America. Floyd's death was not the first time a Black man was killed by law enforcement, and sadly it will not be the last. However, for many of us, both Black and White-bodied alike, his death was a wake-up call to the ongoing injustice and collective apathy that runs rampant. Black-bodied Americans, and Black-bodied citizens throughout the world, experienced a rekindling of fear and anger toward the unbalanced power dynamics of Black and White bodies and law enforcement agencies.

And so the fight-flight-freeze-fawn responses in many bodies of color were reinforced once again, strengthening the synapses that fire when they encounter a similar situation later on. We have witnessed the brutal reality that any of the automatic human responses of fight-flight-freeze-fawn in Black and Brown bodies may result in death. Ahmaud Marquez Arbery, for instance, enlisted the flight and then fight response. Ahmaud was murdered on February 23, 2020, in a neighborhood in Georgia when he was chased down by three men who fatally shot him and recorded his murder. The flight response did not protect him, and the fight response could not save him.

For White bodies, or people who do not identify as Black, Brown, or a person of color, the fight-flight-freeze-fawn responses were affected in a completely different way. Many people who do not identify as a person of color experienced a freeze response when confronted with the murder of George Floyd. The immediate danger of being put in harm's way as a person of color is not a factor in people who identify as White. They can experience a fight response when they find themselves in a similar situation and the body of color being threatened happens to belong to a friend, family member, or person they care for. White-bodied individuals and people who do not identify as a person of color can also have a unique approach to the fawn response; the acquiescence and compliance strategy becomes a justification to turn a blind eye to the injustices behind the actions.

The fight-flight-freeze-fawn response is entirely dependent on the individual and the circumstances surrounding the situation. Take a moment to explore how the Center that your Enneagram Point resides in can affect this response within your own body.

BODY CENTER: EIGHT-NINE-ONE

- Does your dominant Enneagram Point reside in the Body Center (Eight-Nine-One)?

- Where do you experience the anger in your body when confronted by a racialized or othering situation?

- Where do you experience the anger in your body when witnessing a racialized or othering situation?

- Does the anger residing in your Body Center allow for the response to manifest as a protection of your physical form in whatever manner resonates with your Enneagram Point?

- When experiencing a similar situation, do you recall the sensations you felt when faced with the murder of George Floyd and react with a defensive stance anchored in the body?

HEART CENTER: TWO-THREE-FOUR

- Does your dominant Enneagram Point reside in the Heart Center (Two-Three-Four)?

- Where do you experience the shame/guilt in your body when confronted by a racialized or othering situation?

- Where do you experience the shame/guilt in your body when witnessing a racialized or othering situation?

- Does the shame/guilt residing in your Heart Center allow for the response to manifest as a protection of what you care for most in whatever manner resonates with your Enneagram Point?

- When experiencing a similar situation, do you recall the sensations you felt when faced with the murder of George Floyd and react with a compassionate but protective stance anchored in the heart and then filtered through your body?

HEAD CENTER: FIVE-SIX-SEVEN

- Does your dominant Enneagram Point reside in the Head Center (Five-Six-Seven)?

- Where do you experience the fear in your body when confronted by a racialized or othering situation?

- Where do you experience the fear in your body when witnessing a racialized or othering situation?

- Does the fear residing in your Head Center allow for the response to manifest as an avoidance of whatever you may be afraid of in a manner that resonates with your Enneagram Point?

- When experiencing a similar situation, do you recall the sensations you felt when faced with the murder of George Floyd and react with a fearful but alert stance anchored in the head and then filtered through your body?

Continue your exploration and strengthen the connection of your three Centers. Begin with this basic inquiry:

- Explore your underlying biases or obstacles that affect how you may respond to the trauma held within your body. How do these implicit biases affect your Body Center's connection to the Heart and Head Center?

- What is impeding your Heart Center's access for compassion and growth when addressing the connection to your Body and Head Centers? Are you able to identify specific occurrences when you feel unable to see another person as a human being rather than an object?

- How does your Head Center affect the connection to your Heart and Body Centers? Are you able to identify specific moments where you feel a disconnect that may need some additional exploration? Consider your ability to readily access compassion when faced with fear and anger.

No matter how your body shows up in this world, we can learn from how the experience of George Floyd's murder either reinforced or created a fight-flight-freeze-fawn response within all of our bodies; it reinforced the internal trauma held in most Black and Brown bodies, and in some cases created a shift in awareness and engagement in White-bodied people. Every time another body of color is destroyed or a conflict occurs across the dimensions of diversity, we are all subjected to an intensification of the pain and trauma held in our bodies, which then amplifies our unconscious biases. We can use these experiences as a stepping stone to engage in our own inner work; we must address the trauma in order to unravel the web of assumption, belief, bias, and judgment created in our brains.

The concept of holding trauma in our bodies is not a new discovery; in fact, it has been studied, outlined, and proven by countless others—as illustrated earlier in Menakem's *My Grandmother's Hands*, and additionally in *Between the World and Me* by Ta-Nehisi Coates and *The Black Body* by Meri Nana-Ama Danquah. Connecting this concept to the Enneagram and racial healing is how we've built upon their discoveries and expanded the work into the Enneagram community. The intricacies behind trauma exploration in the body from a purely somatic perspective is deep and intentional work; we suggest reading the aforementioned books if you are interested in further exploration behind the development and science of this concept.

LEAD WITH THE HEART

As we explore the connection to the wisdom held in our bodies and our heads, we must also acknowledge the necessity of leading with our heart in this space. One cannot honor the humanity in others or in themselves without first accessing their heart. Despite having trauma passed down through our DNA, as proven in multiple studies, we are brought into this world with a pure heart—free of judgment, bias, bigotry, racism, and hatred. This purity is unfortunately a short-lived phenomenon. From the moment our brains are able to process what is happening around us, we begin to construct the neural pathways that affect our core personality and the inner beliefs and biases. It starts at a young age, and if left unaddressed, the negative connections made by our brains and our bodies begin to inform and affect the way we access our authentic heart space. For instance, an unexamined experience of fear surrounding a negative interaction with an authoritative figure or a person with an unfamiliar dimension of diversity—a certain ethnicity, culture, or religion, for example— may create a shift into a cold and unwelcoming heart space later on in life. This connection of a learned fear response and obstructed access to the heart space creates disconnects when we relate new experiences to the original baseline experience. We project the fear and subsequent reaction in order to distort our perceived reality and align what we believe with what we are experiencing. Our bodies and brains inform our hearts, and when misaligned, the body and head corrupt the authentic access to our heart space. This work is dependent on unobstructed access to our hearts, at which point we are able to honor humanity in others as well as in ourselves.

The Heart Center, where Points Two, Three, and Four reside, holds our capacity for connection, consideration, and love. In this space, we develop the emotional intelligence to connect to our true self and filter the messages we receive around value and othering, and ultimately the way in which we are taught to interact with other people, through the humanity and empathy residing in our heart space. Unfortunately for a lot of us who embark on this journey, access to the Heart Center is often blocked by the anger and fear in our Body and Head Centers. We allow our cognitive processes to inform how our bodies react and respond to challenges and opportunities to stand in authentic Advocacy instead of aligning what we think and what we do with our capacity for empathy. This is where we experience well-intentioned individuals claiming to be Allies and Advocates, but failing to align their impact with their true intention. On paper their actions, behaviors, and beliefs may look good, but when brought out into the real world, they often miss the mark.

Many people who find themselves in the IDEA space express a "pain in the heart" when discussing traumatic events, especially in reference to racially charged incidents or the overt discrimination of "others." Anatomically speaking, we know that pain is processed in the brain; however, the pain people speak of in regard to feeling it in their heart is complex and deeply personal. For some, it's heartbreaking or heart-wrenching to watch another person suffer or be in pain. They describe the pain residing in the heart as a way of expressing a compassionate or empathetic perspective instead of trying to rationalize or act on the pain and suffering. This approach to connection is different in that it demonstrates a desire or need to connect with or alleviate another's pain through aligning oneself with the perspective of the other person. All people possess this ability to compassionately connect with others, though many have difficulty stepping into that space when they find themselves blocked by anger, guilt, and fear. The compassion becomes trapped and is never allowed to extend outward toward other humans, leaving us stuck in inaction and apathy. Only when we have committed to completing our inner work are we able to overcome these barriers and actively engage in our evolution as Allies, Advocates, and Love Warriors.

The key to accessing compassion, empathy, and understanding in the face of bias, bigotry, and hatred is allowing our heart to inform our body and head instead of the other way around. The battle against bias, bigotry, and hatred cannot be won with anger, fear, guilt, and even more hatred. We must choose love. When we find ourselves up against a wall of hatred, we need to become present in the moment and avail ourselves of the opportunity to drop into our hearts and allow ourselves the grace to pause for reflection. When we contact our heart's true nature we become connected to our authentic selves and find our identity as a human being who can honor and value love and connection. The individualism we are predisposed to begins to fade away and make space for the grounded connection we share with our sisters, brothers, and siblings within the human race. Our actions, behaviors, and beliefs become less self-serving and evolve into a shared awareness of our undivided connection as a single species. We take mutually beneficial actions grounded in generosity, we behave in collaborative ways with consideration for our fellow human beings, and we hold beliefs anchored in a compassionate approach to finding common ground. As we covered in the introduction:

> A fundamental flaw in our foundation is the failure to pick up the mirror and do the work of coming to fully understand ourselves as individuals who ultimately become part of a collective community in a societal structure. The foundational aspect of evolution is the survival of the fittest through natural selection, but the broader view of this concept is that *communities rather than individuals are more likely to survive*. Communities rely on cooperation and mutually beneficial practices; generosity, compassion, contribution, and support are key elements in determining a community's survival.

So remember this is how the human species will evolve: as a united community of collaborative Allies, Advocates, and Love Warriors.

———

When we successfully engage our three Centers of Intelligence, we can create a sustainable movement from apathy to empathy in the world of social justice, inclusion, diversity, equity, and anti-racism. If you are ready to commit to becoming an authentic Ally, Advocate, or Love Warrior, begin by listening to what's going on in your head, acknowledging what your body is telling you, and always remembering to lead with your heart.

Chapter 9

WE CAN END OTHERING

Hopefully, you have read this entire book. But if this is the only section of the book that you chose to read or if you're one of those people who reads the last pages first, I have a message for you. The work of social justice and racial healing is not only possible, it is also crucial. We have a fractured society that cannot put itself back together without intentional healing work. The only way that this will be accomplished is if we are all willing to roll up our sleeves and apply the sweat equity that it will take to bring our society back together. Even as I write this, I recognize the flawed nature of my words and the need to correct it. Our society has never been truly together; therefore, what we are working toward is creating a recalibrated baseline. A baseline that starts with truth. A "normal" that is kinder, more compassionate, and less self-serving. It is the transition from "me and mine" to "us and ours." I know this is possible as I have tested the premise for over two decades. The main focus of my work is inclusion, diversity, equity, and anti-racism in combination with the Enneagram, where I have witnessed people wake up and own the truth of how they have shown up in the world. Owning your ignorance and standing in truth is the first step to forging a new path for yourself and for the people that you have chosen to be with on your journey. Ignorance is not bliss. Ignorance is the acceptance of a false reality. If you have lived your life from a false and flawed reality, learning that it is not the truth is painful. If I am repeating myself I can only tell you that this cannot be stated in any other way or often enough. *You cannot go under, around, or over the pain. You must go through it.* And yes, I have been and continue to go through the pain of waking up to my own truth.

As a Black woman, the pain of my ancestors' lived experiences still resides in my body. I am still healing. I can stand with dignity and grace in places where people don't welcome my presence and I endure. When I return to my home, I surround myself with love, human and Divine. I heal from the side-eye glances, and the repetition of my words, rejected from me but accepted by others when received from someone who does not share my Blackness nor my gender. I heal from not being seen when told *"I don't think of you as Black."* This is a perpetual wound as my skin tone is on the lighter end of the spectrum. This makes my acceptance conditional on the part of the human who chooses to judge me by the shade of my skin. It says to me, *"I can stand in this space with you because you are not what I think of as Black; therefore you may be okay."*

Does it make me angry? Yes. Does it hurt? Yes. Do I allow the anger or the pain to stop me? No.

There is too much at stake. All people need to wake up to the truth of what it means to be in your God-given body and to feel and experience everything that comes along with it. We must all become aware of what comes with us when we enter a room and what that energy does to the environment and, more importantly, to the people with whom you may or may not choose to engage.

I have been asked more times than I can count whether or not I hate White people. I know that there are people who would like for me to respond *yes.* That's not my answer and not my truth. I do not like the things that cause the suffering of Love Warriors in the name of Whiteness. The violence that has been, and continues to be, inflicted upon BIPOC humans is beyond my human comprehension, and yet I do not have hate in my heart. The healing from the energy of violence, devastation, and death inflicted or received will be the work of our individual and collective lifetimes. This work must begin with the healing of our hearts and the restoration of love.

It is not uncommon to hear a White-bodied person protest that these heinous acts were not committed by them individually as in "I didn't have anything to do with slavery. Do you see any slaves in my house?" Part of the truth that has to be accepted is that the energy of our ancestors is part of who we are. It enters with each individual when you come into any space, making this *healing* that I refer to a necessary part of the human experience. Some are more removed from or asleep to their own wounding than others. And then there are those among us who are retraumatized over and over again, diminishing the hope that healing is even possible.

I often find myself intentionally engaging in conversations about ending racism and othering when speaking with people who are firmly cemented in passive othering. I am well aware that many consider my approach to this work as an inexorable calling or mission to find a solution, and I do not disagree. I am fully invested in dismantling and ending the practices and policies put in place to force "others" to the margins of society. At times, I am aware that I can be annoying because I believe *we all should be fully invested.* It takes a relentlessly hopeful and persistent mindset to believe that change is entirely possible. The change I hope for may not come during my lifetime; however, I recognize the importance of how together we can create a foundation for others to build upon and continue the work.

Ending bias, bigotry, and hatred is an individual choice that each of us can make—a choice that can be felt on a collective level. The more of us who choose to awaken and stay awake, the closer we come to transforming an idealistic dream to a tangible goal. If you choose to believe that change is possible, let the work begin with you. If you choose to move toward this goal, with the Enneagram as your guide, you will become familiar with your distinct approach to othering. It becomes hardwired into the thoughts we think, the words we speak, and the stereotypes that we hold on to.

It's important for us to become more aware of the damaging outcomes that are rooted in our own narcissism and bias. *Me and mine* versus *us and ours.* Society is fraught with the suffering brought on by the distinct ways in which each of us contributes to the devastating practice of othering. The relentless performance of our selfishness, greed, and arrogance only perpetuates racism, sexism, xenophobia, homophobia, and all forms of othering. We must become selfless, compassionate, respectful humans who intentionally strive for a better tomorrow. Hopefully you will continue to educate yourself about how racism came to be an insidious and prolific blight that continues to thrive, despite the struggles and sacrifices to contain and destroy it. This exploration will open your eyes to the dark reality of the detrimental effects of our historical transgressions against humanity, and ultimately reveal a path forward for us to restore and reclaim our humanity.

We must face the challenge of opening our minds and hearts to release the lies that we embraced as truth as we come together to accept our shameful history. The pain of the acceptance of the truth, at times, is unbearable. We cannot move forward without reeducating ourselves and restoring our world as one unified human race. This is a daunting task when we consider the broad spectrum of divisions that stretch across the globe. In so many parts of the world, the social dominance hierarchies and the competition for limited resources are considered essential to human survival. Nonetheless, we must remember the intrinsic element that truly determines human evolution: *communities rather than individuals are more likely to survive.* Our world is abundant. There is more than enough for everyone; however, if we do not move beyond "me and mine" to get to "us and ours," the reality of truly knowing justice and peace will remain out of reach. We will continue to have corruption, poverty, societal disparities, and dysfunctional legal systems as the very foundation of what we identify as *justice* remains biased and inequitable.

Peace comes to those who seek to know peace; it doesn't just happen. We must learn how to intentionally nurture the practice of peace. If we work toward the cultivation of peace, we can begin the process of dismantling systemic racism and othering in all its twisted forms, but we must know love first. Love is the only way to transmute the distortions created by racism. We must choose to love one another, choose to love ourselves, choose love even in the face of hatred. It is vital for us to embrace this message together. I think of the staggering communities of people who are marginalized based on the color of their skin, who they choose to share their lives with, what part of town they were born in, how they worship, and so forth. People will suffer and go without as if it were our choice to not be born into a family with a higher socioeconomic status—a status that would have eliminated hunger and made it possible for education to be a core value accessible to all. I weep when I see humans who are denied the simple right to fall in love with someone based on antiquated parameters of who is and who is not acceptable to be loved. My heart breaks for the children trapped in the seemingly inescapable prison pipeline created by centuries of systemic inequities.

I know the absence of peace, because I know the absence of justice. In spite of the state of our world, I can see the way back. I see the path of hope and love and light. It is time to reclaim and know justice and to find a way to restore and know peace.

Who is the observer of our destiny? Who is the "they" that decides and has the power to determine where we fit in the Humanity Mosaic? The response to this inquiry is you. You are the observer of your own destiny. You are the only one that has the power to determine where you fit in the Humanity Mosaic. Each individual who finds their authentic self and chooses the path of love, hope, and compassion will contribute to the re-creation of our collective Humanity Mosaic; one human and one choice at a time. We can change the flawed worldview and pernicious mindset of cruel disparities and inequity. Human to human, moment by moment. We can bring "others" back in from the margins and it all begins by respecting and loving one another. The Love Warriors, Allies, and Advocates coming together to create, in the words of Eckhardt Tolle, *A New Earth*.

When I wrote the preface for this book, I knew I had painted a pretty bleak picture of my comfort level within the Enneagram community. The story doesn't end there because change truly does happen. I now have a seat on the board of the International Enneagram Association (IEA).

In the span of time between 2016 and 2022, the IEA has taken a look in the mirror and many members of the board saw exactly what I did in 2016. A sea of White faces. The board is presently much more representative of a global organization. We have intentionally sought out ways the IEA can serve the Enneagram community. Moving away from the paradigm of having one person of color means we can now call ourselves diverse. We consciously and respectfully examine who is not represented on the board based on ethnicity, language, age, gender, sexual diversity, nationality, socio-economics, learning styles, education etc. We are quite the mixed bag of humans trying to evolve to meet the needs of a global community. Diversity, Equity, and Inclusion (DEI) is part of the ongoing learning of the board to include special sessions on implicit bias. There is a DEI team that proactively scans for ways to be more inclusive right down to some of the things that might not come up on the radar of a monolithic board, like pronouns. Our board launched a mentorship program in 2022 to allow more opportunities for individuals who may not have access to the schools or deeper levels of training. Enneagroups have formed to allow people to self-organize around inclusive topics of interest to cultivate safe spaces for growth and learning with the Enneagram. Pre-pandemic we brought together diversity roundtable discussions at the conferences, and I was no longer the only Black person talking about "rebuilding the bridges that differences broke." Jessica Dibb opened the doors at The Shift network where I became a regular guest teacher along with other BIPOC teachers. Sightings of BIPOC individuals in the Enneagram community are no longer a rare occurrence; just check out Instagram, Facebook, TikTok, and YouTube and you'll see this diverse Enneagram generation taking the work to a whole new level.

The numbers are growing and the conversations are happening. The platforms are expanding and people who used to not have a voice, or even a seat at the table, are being brought in and the space has intentionally been shared. I was invited to start a podcast on Voice America, and in 2020, the IEA certified my Enneagram and Inclusion, Diversity, Equity, & Anti-Racism (IDEA) Certification Training. A few years ago if you told me the IEA had a training program for honoring the diverse spectrum of human diversity and our need to understand the implications of this when doing our inner work, I would have never believed it given my past experiences. But today the IEA has more programs, teachers, schools, and seminars on topics related to human diversity and "rebuilding the bridges that differences broke" than I ever imagined possible.

The intentional weaving of diversity into the Enneagram community was embraced by people who were willing to make the ripples in the pond. I have worked with Enneagram schools who desire to walk the talk and move beyond the hollow actions so often engaged as a temporary checking off the box. I have spoken at Enneagram chapters, conferences, podcasts, and panels, and I am beyond grateful to see the generations after me moving this work forward. It's happening and I am grateful to experience this fresh new air that is breathing life back into the Enneagram community.

CONCLUSION

Continuing to Walk Each Other Home

The completion of the last chapter of this book happened to coincide with the culmination of the first Enneagram Social Justice and Racial Healing Seminar held at the Esalen Institute in Big Sur, California, facilitated by Russ Hudson and myself. I believe the people who came to the week-long workshop were divinely selected by the universe. In Scripture, it is written that "many are called but few are chosen." The people who attended and chose to stay engaged were human beings who will now go out into the world with an open heart, intuitive wisdom brought to life, and an informed lens for truth and justice in a way that they have not experienced before.

What I witnessed as we facilitated this workshop was the true power of inner work. We collectively discovered that when we successfully transcend the surface dimensions of our diversity what remains is our essence—which is pure love. The sharing that took place rose from the deepest places in everyone's heart. The desire to be a part of the solution arrived from the core of everyone's being and the light and love that radiated from the eyes, which are the windows to the soul after all, could not be missed by even a passing stranger. As we explored the dimensions of diversity in the room, we all began to love one another as we learned to love ourselves. In this space, we saw how often these dimensions are demonized, demeaned, and disrespected in the world—Black, White, Brown, gay, straight, male, female, nonbinary, spiritual, religious, and too many other deep dimensions of diversity to share.

We cohabitated for a full week together in our love and our pain. We laughed, cried, danced, hiked, ate, slept, and learned together, even as we explored the deep divisions of race and othering. We acknowledged the insidious nature of othering, and we went deep. We were fearless. We acknowledged shame, fear, guilt, frustration, anxiety, and yet we let nothing stop us from surfacing our individual and collective truths. We grieved the reality of the differences and the experiences of those who are categorized as "other," suffering moments of helplessness in the process. I vividly remember the day that the systemic racism timeline was presented to the group. The images and the narrative are excruciatingly painful. It is still difficult for me to simultaneously hold the energy of the group and present the timeline of the historical systematic destruction, brutalization, and death of my people. On this day, Tracy, my colleague who keeps a pretty close watch on me, stepped in to present the timeline. Russ and I held the energy in the room, responding to questions and watching the opening of hearts. The internal shift was manifesting for the transformative process of the activation of Allies and Advocates to stand with Love Warriors. This all occurred as scheduled so that everyone would have their private time for the rest of the evening. The experience created an opening that resulted in these humans wanting to know more and to do more, and they were resolute. We stayed in the room talking long past the time of dismissal. A cohort of humans having an inner room experience together.

The people who participated in the course throughout the week were changed; they were no longer the same people who had come to Esalen just a week before. We witnessed what would be called true conversion moments. You might question how I can possibly be so certain that people were truly changed. All I can tell you is that the Divine was present in the details of this inner work. We remained present and witnessed something miraculous.

At our final session, we all stood in the middle of the room. It felt a little awkward and a lot more uncomfortable than how we felt knowing we could reconvene again to stay connected. On this day, we knew we had to depart from one another. Somehow the feeling of departure was a challenge to the very thing we had cultivated that week. So we stood in the center of the floor and, without words, laughed at the fact that we were about to have that funny moment where we all held hands and said our goodbyes.

Tracy, who participated as well as assisted for this seminar, was suddenly brought down by the onset of a terrible migraine. I have no doubt she was still holding on to the energy from presenting the systemic racism timeline, which in my experience is both physically and mentally taxing. She was unable to physically join us in the middle of the floor, so we made her comfortable with some pillows against the wall as she lifted up her sunglasses to block the light. We were all acutely aware of her pain that day. She is much beloved by all of us, as we are to one another. Tracy happens to be a radiant Black woman—the sun rises in her eyes and the moon is present there when the sun sets. She is an unmistakably beautiful human, inside and out. As we stood on the floor holding hands, I glanced over to see if she was okay. Without speaking a single word or breaking our joined hands, we all began to move in the circle together as one. Our group had moved toward Tracy. As she sat in the corner, a person on either side of her positioned themselves to hold her hands.

I felt the tears welling up from a deep place inside me, and in a shaky voice I said, "It is not lost on me that one of our sisters is down today, and it is not lost on me that without words we have all moved toward her to make sure that she is included in this circle of love."

Perhaps you needed to have been there to feel the full power of this moment, though I am sure this image will live within you as it lives within each of us who were present that day. It was demonstrative of our hope for the world. The hope that as one of us falls, the rest of us will come to stand beside and lift up someone who may be hurting, marginalized, or dismissed in any part of society—to venture to the margins, acknowledge the people who reside in the periphery, and work to bring them back in with love, respect, and compassion. God gave us a silent nod that day and let us know that we were on the right path. Being inclusive and not casting our eyes away.

If that were to be the last workshop that I ever facilitated in my lifetime, it would have been enough. I know that the people present will always remember that experience. We will remember the love that we cultivated and nurtured. We will remember the laughter and the tears. We will remember expressing some of our deepest fears and our insecurities and feeling safe in expressing our deepest truths. None of the things that we shared were foreign to us, and the hierarchy of White-body/Black-body, gay/straight, religious/spiritual, man/woman/nonbinary, wealthy/poor did not matter. We all felt our wounds together and recognized that we were capable of healing ourselves and of healing one another.

Shortly after this group returned home, I was invited to host another Enneagram and IDEA workshop at Esalen. This time there were twice as many people in attendance. It is my full intention to continue doing these workshops around the world, and though it may be a slow process, I know in my heart it is a process that works. I am well aware that there are people who have no interest in healing the divisions that have been created, and I have empathy and compassion for them. I recognize that if you do not know this type of deep love, it is not possible for you to heal your own wounds. Healing will only occur by acknowledging your woundedness, the places where you feel the most broken and vulnerable, and then allowing yourself the gift of grace to be healed. You can be comforted, and you can enter the circle of love. Withholding is something that we do and are often unaware of; we withhold love from others, and we also withhold it from ourselves. We must learn to open our hearts to give and receive love.

You are part of the journey, and whether you take a stand or a position is your choice.

During this workshop, Russ spoke about the difference between taking a position and taking a stand. Taking a position can often be superficial and binary: right, wrong, good, bad. Taking a stand requires some depth of knowledge and mindfulness. Perhaps it is more accurately described as *wisdom*. People can shift positions on a dime, but taking a stand allows you to grow deep roots in a way where your nourishment in that stand becomes grounded in your being.

I wish all of you had been in our workshop. Esalen is a healing space, unsurpassed as a place of beauty steeped in spiritual traditions. Many have come there for hope and healing, and I hope you have the opportunity to visit one day. I am grateful that this particular workshop began and will continue at the very center of a place that has held spiritual wisdom traditions for many years. For those of you who are reading this, perhaps you can join me there sometime and begin your journey. In the meantime, I boldly ask that you open your eyes to what may be happening in your corner of the world. Research and honor what may have happened on the land that you are currently residing upon. Look around your neighborhood and see who is there and who is not, and ask yourself why. Pay attention when you go to work and take note of the people who occupy the positions at the top of a hierarchy in your workplace. If you see a person living on the streets, think about the circumstances behind their story, and consider the factors that may have pushed this person to the very edge of society. Research the inequities in your communities and find ways to become part of the solution. And the most important questions that you can ask yourself are: Where do I fit in the Humanity Mosaic? How can I be a part of making sure that everyone has a place where love, value, respect, dignity, and equity are available to all? What am I willing to do to make the world a better place for future generations?

Whether we are ready to accept it or not, we are all on a journey together, and hopefully this path will heal more of us so that we can ensure less of us are subjected to unnecessary suffering, discrimination, and untimely death. The journey deep into the heart of humanity is not for the faint of heart. It is a journey of Love Warriors, Allies, and Advocates who have opened their minds and hearts and accepted the intuitive wisdom of the body to recognize that we must keep one another safe as we walk each other home. This is a message that has been delivered to us over and over again and comes from many different sources. The message that "love is the only way" rings true today as it has in spiritual traditions for centuries. We must also be mindful of the fact that hatred extracts a heavy toll for all of us. It brings suffering and pain, death and destruction. We must be willing to choose love and light in the face of hatred and darkness if we expect to journey into the heart of humanity and heal our divides.

I am deeply grateful for those of you who chose to read this book. I hope that you have been affected by the words you've read, and I call on you as an Ally, Advocate, or Love Warrior to share this message of love, connection, and hope with anyone who may be pushed to the margins of society, or anyone who may be paralyzed by apathy as they turn a blind eye to the current state of the world. If you have been wounded in any way, I hope that you will take the time to heal your own wounds. It will be that healing that allows you to open your heart to all of humanity. Once you become whole, my prayer for you is that there will be a strong desire to help others become whole as well. Always remember: We walk this path together.

Some of you may read this book and recognize yourself somewhere in the pages, and some of you will take action. Those actions demonstrate that every step taken in this direction is another step toward healing a heart. It is the activation of another Ally, Advocate, or Love Warrior waking up. Some of you reading this book may feel disheartened by the thought of others not being able to see the same path. It is important to realize that you cannot control the actions, behaviors, or beliefs of other humans. Your purpose and journey is to live your life with compassion, courage, connection, and love; the outcome will hopefully allow your light and love to extend to others and eventually bring everyone you meet into the warmth of your heart. The way in which we treat other humans matters, and yet we still argue and disagree over the simple common sense construct of whose lives matter and whose lives do not. Enough is enough.

We all have value, purpose, meaning, and dreams in this lifetime. To honor one another is the greatest gift that we can give to ourselves. And I know that it is the greatest gift that we can pay forward for future generations to build on. I love my children. I love my grandchildren. I love your children and grandchildren as well as I know the feelings in the hearts of parents and grandparents that I speak with all over the world. These words ring true. I have spoken to so many who share this concern for the future. We can move beyond concern to action. We can see and experience and understand how deep those feelings go for those of us who are engaged in this love battle for the healing and hope of our humanity. We should all acknowledge this love battle; for those of us who live on the margins of society and are without the protection of certain automatic advantages, or those who may be at risk of harm to our bodies and to the bodies of those around us.

If we are to build a better world for all of us to inhabit together, I will repeat words that I often say to Allies and Advocates trying to find their place in this space: to know justice and peace will require work. Consistent work. We cannot reap the rewards of the manifestation of love without doing our inner work. The manifestation of what we do internally will reveal an external outcome. The external outcome of our inner work is what will bring us back together as connected loving, kind, and peaceful human beings.

We can walk this earth as ambassadors of intentional peace.
There is no peace without justice.
There is no peace where there is division.
There is no peace without intentional effort toward peace
brought forward by love.
To know justice and to know peace is to first know love.
God willing, we will learn to walk side by side. As Allies,
Advocates, and Love Warriors.
We will find our way home together.

INDEX

RESOURCES FOR CONTINUED LEARNING

If you'd like to delve deeper into the Enneagram, I invite you to visit **deborahegerton.com** where you will find an updated list as more resources become available.

BOOKS

The Wisdom Of The Enneagram: The Complete Guide To Psychological And Spiritual Growth For The Nine Personality Types, by Don Richard Riso and Russ Hudson

The Complete Enneagram: 27 Paths to Greater Self-Knowledge, by Beatrice Chestnut Ph.D.

The Enneagram: A Christian Perspective, by Richard Rohr and Andreas Ebert

The Enneagram: Nine Gateways to Presence, by Russ Hudson

The Awakened Company, by Catherine Bell

SCHOOLS, GROUPS, TRAINING PROGRAMS

Enneagram and Inclusion, Diversity, Equity, and Anti-Racism Certification Program by Dr. Deborah Egerton

Alternatives UK

Be Mindfully Well

Chestnut Paes Enneagram Academy

Deep Coaching Institute

Enneagram Georgia

The Enneagram Institute

Integrative Enneagram Solutions

International Enneagram Association

The Narrative Enneagram

REFERENCES

Coates, Ta-Nehisi. *Between the World and Me*. New York, NY: Spiegel & Grau, 2015.

Danquah, Meri Nana-Ama. *The Black Body*. New York, NY: Seven Stories Press, 2009.

DiAngelo, Robin. *White Fragility: Why It's So Hard For White People To Talk About Racism*. Boston, MA: Beacon Press, 2018

The Enneagram Institute. Stone Ridge, New York. Established 1997. www.enneagraminstitute.com

The Esalen Institute. Big Sur, California. Established 1962. www.esalen.org

Jackson, Michael. "The Man in the Mirror," Bad. Epic Records, 1987.

Kendi, Ibram X. *How to Be an Antiracist*. London: Bodley Head, 2019.

Menakem, Resmaa. *My Grandmother's Hands: Racialized Trauma and the Pathway to Mending our Hearts and Bodies*. London: Penguin Books, 2017.

Oluo, Ijeoma. *So You Want to Talk about Race*. New York, NY: Seal Press, 2018.

Riso, Don Richard, and Russ Hudson. *The Wisdom of the Enneagram: The Complete Guide to Psychological and Spiritual Growth for the Nine Personality Types*. New York, NY: Bantam Books, 1999.

Sussman, Robert Wald. *The Myth of Race: The Troubling Persistence of an Unscientific Idea*. Cambridge, MA: Harvard University Press, 2016.

Tolle, Eckhart. *A New Earth: Awakening to Your Life's Purpose*. New York, N.Y: Dutton/Penguin Group, 2005.

ACKNOWLEDGMENTS

This book would not have seen the light of day without the partnership of Lisi Mohandessi. Thank you to the entire Mohandessi family for sharing Lisi. She kept track of practically every word I have ever spoken over the past 15 years. Her research and authentic desire and determination to put this message out into the world was awe-inspiring. We worked together to give our readers something that just might help to create a kinder and more loving and compassionate world.

Special thanks to all of my friends and family who supported us on this journey. My husband, Gene, can probably recite this book from memory, having been so patient and kind with the reading of revisions. This work is also dedicated to my ancestors who came before me (especially my parents, Margaret and Walter), my children and grandchildren, and the entire Threadgill-Egerton family. Thank you for your love which sustains everything that I do. Also Tracy Cooper, who wore multiple hats during this project—proofreader, organizer, chief of all things at my company, Trinity Transition Consultants—thanks for keeping everything stable and on track. None of this would have been possible without you stepping in and stepping up without being asked and without any hesitation. Every human should be so blessed as to have this caliber of colleague and friend.

I must also acknowledge and honor a remarkable group of humans who ventured into this work with me as the first-ever Enneagram and IDEA class to be certified. Our pioneering group consisted of an incredibly diverse cross-section of communities with people from different cultural and ethnic backgrounds, gender and sexual diversities, geographical locations, ages and experiences, occupations, Enneagram Points, and a wide spectrum of other dimensions. No single participant was like another, and yet we all came together to do the inner work and find common ground, even with our obvious differences. We discovered that, while we were all very different, we had similarities that brought us together: our love for the Enneagram; our desire to do more in this world; the realization that we all had a calling to bring our work out into the world to create sustainable change and move toward a more fair and equitable society. We laughed, we cried, we connected. We didn't let the pandemic stop us from meeting on Zoom to continue our work. We managed to create a safe and healing space while never once being in the same room as one another. I am grateful for each and every one of these humans: Tracy, Emilie, Brian, Joyce, Erlina, Donna, Lynda, Milton, Christy, Linda, Ben, Pegah, Yasmina, Emily, Christine, and Matt.

I also acknowledge all of my colleagues, students and friends, who I continue to learn from every day. The list could fill this entire book, but I want to mention additional active Allies and Advocates who show up to encourage me in challenging the status quo to work toward the elimination of "othering": Catherine Bell, for setting the intention for collaboration; Ginger Lapid-Bogda, for bringing this work into your business community and your heart for diversity; Marion Gilbert, for the healing work that is the desire of our hearts to continue; Dirk Cloete and Shawn Smith, for giving me a key to open doors that otherwise might not be accessible; Tom Condon, for peeking in and always having a word of encouragement; Deborah Ooten, who had my back from day one; Bernadette Galea, who has the voice of an angel and inspires me with every note from afar; Jan Shegda, for driving to Fresno to find me. You certainly set some Good Trouble in motion.

Finally to the Enneagram community, I thank you for your efforts toward opening the doors to make the Enneagram more accessible to all people. You know who you are and I see you acknowledging the broad spectrum of diversity. For those of us who have studied the Enneagram, we know that we have been given a gift. All of you are the bearers of the pebble that creates the ripples in the pond. We never know how far they will reach, but if you throw it into the pond there will be ripples.

I have many Allies and Advocates who stand with me and my community of Love Warriors. They all have one thing in common that touches my heart and keeps hope alive: each of them entered the Love Battle with no questions asked, but if there was a question asked of me it was, "How can I help?"

I frequently walk myself around the Enneagram to experience the energy at each Point and remind myself of and remember to be encouraged by the people who are at their dominant Point in this Love War. I start at Point One, my dominate Enneagram energy. To access the encouragement and the spiritual nourishment that I need, I go to Fr. Richard Rohr. I have to go to YouTube or my bookshelf to find him, but he is always there for me. His words speak directly to my spirit. Fr. Rohr is also a One. He gets me.

I continue my walk through the Enneagram to arrive at Point Two. There I find the warmth of Beatrice Chestnut. My friend, my Ally, and my Advocate. Bea has literally packed her bags and flown across the country to work with me. I know when I have clients who are ready for the next level of depth that is going to help them decide whether or not they want to continue the journey, and she will be at my side to help get them there. She also holds my hand and my heart when I need someone who will listen. Also at Point Two stands Jessica Dibb. It was Jessica who has been an early Ally and Advocate. She was the woman who stood up for me in Minneapolis where this all began. She has slayed dragons and cleared the thorns and thistles out of the way to make sure that my voice is heard. At every given opportunity, Jess has opened a door to allow me to bring light into spaces that might have remained unenlightened. And she will answer the phone or respond to a frustrated text when I've had to deal with painful adversity, responding with loving-kindness.

I move on to Point Three. There I feel the loving energy of Robert Holden. A friend like this I wish for all Love Warriors. Robert never hesitated, never wavered, got on the Ally train and headed straight into the battle. He has been by my side from the day we met. He holds my feet to the fire. Always encouraging, motivating, and lovingly nudging me forward. I have always been on the front lines of this war, but there is something powerful about that Three energy that catapults me to higher levels of looking at what is possible. I pivot a little still at Point Three and Brian Mitchell-Walker is staring back at me. I meet Brian's gaze and I'm grateful for all that he brings to this Love Battle. We have been assigned to the same battle for decades, and we are both still standing. We learn from one another and exchange war stories. It feels good, supportive and consistent, persistent and dependable. He reminds me that we are in this for the long haul, but we've got each other's back. And we will win. I'm with him in the energy of Point Three.

As I reach Point Four, I find myself longing to linger in the space for a while. There is so much healing that is happening in my spirit. Allies and Advocates, old and new, are here. My loving sister-in-law, Marianne Niles, is here. She is my safe haven and fountain of wisdom. She sees the world through different eyes at Point Four, and the energy of her empathy and compassion holds me together. Also here at Point Four is Hollie Holden, with her appreciation for beauty in the broken places and the desire to make them whole again and love them exactly as they are. I can feel her energy as she transmits another beautiful way for us to make a difference in this world. It's real, and true, and authentic. I am just leaving the beauty at Point Four, when a wave of gratitude washes over me. I recognize this energy of friendship and collaboration. Jan Shegda is here holding the energy of possibility before me. I try to move on, but the energy has come into my heart and my home. I feel the resolve of a powerful Ally and Advocate who I know will energize me and make me smile while we do what must be done.

The journey to Point Five is eye-opening. I acknowledge the shift in my centers, and I am met with energy coming from two powerful Allies and Advocates. Russ Hudson is standing with me, bringing the wisdom and the power of his knowledge to help me gain entryway to find the inner strength to keep moving forward. His energy is comfortable, funny, and familiar. I am suddenly feeling very intense healing energy that is making me aware of wounds that I still need to heal. I smile. I know this is the healing energy of Uranio Paes. He reminds me, as does Russ: *Deborah, you are not alone.*

And I realize those words are true when I move on to Point Six. The loyal and loving energy that greets me here allows me a brief respite. I know that I'm on the path with Lynda Roberts. We've been together from the beginning of our Enneagram journeys. Here, I am reminded of her determination and resolve. Lourdes is here. Living proof of the power of love and friendship across differences. We may speak different languages, but we understand every word that is spoken from our hearts. I know the battle will always have Allies and Advocates at this Point.

At Point Seven, I step into an energy where I can let go of the weight of the journey. I am surrounded by familiar love and joy. My brother Walter Threadgill's energy is here. I soak it in and remember how he showed me to follow my own path and that he would find me if I got lost. My dear friend Deni Mineta is also here at Point Seven, smiling at me and bringing light into everything that she does. I recognize her stepping into this energy, which brings me immediately to a place of joy and laughter and mischief. These are Allies and Advocates who have been with me throughout my life.

I arrive at Point Eight. I have many familiar Allies and Advocates here. I feel the strength and the goodness that surrounds me. I feel protected and powerful simultaneously. I have two strong women standing beside me. Catherine Bell is clearing a path forward. I feel the intentionality of the steps that are being taken. Marion Gilbert is holding and healing a wounded place in me. I feel the connection and force that is moving us forward together. Nothing can defeat the strength of this energy. Strong and powerful, intertwined with loving-kindness.

I ease over to Point Nine, the last stop before I return to my home Point. Another familiar energy meets me. An Ally and Advocate and a Love Warrior that I watched and learned so much from the gentle way that he moves through the world: Norman Y. Mineta. I linger here deliberately and send up a little prayer that I can endure as a Love Warrior with his dignity and grace as my model. I'm not ready to leave Point Nine. Another wing space for me. The energy is amazing here. It's my safe space to land. There is a love here that pulls me in, and I never want this energy to let me go. Walter Eugene Egerton III is here. My husband. My favorite Love Warrior. My Ally, Advocate, and my heart. I feel calm and held and unshakable here. Fortunately, when I slide back over to Point One, we can still hold hands.

ABOUT THE AUTHOR

Deborah Threadgill Egerton, MA, Ph.D. is an internationally respected psychotherapist, spiritual teacher, an IEA certified Enneagram practitioner, and a consultant and coach. "Dr. E," as she is affectionately referred to, is the founder and president of Trinity Transition Consultants LLC. She works with individuals and organizations—both large and small—to help them release false historical narratives and to open their minds and hearts to a new IDEA (Inclusion, Diversity, Equity, and Anti-Racism).

For more than two decades, the focus of her work has been teaching the Enneagram as a valuable tool for social justice and anti-racism and using it as a blueprint to reunite people. Her visionary approach to IDEA work expands the traditional scope of the DEI (Diversity, Equity, and Inclusion) method and allows for the honoring of every individual with respect to all dimensions of their unique self-identification. She is a current board member of the International Enneagram Association, and her greatest passion is leading others to understand their own humanity.

To learn more about Dr. Egerton and her powerful work, visit deborahegerton.com and trinitytransition.com.

Hay House Titles of Related Interest

YOU CAN HEAL YOUR LIFE, the movie, starring Louise Hay & Friends
(available as an online streaming video)
www.hayhouse.com/louise-movie

THE SHIFT, the movie,
starring Dr. Wayne W. Dyer
(available as an online streaming video)
www.hayhouse.com/the-shift-movie

———

*108 PEARLS TO AWAKEN YOUR HEALING POTENTIAL: A Cardiologist
Translates the Science of Health and Healing into Practice,*
by Mimi Guarneri, M.D.

*BLACK GIRL IN LOVE (WITH HERSELF): A Guide to Self-Love, Healing, and
Creating the Life You Truly Deserve,* by Trey Anthony

*DREAM TO FREEDOM: A Handbook for Integrating Dreamwork and Energy
Psychology,* by Robert and Lynne Hoss

GOOD VIBES, GOOD LIFE: A Real-World Guide to Achieving a Greater Life,
by Vex King

LIFE LOVES YOU: 7 Spiritual Practices to Heal Your Life, by Louise Hay and
Robert Holden, Ph.D.

All of the above are available at your local bookstore,
or may be ordered by contacting Hay House (see next page).

We hope you enjoyed this Hay House book. If you'd like to receive our online catalog featuring additional information on Hay House books and products, or if you'd like to find out more about the Hay Foundation, please contact:

Hay House, Inc., P.O. Box 5100, Carlsbad, CA 92018-5100
(760) 431-7695 or (800) 654-5126
(760) 431-6948 (fax) or (800) 650-5115 (fax)
www.hayhouse.com® • www.hayfoundation.org

———

Published in Australia by: Hay House Australia Pty. Ltd.,
18/36 Ralph St., Alexandria NSW 2015
Phone: 612-9669-4299 • *Fax:* 612-9669-4144
www.hayhouse.com.au

Published in the United Kingdom by: Hay House UK, Ltd.,
The Sixth Floor, Watson House, 54 Baker Street, London W1U 7BU
Phone: +44 (0)20 3927 7290 • *Fax:* +44 (0)20 3927 7291
www.hayhouse.co.uk

Published in India by: Hay House Publishers India,
Muskaan Complex, Plot No. 3, B-2, Vasant Kunj, New Delhi 110 070
Phone: 91-11-4176-1620 • *Fax:* 91-11-4176-1630
www.hayhouse.co.in

———

Access New Knowledge.
Anytime. Anywhere.

Learn and evolve at your own pace
with the world's leading experts.

www.hayhouseU.com

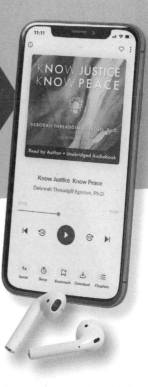

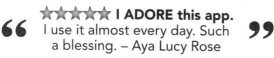